Robert K. Massie was born in Lexington, Kentucky, 1929. He studied American history at Yale University and modern European history at Oxford University, which he attended as a Rhodes Scholar. He served from 1987 to 1991 as president of the Authors Guild. His previous books include *Nicholas and Alexandra*, *Peter the Great*, *Journey* and *Dreadnought*.

Praise for *The Romanovs: The Final Chapter*

'Robert K. Massie . . . has produced . . . what deserves to be the last word on the question of identification [of the bones] . . . his version of the verifiable fact is magisterial, and it is hard to see how any further investigation could produce anything to supersede it.'
Night & Day

'Massie writes very well and . . . this book is a proper, if harrowing, pendant to his earlier books on the Romanovs.'
The Times

'A compelling conclusion to the Romanov story . . . a powerful explanation of one of the most fascinating mysteries of the 20th Century.'
Irish Times

'An admirable scientific chronicle . . . a complex historical thriller . . . macabre historical irony, subtly intimated, give(s) this often masterly book a tone of dignity and horror.'
New York Times Book Review

'This tangled, extraordinary tale of intrigue . . . is the subject of a masterful and enthralling new book . . . Massie has constructed a narrative as gripping as a well-wrought murder mystery, told in vividly realised, densely atmospheric scenes, rich with moments of grim fascination.'
Washington Post

'Part political thriller, part scientific analysis, the intriguing story is a masterpiece of investigative reporting. Massie's dramatic use of detail makes for highly readable history.'
San Francisco Chronicle

'Absorbing . . . The book is a mesmerising mix of forensic medicine, historical detective work, contested royal succession and political, scientific and religious in-fighting that reads like a high-octane novel of suspense . . . A must read.'
Flint (Michigan Journal)

'Untangles the web of mystery surrounding the slaughter of Russia's romantically tragic royal family.'
Vanity Fair

Also by Robert K. Massie

Nicholas and Alexandra
Peter the Great
Dreadnought
Journey (co-author)

THE ROMANOVS:
THE FINAL CHAPTER

Robert K. Massie

ARROW

Published in the United Kingdom in 1996 by Arrow Books

1 3 5 7 9 10 8 6 4 2

Copyright © Robert K. Massie 1995

The right of Robert K. Massie to be identified as the author
of this work has been asserted by him in accordance
with the Copyright, Designs and Patents Act, 1988

First published in the United Kingdom in 1995 by Jonathan Cape

Arrow Books Limited
Random House UK Ltd
20 Vauxhall Bridge Road, London SW1V 2SA

Random House Australia (Pty) Limited
16 Dalmore Drive, Scoresby, Victoria 3179

Random House New Zealand Limited
18 Poland Road, Glenfield
Auckland 10, New Zealand

Random House South Africa (Pty) Limited
PO Box 2263, Rosebank 2121, South Africa

Random House UK Limited Reg. No. 954009

A CIP catalogue record for this book
is available from the British Library

Papers used by Random House UK Limited
are natural, recyclable products made from wood grown in
sustainable forests. The manufacturing processes conform to
the environmental regulations of the country of origin

ISBN 0 09 960121 4

Printed and bound in Great Britain by
Cox & Wyman Ltd, Reading, Berkshire

For Christopher

CONTENTS

III: THE SURVIVORS

IV: THE IPATIEV HOUSE

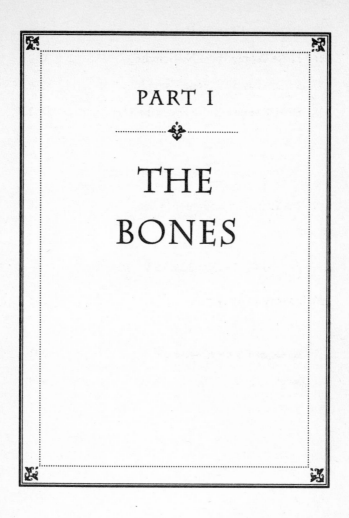

PART I

THE
BONES

CHAPTER 1

·········· ❖ ··········

DOWN
TWENTY-THREE
STEPS

At midnight, Yakov Yurovsky, the leader of the executioners, came up the stairs to awaken the family. In his pocket he had a Colt pistol with a cartridge clip containing seven bullets, and under his coat he carried a long-muzzled Mauser pistol with a wooden gun stock and a clip of ten bullets. A knock on the prisoners' door brought Dr. Eugene Botkin, the family physician, who had remained with the Romanovs for sixteen months of detention and imprisonment. Botkin was already awake; he had been writing what turned out to be a last letter to his own family.

Quietly, Yurovsky explained his intrusion. "Because of unrest in the town, it has become necessary to move the family downstairs," he said. "It would be dangerous to be in the upper rooms if there was shooting in the streets." Botkin understood; an anti-Bolshevik White Army bolstered by thousands of Czech former prisoners of war was approaching the Siberian town of Ekaterinburg, where the family had been held for seventy-eight days. Already, the captives had heard the rumble of artillery in the distance and the sound of revolver shots fired nearby on recent nights. Yurovsky asked that the family dress as soon as possible. Botkin went to awaken them.

They took forty minutes. Nicholas, fifty, the former emperor, and his thirteen-year-old son, Alexis, the former tsarevich and heir to the throne, dressed in simple military shirts, trousers, boots, and forage caps. Alexandra, forty-six, the former empress, and her daughters, Olga, twenty-two, Tatiana, twenty-one, Marie, nineteen, and Anastasia, seventeen, put on dresses without hats or outer wraps. Yurovsky met them outside their door and led them down the staircase into an inner courtyard. Nicholas followed, carrying his son, who could not walk. Alexis, crippled by hemophilia, was a thin, muscular adolescent weighing eighty pounds, but the tsar managed without stumbling. A man of medium height, Nicholas had a powerful body, full chest, and strong arms. The empress, taller than her husband, came next, walking with difficulty because of the sciatica which had kept her lying on a palace chaise longue for many years and in bed or a wheelchair during their imprisonment. Behind came their daughters, two of them carrying small pillows. The youngest and smallest daughter, Anastasia, held her pet King Charles spaniel, Jemmy. After the daughters came Dr. Botkin and three others who had remained to share the family's imprisonment: Trupp, Nicholas's valet; Demidova, Alexandra's maid; and Kharitonov, the cook. Demidova also clutched a pillow; inside, sewed deep into the feathers, was a box containing a collection of jewels; Demidova was charged with never letting it out of her sight.

Yurovsky detected no signs of hesitation or suspicion; "there were no tears, no sobs, no questions," he said later. From the bottom of the stairs, he led them across the courtyard to a small, semibasement room at the corner of the house. It was only eleven by thirteen feet and had a single window, barred by a heavy iron grille on the outer wall. All the furniture had been removed. Here, Yurovsky asked them to wait. Alexandra, seeing the room empty, immediately said, "What? No chairs? May we not sit?" Yurovsky, obliging, went out to order two chairs. One of his squad, dispatched on this mission, said to another, "The heir needs a chair...evidently he wants to die in a chair."

Two chairs were brought. Alexandra took one; Nicholas put Alexis in the other. The daughters placed one pillow behind their mother's back and a second behind their brother's. Yurovsky then began giving directions—"Please, you stand here, and you here...that's it, in a row"—spreading them out across the back wall. He explained that he needed a photograph because people in Moscow were worried that they had escaped. When he was finished, the eleven prisoners were arranged in two rows: Nicholas stood by his son's chair in the middle of the front row, Alexandra sat in her chair near the wall, her daughters were arranged behind her, the others stood behind the tsar and the tsarevich.

Satisfied by this arrangement, Yurovsky then called in not a photographer with a tripod camera and a black cloth but eleven other men armed with revolvers. Five, like Yurovsky, were Russians; six were Latvians. Earlier, two Latvians had refused to shoot the young women and Yurovsky had replaced them with two others.

As these men crowded through the double doors behind him, Yurovsky stood in front of Nicholas, his right hand in his trouser pocket, his left holding a small piece of paper from which he began to read: "In view of the fact that your relatives are continuing their attack on Soviet Russia, the Ural Executive Committee has decided to execute you." Nicholas turned quickly to look at his family, then turned back to face Yurovsky and said, "What? What?" Yurovsky quickly repeated what he had said, then jerked the Colt out of his pocket and shot the tsar, point-blank.

At this, the entire squad began to fire. Each had been told beforehand whom he was to shoot and ordered to aim for the heart to avoid excessive quantities of blood and finish more quickly. Twelve men were now firing pistols, some over the shoulders of those in front, so close that many of the executioners suffered gunpowder burns and were partially deafened. The empress and her daughter Olga each tried to make the sign of the cross but did not have time. Alexandra died immediately, sitting in her chair. Olga was killed by a single bullet through her head. Botkin, Trupp, and Kharitonov also died quickly.

Alexis, the three younger sisters, and Demidova remained alive. Bullets fired at the daughters' chests seemed to bounce off, ricocheting around the room like hail. Mystified, then terrified and almost hysterical, the executioners continued firing. Barely visible through the smoke, Marie and Anastasia pressed against the wall, squatting, covering their heads with their arms until the bullets cut them down. Alexis, lying on the floor, moved his arm to shield himself, then tried to clutch his father's shirt. One of the executioners kicked the tsarevich in the head with his heavy boot. Alexis moaned. Yurovsky stepped up and fired two shots from his Mauser directly into the boy's ear.

Demidova survived the first fusillade. Rather than reload, the executioners took rifles from the next room and pursued her with bayonets. Screaming, running back and forth along the wall, she tried to fend them off with her armored pillow. The cushion fell, and she grabbed a bayonet with both hands, trying to hold it away from her chest. It was dull and at first would not penetrate. When she collapsed, the enraged murderers pierced her body more than thirty times.

The room, filled with smoke and the stench of gunpowder, became quiet. Blood was everywhere, in rivers and pools. Yurovsky, in a hurry, began turning the bodies over, checking their pulses. The truck, now waiting at the front door of the Ipatiev House, had to be well out of town before the arrival in a few hours of the July Siberian dawn. Sheets, collected from the beds of the four grand duchesses, were brought to carry the bodies and prevent blood dripping on the floors and in the courtyard. Nicholas's body went first. Then, suddenly, as one of the daughters was being laid on a sheet, she cried out. With bayonets and rifle butts, the entire band turned on her. In a moment, she was still.

When the family lay in the back of the truck, covered by a tarpaulin, someone discovered Anastasia's small dog, its head crushed by a rifle butt. This little body was tossed into the truck.

The "whole procedure," as Yurovsky later described it, including feeling the pulses and loading the truck, had taken twenty minutes.

Two days before the executions, Yurovsky and one of the other executioners, Peter Ermakov, a local Bolshevik leader, had gone into the forest looking for a place to bury the bodies. About twelve miles north of Ekaterinburg, in an area of swamps, peat bogs, and abandoned mine shafts, there was a place known as the Four Brothers because four towering pine trees had once overlooked the site. Around the stumps of these old trees, and among the birches and pines which grew there now, were empty pits, some shallow, some deeper, from which coal and peat had once been dug. Abandoned, some had filled with rainwater and become small ponds. The largest of these, named after a peasant prospector, was called Ganin's Pit. Nearby, other smaller, deeper mines were nameless. It was to this place that Yurovsky brought the bodies.

Already deep in the forest, jouncing through the darkness along a muddy, rutted road, Yurovsky's truck suddenly encountered a party of twenty-five men on horseback and in peasant carts. Most were drunk. They were factory workers from the town, some of them members of the new Ural Regional Soviet, tipped off by their comrade, Ermakov, that the Imperial family would be coming down that road. But they had expected to see the family alive; Ermakov had promised his friends the four grand duchesses as well as the thrill of killing the tsar. "Why didn't you bring them alive?" they shouted.

Yurovsky, in control, calmed the angry men and ordered them to shift the bodies from the truck into the carts. In the process, the workers began stealing from the victims' clothing and pockets. Yurovsky halted this by threatening an immediate firing squad. Not all of the bodies would fit into the small carts, and some remained on the truck; in tandem, this macabre procession continued into the forest.

In the darkness, surrounded by dense pines and birches, the party could not find the Four Brothers. Yurovsky sent horsemen up and down the road looking for the turnoff to the site. When the sun began to rise and the forest grew light, they located it. The road became only a track, and soon the truck had wedged itself between two trees and could go no farther. More bodies were heaped into the carts. At six in the morning, the procession reached the Four Brothers. Ganin's Pit, nine feet deep, had a foot of water in the bottom. Not far away, in another, narrower mine shaft, cut thirty feet into the earth, the water was deeper.

Yurovsky ordered the corpses laid out on the grass and undressed. Two fires were built. As the men were stripping one of the daughters, they found her corset torn by bullets. From the ripped slash gleamed rows of diamonds sewed tightly together—the "armor" which initially had shielded her from bullets and astonished her executioners. Sight of the jewels excited the men; again, Yurovsky moved quickly and dismissed all but a few, sending them back down the road. The undressing continued. Eighteen pounds of diamonds were collected, mostly from the corsets worn by three of the grand duchesses. The empress was found to be wearing a belt of pearls made up of several necklaces sewed into linen. Each of her daughters wore around her neck an amulet bearing Rasputin's picture and a prayer by the peasant "holy man." These jewels, amulets, and anything else of value were placed in sacks, and everything else, including all clothing, was burned.

The naked bodies lay on the grass. All had been violently disfigured. At some point in the carnage, perhaps in maniacal rage, perhaps in a deliberate attempt to make the corpses unrecognizable, the faces had been crushed by blows from rifle butts. Nevertheless, as the six women—four of them young and, twelve hours earlier, beautiful—lay on the ground, their bodies were touched. "I felt the empress myself and she was warm," said one of the party later. Another said, "Now I can die in peace because I have squeezed the empress's ——." The last word in this sentence is crossed out.

Once the bodies were stripped, the jewels collected, and the clothing burned, Yurovsky was almost finished. He ordered the bodies thrown down the smaller, deeper mine shaft. Then, attempting to collapse the pit, he dropped in several hand grenades. By ten in the morning, his work was done. He returned to Ekaterinburg to report to the Ural Regional Soviet.

Eight days after the murders, Ekaterinburg fell to the Whites and a group of White officers rushed to the Ipatiev House. The building was mostly empty. Toothbrushes, pins, combs, hairbrushes, and smashed icons were scattered on the floors. Empty hangers hung in the closets. Alexandra's Bible still was there, heavily underlined, containing dried flowers and leaves pressed between its pages. Many religious books also remained, along with a copy of *War and Peace,* three volumes of Chekhov, a biography of Peter the Great, a volume of *Tales from Shakespeare,* and *Les Fables de la Fontaine.* In one bedroom, the officers found a smooth-edged board on which the tsarevich had eaten and played games in bed. Nearby was a handbook of instructions for playing the balalaika. In the dining room near the fireplace stood a wheelchair.

The room in the cellar seemed sinister. A few traces of dried blood still clung to the baseboards. The yellow floor, thoroughly mopped and scrubbed, bore scratches and dents from bullets and lunging bayonets. The walls were scarred by bullet holes; from the wall against which the family had been standing, large pieces of plaster had fallen away.

An immediate search for the family led nowhere. Not until six months later, in January 1919, did a thorough investigation begin when Admiral Alexander Kolchak, "Supreme Ruler" of the White Government in Siberia, assigned Nicholas Sokolov, a thirty-six-year-old professional legal investigator, to the task. As soon as the snow melted, Sokolov began working at the Four Brothers. The track through the forest still showed deep ruts from the carts and the truck. The earth around the pits had been trampled by horses' hooves. Cut branches and burned wood floated on the surface of Ganin's Pit and the narrow mine shaft. The walls of the deeper pit showed evidence of grenade explosions. There were traces of two bonfires, one at the edge of the narrow mine, the other in the middle of the forest road.

Sokolov ordered the water pumped out of Ganin's Pit and the nameless mine shaft and began to excavate. In Ganin's Pit he found nothing, but from the other he collected dozens of articles and fragments. In this grim work he was assisted by two of the tsarevich's tutors: Pierre Gilliard, whose subject had been French, and Sidney Gibbes, who had taught English. Both had remained in Ekaterinburg after the Imperial family was sent to the Ipatiev House. Among the evidence identified and cataloged by these heartbroken men was the tsar's belt buckle; a child's military belt buckle which the tsarevich had worn; a charred emerald cross which the Dowager Empress Marie had given to Empress Alexandra; a pearl earring from a pair always worn by Alexandra; the Ulm Cross, a jubilee badge adorned with sapphires and diamonds, presented to the empress by Her Majesty's Own Uhlan Guards; a metal pocket case in which Nicholas always carried his wife's portrait; three small icons carried by the grand duchesses; the empress's spectacle case; six sets of women's corsets; fragments of the military caps worn by Nicholas and his son; shoe buckles belonging to the grand duchesses; and Dr. Botkin's eyeglasses and upper plate with fourteen false teeth. There were also a few charred bones, partly destroyed by acid but still bearing the marks of an ax; revolver bullets; and a severed human finger, slender and manicured as Alexandra's had been.

Sokolov also collected an assortment of nails, tinfoil, copper coins, and a small lock, which puzzled him until they were shown to Gilliard. The tutor immediately identified them as part of the pocketful of odds and ends always carried by the tsarevich. Finally, at the bottom of the pit, mangled but unburned, the investigators found the decomposed corpse of Anastasia's spaniel, Jemmy.

But other than the finger and the charred bones in the pit, Sokolov found no human bodies or bones. He interrogated one of the executioners and numerous corroborating witnesses and established that eleven people had been killed at the Ipatiev House. He knew that the bodies had been brought to the Four Brothers. He learned that on the day following the murders, two more trucks carrying three barrels had gone down the Koptyaki road into the forest. He discovered that two of those barrels had been filled with gasoline and one with sulfuric acid. Accordingly, Sokolov concluded that on July 18, the day after the execution, Yurovsky had destroyed the bodies by chopping them up with axes, dousing them repeatedly with gasoline and sulfuric acid, and burning them to ash in bonfires near the mine shafts. These ashes and bones he declared to be the remains of the Imperial family, the site of the bonfires to be their grave.

Reverently, Nicholas Sokolov placed the physical results of his investigation—the charred bones, the finger, and the principal personal articles—inside a suitcase-sized box. In the summer of 1919, when the Red Army surged back into Ekaterinburg, Sokolov traveled across Siberia to the Pacific and went by boat to Europe. His box, later to become an object of mystery and contention, went with him.

When in 1924 he published his conclusion, skeptics argued that it was not possible to burn eleven corpses so completely in a bonfire. Nevertheless, Sokolov's story was buttressed by his simple, seemingly indisputable statement: there were no bodies.

For most of the twentieth century, this is what the world believed.

·············· ❧ ··············

CHAPTER 2

APPROVED
BY MOSCOW

From the beginning, the annihilation of the Romanovs—their execution and the disappearance of their bodies—had been approved by Moscow. As late as June 1918, the Bolshevik leadership had been uncertain what to do with the Imperial family. The Ural Soviet, in actual possession of the prisoners in Ekaterinburg, was vehemently in favor of execution. Leon Trotsky, the mercurial Red commissar for war, wanted a public trial of the former tsar in Moscow to be broadcast by radio throughout the country with himself as prosecutor. Lenin, always pragmatic, preferred to keep the family in hand as pawns in the game he was playing with Germany. In April, Soviet Russia had signed the Treaty of Brest Litovsk with Imperial Germany, achieving peace by handing over one third of European Russia and all of the western Ukraine to German occupation. Millions of Russians were dismayed by this decision, which they considered a betrayal. For a while, Lenin hoped that Nicholas could be persuaded to sign or at least to endorse the treaty, thereby partially legitimizing the document and diminishing the furor. Another complication was that the Empress Alexandra was a German princess and the Kaiser Wilhelm's first cousin. Now that Russia was out of the war, the new German ambassador in Moscow, Count Wilhelm Mirbach, had made clear his government's concern for the safety of Alexandra and her four daughters. Lenin had no wish to antagonize the Germans—particularly at this moment.

By early July, civil war and foreign intervention were threatening Bolshevism's grip on Russia. In addition to the Germans in the west and south, American marines and British soldiers had landed in the north, at Murmansk. In the eastern Ukraine, Generals Alekseyev, Kornilov, and Deniken had organized a White Volunteer Army. In Siberia, the Czech Legion of forty-five thousand men, former prisoners of war taken from the Austro-Hungarian Army, had taken Omsk and was advancing westward toward Ekaterinburg. When the Bolsheviks made peace, Trotsky had agreed that the stranded Czechs be permitted to leave Russia by way of the Pacific in order to return to Europe to fight for a Czech homeland. The Czechs were already in Siberia headed eastward in a string of trains when the German General Staff sternly objected to their passage and demanded that the Bolsheviks stop and disarm them. The Bolsheviks tried, but the Czechs fought back and, strengthened by anti-Bolshevik Russian officers and soldiers, began to prevail. It was the approach of this Czech-White army to Ekaterinburg that forced Lenin and his deputy Yakov Sverdlov (Trotsky had been called to the front) to change their plans for the former tsar and his family imprisoned in the Ipatiev House.

On July 6, the Bolsheviks suffered another blow. In Moscow, two Left Social Revolutionaries, passionately opposed to the Brest Litovsk Treaty, assassinated the German ambassador. Lenin and Sverdlov feared that German troops would enter the capital. In the midst of this confusion, talk of a show trial for Nicholas, of persuading him to sign a treaty, of using his family as bargaining chips, appeared senseless, irrelevant. The Romanovs themselves began to seem superfluous, almost an encumbrance. Sverdlov described this situation to his friend Filipp Goloschekin, a member of the Ural Regional Soviet, who happened to be staying that week in Sverdlov's house in Moscow.

On July 12, Goloschekin returned to Ekaterinburg and told his comrades of the Ural Soviet that the government had no further use for the Romanovs and was leaving to them the timing and manner of the family's disposition. The Ural Soviet immediately voted to execute the entire family. Yurovsky, the commandant at the Ipatiev House, was ordered to shoot all the prisoners and to destroy the evidence of what had happened.

In the days immediately following the executions, Moscow tightly controlled the release of all information about the event in Ekaterinburg. At nine o'clock on the night of July 17, the Kremlin received a coded telegram from the Ural Regional Soviet saying, "Tell Sverdlov that the whole family has suffered the same fate as the head. Officially the family will perish during the evacuation." Sverdlov, expecting this message, telegraphed in reply: "Today [July 18] I will report your decision to Presidium of Central Executive Committee. There is no doubt it will be approved. Notice about the execution must follow from the central authorities. Refrain from publication until its receipt." Sverdlov, whose title was Chairman of the Central Executive Committee, informed the Presidium and, unsurprisingly, obtained its approval.

The pretense that Moscow did not know until after the event was continued that evening, when Sverdlov arrived late at a meeting of the Soviet of People's Commissars. Lenin was presiding over discussion of a public health project. Sverdlov entered, took a chair behind Lenin, leaned forward, and whispered into his ear. Interrupting the commissar for people's health, Lenin said, "Comrade Sverdlov asks the floor to make an announcement."

"We have received information," Sverdlov announced in a calm, matter-of-fact voice, "that in Ekaterinburg, by decision of the Ural Regional Soviet, Nicholas has been shot. Alexandra Feodorovna and her children are in reliable hands. Nicholas wanted to escape. The Czechs were getting close. The Presidium of the Executive Committee has given its approval." When Sverdlov finished, the hall was silent. After a pause, Lenin said, "We shall now proceed to read the project, article by article."

The official announcement that Sverdlov drafted and gave to *Pravda* and *Izvestia* again omitted to mention that Nicholas's wife, son, and daughters had been killed along with the tsar. On July 20, papers appeared in Moscow and St. Petersburg declaring, EX-TSAR SHOT AT EKATERINBURG! DEATH OF NICHOLAS ROMANOV! That same day, the Ural Soviet drafted an announcement and asked Moscow's permission to publish it: "The ex-tsar and autocrat Nicholas Romanov has been shot along with his family.... The bodies have been buried." The Kremlin forbade release of this statement because it mentioned the death of the entire family. Only on July 22 were Ekaterinburg editors permitted to publish a Moscow-drafted version of what had happened in their city. On that day, newspaper broadsheets were plastered around the Siberian city declaring:

DECISION OF THE PRESIDIUM OF THE DIVISIONAL
COUNCIL OF DEPUTIES OF WORKMEN, PEASANTS,
AND RED GUARDS OF THE URALS:

In view of the fact that Czechoslovak bands are threatening the Red capital of the Urals, Ekaterinburg; that the crowned executioner may escape from the tribunal of the people (a White Guard plot to carry off the whole Imperial family has just been discovered), the Presidium of the Divisional Committee in pursuance of the will of the people has decided that the ex-tsar Nicholas Romanov, guilty before the people of innumerable bloody crimes, shall be shot.

The decision ... was carried into execution on the night of July 16–17. Romanov's family has been transferred from Ekaterinburg to a place of greater safety.

Eight days after the massacre, on July 25, the White and Czech armies entered Ekaterinburg.

In 1935, Leon Trotsky published his *Diary in Exile*. The former Bolshevik leader, who had been forced into exile by Stalin, described the link between Lenin and Sverdlov, who had authorized the Ekaterin-

burg massacre, and the Ural Soviet, which had determined the time
and method of execution:

> My next visit to Moscow [Trotsky had been at the front] took
> place after the fall of Ekaterinburg. Talking to Sverdlov, I asked in
> passing: "Oh, yes, and where is the tsar?"
> "It's all over," he answered. "He has been shot!"
> "And where is the family?"
> "And the family along with him."
> "All of them?" I asked, apparently with a touch of surprise.
> "All of them," replied Sverdlov. "What about it?" He was wait-
> ing to see my reaction. I made no reply.
> "And who made the decision?" I asked.
> "We decided it here. Ilych [Lenin] believed that we shouldn't
> leave the Whites a live banner to rally around, especially under
> the present difficult circumstances."
> I did not ask any further questions and considered the matter
> closed. Actually, the decision was not only expedient but neces-
> sary. The severity of this summary justice showed the world that
> we would continue to fight on mercilessly, stopping at nothing.
> The execution of the tsar's family was needed not only in order to
> frighten, horrify and dishearten the enemy, but also in order to
> shake up our own ranks to show that there was no turning back,
> that ahead lay either complete victory or complete ruin.... This
> Lenin sensed well.

The report that Nicholas was dead, killed by the decision of a
provincial soviet, and that his family was still alive spread quickly
around the world. In Moscow, the counselor of the German Embassy,
acting in place of the murdered ambassador, officially condemned
the execution of the tsar and expressed concern about the fate of the
German-born empress and her children. The Soviet government
began telling the lie to foreigners which it continued to tell for the
next eight years. On July 20, Karl Radek, head of the European Department of the Bolshevik Foreign Commissariat, informed the German counselor that it might be possible for the survivors to be

granted freedom "on humanitarian grounds." On July 23 and July 24, Radek's superior, Georgy Chicherin, head of the Foreign Commissariat, assured the German envoy that Alexandra and her children were safe. Through August and most of September, the German government continued to press and was continually reassured. On August 29, Radek proposed an exchange of the Imperial family for prisoners the Germans were holding; a few days later Chicherin again gave assurances that the empress and her children were safe; on September 10, Radek again discussed release of the prisoners; in the third week of September, Berlin was told that the Soviet authorities now were thinking of "moving the whole Imperial family to the Crimea."

The British government, meanwhile, was receiving more ominous information. On August 31, British Military Intelligence received a report, passed to the War Cabinet and to King George V at Windsor Castle, that the Empress Alexandra and all five of her children probably had been murdered at the same time as the tsar. The king accepted the authenticity of this report and sat down to write to his cousin, Alexandra's sister, Princess Victoria of Battenberg:

> My dear Victoria:
> May and I feel most deeply for you in the tragic end of your dear sister and her innocent children. But perhaps for her, who knows, it is better so; as after dear Nicky's death she could not have wished to live. And the beautiful girls may have been saved from worse than death at the hands of those horrible fiends. My heart goes out to you.

Despite the king's dispatch of condolences, the Foreign Office decided to investigate the matter further. Sir Charles Eliot, the British high commissioner for Siberia, was sent from Vladivostok to Ekaterinburg, and on October 15, his confidential report, addressed directly to Foreign Secretary Arthur Balfour, arrived in London. Eliot's dispatch seemed to offer hope. "On July 17," he wrote, "a train with the blinds down left Ekaterinburg for an unknown destination and it is believed that the surviving members of the Imperial family were in it.... It is the general opinion in Ekaterinburg that the empress, her son and daughters were not murdered."

Thereafter, the survivors—if there were survivors—seemed to disappear. Four years later, at an international conference in Genoa, a foreign journalist asked Chicherin whether the Bolshevik government had killed the tsar's four daughters. Chicherin replied, "The fate of the four young daughters is unknown to me. I have read in the press that they are now in America."

In 1924, the mystery appeared solved when the White investigator Nicholas Sokolov, then living in Paris, presented his findings and conclusions in a book published first in French and then in Russian. The book, *Judicial Enquiry into the Assassination of the Russian Imperial Family*, provided the world with an eyewitness description of eleven bodies lying in pools of blood on the floor of the Ipatiev House cellar. Sokolov also printed photographs of the bones, severed finger, jewelry, corset stays, false teeth, and other articles and objects he had gathered from the Four Brothers mine shaft. He gave not only a brutal description of the actual massacre but a detailed, seemingly plausible account of the destruction of the bodies by acid and fire: "The bodies were chopped in pieces with cutting instruments... the bodies were destroyed with sulfuric acid and by burning on the bonfires with the aid of gasoline.... The fatty matter in the corpses melted and spread over the ground where it became mixed with the earth." Evidence that the entire family was dead appeared overwhelming.

Sokolov's path had not been smooth. He had been forced to give up his work in Ekaterinburg when the Red Army approached and recaptured the city in July 1919. Traveling east on the Trans-Siberian Railroad, he took with him, along with his box of charred bones and other physical evidence, seven fat folios of written material. In the West, Sokolov continually added to these volumes, endlessly interviewing emigres who had escaped the revolution and who might know something—anything—about the death and disappearance of the Imperial family. He received little assistance. His appearance and manner were not in his favor. Small with dark, thinning hair, he possessed a cracked glass eye that gazed disconcertingly from an intensely nervous face. While talking, he swayed from side to side, continually rubbing his hands or tugging at his stringy mustache. But his appearance and tics had nothing to do with the rebuff he received from the most important of all Russian emigres: Nicholas's mother, the Dowager Empress Marie Feodorovna. Although Marie had made a financial contribution to Sokolov's work when he was in Siberia, once she learned that he believed the entire family was dead, she refused to see him or to receive his dossier or box of relics. Until the day of her death in October 1928, Marie insisted that her son and his family remained alive.

Obsessed, Sokolov continued interviewing and writing. For a while, he was supported by Prince Nicholas Orlov, who moved the investigator and his papers from the Hotel du Bon La Fontaine in Paris to an apartment in Fontainebleau. Here, Sokolov finally completed his book. A few months after its publication, he suffered a heart attack and died, still only forty-two. Sokolov's reward was posthumous: for six and a half decades, until 1989, his work was the accepted historical explanation of how the Russian Imperial family had died and what had happened to their bodies.

Publication and worldwide acceptance of Sokolov's book forced the Soviet government to change its story about the fate of the empress and her children. By 1926, after eight years of denying any knowledge as to their whereabouts, Moscow's credibility on the subject had been unraveled by the details and photographs in Sokolov's book. In addition, times had changed: German concern for a former German princess no longer existed; Lenin was dead; Stalin, his successor, possessed an even greater appreciation of the tonic nature of ruthlessness. Accordingly, a Soviet version of Sokolov's book, *The Last Days of Tsardom*, was authorized. Written by Pavel M. Bykov, a new chairman of the Ural Soviet, and largely plagiarized from Sokolov's work, it admitted that Alexandra, with her son and daughters, had been murdered along with Nicholas.

Now Reds and Whites agreed that the entire Imperial family was dead. But to Sokolov's description of the destruction of the bodies, Bykov added what seemed a minor editorial variation:

Much has been said about the absence of corpses. But...the remains of the corpses, after being burned, were taken quite far away from the mines and buried in a swampy place, in an area where the volunteers and investigators did not excavate. There the corpses remained and by now have rotted.

In a single sentence, Bykov had offered five fresh clues: There were *remains which had survived the fires;* these *remains had been buried;* they had been buried "*quite far away from the mines*"; "*in a swampy place*"; "*in an area where the volunteers and investigators did not excavate.*" In other words, something had been hidden, but it was nowhere near the Four Brothers site where Sokolov had searched.

Bolshevism's grip on Russia intensified, and the revolution appeared permanent. Famous cities were renamed after its heroes: St. Petersburg became Leningrad, Tsaritsyn became Stalingrad, Ekaterinburg became Sverdlovsk. Lesser men sought recognition of their revolutionary heroism in recording their personal participation in the massacre in the cellar. In 1920, Yakov Yurovsky gave the Soviet historian Michael Pokrovsky a detailed account of what he had done in Ekaterinburg in July 1918 "so history would know." In 1927, he presented his two revolvers, the Colt and the Mauser, to the Museum of the Revolution on Red Square. Peter Ermakov, the local Ural commissar, sometimes challenged Yurovsky for "the honor of having executed the last tsar" and gave his revolver, also a Mauser, to the Sverdlovsk Museum of the Revolution. In the early 1930s, near Sverdlovsk, Ermakov liked to appear before groups of boys gathered around campfires on summer nights. His enthusiasm fueled by a bottle of vodka, he would describe how he had killed the tsar. "I was twelve or thirteen," recalled one of these listeners, a member of the Chelyabinsk Tractor Pioneer Camp in 1933. "He was presented to us as a hero. He was given flowers. I watched him with envy. He ended his lecture by saying, 'I personally shot the tsar.' "

Sometimes, Ermakov modified his story. In 1935, the journalist Richard Halliburton visited Ermakov, supposedly dying of throat cancer, in his Sverdlovsk apartment: "On a low, crude Russian bed...piled with red cotton quilts...a huge...fat man of fifty three [was] turning restlessly in his feverish efforts to breathe.... His mouth hung open and from one corner there was a trickle of blood.... Two bloodshot and delirious black eyes gleamed at me." During a three-hour conversation, Ermakov admitted to Halliburton that it was Yurovsky who had killed Nicholas. His own victim, he said, was Alexandra: "I fired my Mauser at the tsarina—only six feet away—couldn't miss. Got her in the mouth. In two seconds she was dead."

Ermakov's account of the destruction of the bodies buttressed Sokolov's assumptions: "We built a funeral pyre of cut logs big enough to hold the bodies, two layers deep. We poured five tins of gasoline over the corpses and two buckets of sulfuric acid and set the logs afire.... I stood by to see that not one fingernail or fragment of bone remained unconsumed.... We had to keep the fire burning a long time to burn up the skulls." Ultimately, Ermakov said, "we didn't leave the smallest pinch of ash on the ground.... I put the tins of ashes in the wagon again and ordered the driver to take me back toward the high road.... I pitched the ashes into the air—and the wind caught them like dust and carried them out across the woods and fields." Back in New York, Halliburton published his interview as Ermakov's deathbed confession; in Sverdlovsk, however, Ermakov arose from his red quilts and lived another seventeen years.

In 1976, forty-one years after Halliburton's book appeared, two journalists working for BBC Television asked new questions about the disappearance of the Romanovs. In their book *The File on the Tsar,* Anthony Summers and Tom Mangold challenged Sokolov's conclusion that, in two days, even with a plentiful supply of gasoline and sulfuric acid, the executioners had been able to destroy "more than half a ton of flesh and bone" and, as Ermakov had claimed, "[pitch] the ashes into the air." Professor Francis Camps, a British Home Office forensic pathologist with thirty years' experience, explained to the authors how difficult it was to burn a human body. Fires char bodies, he said, "and the charring itself prevents the rest of the body being destroyed." Professional cremation, performed in closed, gas-fired ovens at temperatures up to two thousand degrees, can reduce a body to ashes, but this technique and equipment were not available in the Siberian forest. As for sulfuric acid, Dr. Edward Rich, an American expert from West Point, told the authors that with "eleven fully-grown or partly-grown bodies... merely pouring acid on them would not do too much damage other than disfigure the surface."

The most glaring forensic discrepancy in Sokolov's findings, both the Home Office and the West Point experts agreed, was the total absence of human teeth. "Teeth are the only components of the human body which are virtually indestructible," wrote Summers and Mangold. "If the eleven members of the Romanov household were really taken to the mine, there are about 350 missing teeth." The West Point expert told them that he had once left several teeth completely immersed in a beaker of sulfuric acid, not for two days but for three weeks. They emerged as teeth.*

During the Second World War, Sverdlovsk grew from a town to a large city. As the German Army rolled eastward across Russia and the Ukraine, whole factories and thousands of workers were moved be-

---

*Although *The File on the Tsar* attracted wide attention, it also drew strong criticism onto itself and its authors. In part, this was because of its style, which breathlessly announced the discovery of "new evidence... deliberately suppressed at the time... [which] has lain hidden for nearly sixty years." The villain in this thesis was Sokolov, who, the authors charged, "meticulously included all evidence that supported his premise that the entire family had been massacred at the Ipatiev House, but omitted evidence that hinted or stated categorically that something else had happened." This "something else" was that the empress and her daughters had been taken to Perm, been imprisoned there from July to November, and then disappeared. Authority for this was a woman in Perm who had said, "In the poor candle light I could make out the former Empress Alexandra Feodorovna and her four daughters.... They slept on pallets on the floor without sheets or bedding. The weak light of a tallow candle was the only illumination." Sokolov had read this statement, along with reports of numerous other Romanov "sightings," during his investigation. He did not include it in his

hind the Urals. By the end of the war, Sverdlovsk produced tanks and battlefield Katyusha rockets. After the war, once the Soviet Union acquired the knowledge to build an atomic bomb, secret new towns, ringed by barbed wire and watchtowers, mushroomed near Sverdlovsk and Chelyabinsk to the south. Both of these cities and the entire region were declared off-limits to foreigners, and a generation grew up in the Urals without ever meeting anyone from another country. It was to probe the secrets of Sverdlovsk and Chelyabinsk that CIA pilot Gary Powers flew his U-2 spy plane over these cities in 1960.

During these years, the Ipatiev House became a museum of the revolution, an antireligious museum, the home of the Council of Atheists Society, the Regional Party Archive, and the Rector's Office of the Ural-Siberian Communist University. Pictures of Bolshevik leaders lined the walls; if they had been natives of the Urals, their hats, coats, and medals were displayed in glass cases. Posters and diagrams proclaimed the glories of Communism, showing how many more tractors, airplanes, tons of steel, and suits of underwear were made under Stalin than under the tsar. An upstairs room was devoted to the Romanovs. There were selections from Nicholas's diary, pages of Alexis's diary, and the front page of an Ekaterinburg newspaper with these headlines: EXECUTION OF NICHOLAS, THE BLOODY CROWNED MURDERER—SHOT WITHOUT BOURGEOIS FORMALITIES BUT IN AC-

---

conclusions because he believed it to be false. But he did keep it in his papers. Summers and Mangold found it, not hidden or suppressed, in the Houghton Library at Harvard.

When the book appeared, Secretary of State Henry Kissinger was asked, "What about the Romanov rescue and those sensational documents?" Inimitably, the secretary replied, "That whole story is a lot of crap." Professor Richard Pipes of Harvard, reviewing the book in *The New York Times*, was so indignant at Summers and Mangold's claim to have discovered fresh evidence and so scornful of a claim of identification in Perm by "the weak light of a tallow candle," that he applied Kissinger's statement to the book as a whole.

Nevertheless, the two authors did perform a service by asking questions of the Home Office's Professor Camps and West Point's Dr. Rich. One did not have to think Sokolov dishonest or believe in the woman in Perm to wonder what had happened to the bones and teeth, which are difficult to destroy with acid or fire.

CORDANCE WITH OUR NEW DEMOCRATIC PRINCIPLES. The cellar room
was not part of the museum; piled to the ceiling with old packing
cases, it became a storeroom.

Visitors to the Ipatiev House, perforce Soviet citizens, stared at the
pictures, posters, and diaries, and then shuffled out into the Square of
the People's Revenge. They displayed no particular sympathy for the
Romanovs; the Imperial family was a part of history, condemned, its
diaries placed in glass cases, no longer relevant. But the Party and the
KGB never forgot. In 1977, KGB chairman Yuri Andropov convinced
aging President Leonid Brezhnev that the Ipatiev House had become
a site of pilgrimage for covert monarchists. An order flashed from the
Kremlin to the first secretary of the Sverdlovsk Region, a native
Siberian named Boris Yeltsin. Yeltsin was commanded to destroy the
Ipatiev House within three days. On the night of July 27, 1977, a giant
ball wrecker accompanied by bulldozers arrived in front of the house.
By morning, the building, reduced to bricks and stones, had been carried off to the city dump. Subsequently, although Brezhnev and Andropov gave the orders, Yeltsin was blamed for carrying them out. In
his autobiography, *Against the Grain,* he accepted his share of responsibility: "I can well imagine that sooner or later we will be ashamed of
this piece of barbarism."

.... ❖ ....

CHAPTER 3

LET ME FIND
NOTHING

"I had never imagined that I would find the remains of the Romanovs. I was not planning to get involved with this whole thing in any way. All of it somehow happened by itself."

Alexander Avdonin was speaking truthfully and, at the same time, telling only part of the truth. It is true that fifty years ago, when he set out on the journey that would lead to his remarkable historical discovery, he did not know where this journey would end. But the finding of nine skeletons in a shallow grave four and a half miles from the Four Brothers mine shaft did not happen by itself. It was a purposeful enterprise, carried out over many years, successful in spite of towering obstacles. It was a team effort, but the team was small, and Alexander Avdonin was its leader and motive force.

Avdonin, now sixty-four, is an intense, silver-haired man of average height, with light blue eyes which gaze out through thick, steel-framed glasses. His tanned skin and sturdy, resilient body are not surprising: he was a geologist—he is now retired—and most of his life has been spent outdoors, tramping the meadowlands and forests near his native city. He was born and grew up in Ekaterinburg, then called Sverdlovsk. As an adolescent in school, he was drawn to the natural sciences—geology and biology—and also to the history and folklore of this rolling country east of the Urals. There were dark strands woven into this history: rumors that the floor of the forest was filled with the bodies of people shot by the Cheka; legends about the Romanovs; tales about the execution, about Sokolov, about pretenders reappearing. As a boy, Avdonin saw Ermakov walking about the town. Curious, young Avdonin went to the Ipatiev House, visited other museums, and read what he could about the Romanovs. "Whenever I heard anything, I would somehow accumulate it, just for my own knowledge, not for any other purpose. But as I collected information and documents, material evidence and other historical facts, my thoughts began to change. Our Soviet history was so restricted and boring that I began to think of restoring unknown spots in the history of our region, not for use at that time, but for the future."

Because the subject was forbidden, most of what Avdonin learned came by word of mouth. He spoke to a niece of one of the guards at the Ipatiev House, to the wife of a member of the Ural Soviet who had voted to shoot the Romanovs, to the son of one of the executioners, and to a reporter for the newspaper *The Urals Worker* who, as a teenager, had participated in Sokolov's investigations. In 1919, this man, Gennady Lissine, had been one of twenty children and adolescents whom Sokolov gathered and brought to the woods at the Four Brothers. He lined them up six feet apart and sent them walking in a row through the woods, picking up everything they found. Near Ganin's Pit, they found a button, the remains of a small scarf, and another rag. More important to Sokolov, they found nothing anywhere else; for this reason the investigator concentrated his work near Ganin's Pit and the Open Shaft. In 1919, Lissine was fifteen; in 1964, when he was sixty, he took Avdonin to the Four Brothers and told him what he remembered about Sokolov and his work. Neither man had ever seen Sokolov's book, which was banned. Avdonin read Bykov's book, which said that there had been remains that had been burned, but not completely burned, and that had been taken some distance from the Four Brothers and buried in "a swampy place."

Over time, Alexander Avdonin became known in Sverdlovsk for his particular interest and knowledge, but his work was stymied. "It was not simple to gather information in the sixties and seventies," Avdonin said, looking back from the vantage of the mid-1990s. "There were no tape recorders, it was all word of mouth. And people were afraid to talk."

Then, out of the blue, Avdonin found a powerful ally. Geli Ryabov was an important man in Moscow, a famous filmmaker and writer of detective thrillers. One of his films, a well-known ten-part series, *The Birth of the Revolution,* was about the MVD, the ordinary Soviet police, or militia, who handle nonpolitical crime (as opposed to the more sinister KGB, the Office of State Security, responsible for dealing with political dissent). In 1976, Ryabov came to Sverdlovsk to show his film. Out of "pure human curiosity," he went to the Ipatiev House, then closed to visitors (and only a year away from destruction). He persuaded the police to let him in. He went down to the cellar room. When he came out, Ryabov remembered, "I decided that I must get involved with this story. I felt a moral obligation, a mission, that will stay with me until I die, to write about all that happened to those people."

Ryabov needed somewhere to start. He asked the local MVD chief whether anyone in the city knew anything about the Romanovs. He was told, "If anyone, Avdonin." A year later, the two men were introduced. Avdonin's first reaction was dismissive (he says "cautious"). He told Ryabov that it would be impossible to find anything; looking would be a waste of time; houses and a factory had been built over the places where everything had happened. In time, Avdonin—whose first reaction to newcomers remains a strained politeness—began to mellow. He said he found Ryabov "a very intelligent and interesting person. I liked him."

They talked at length about their motives: why should they look for the remains? "We both had only honorable goals," Avdonin recalled. "We wanted to do this in order to restore one of the pages of our history. In principle, the question of the tsar's remains should have been handled by the government. But the government had just knocked down the Ipatiev House. We thought it was possible that they would liquidate the remains as well. We didn't know where they were, but we thought that if we didn't find them, they could easily be destroyed. We decided that we *had* to look for them."

There was another consideration to be discussed. "This is very dangerous," Avdonin told Ryabov. "If anyone finds out about this, if it reaches 'the organs' [the KGB], this will end up being very lamentable for me. I have a family and two sons. Ryabov told me that he worked for Sholokhov, the minister of internal affairs, and so, what do I have to worry about? 'I will always cover for you,' he said. So I said, 'Under those conditions, let's start. You supply me with materials from the archives and I will search for the spot.' "

Ryabov returned to Moscow and told Sholokhov that in order to continue writing his history of the Soviet militia, he needed greater access to secret archives for books, memoirs, and documents. Sholokhov wrote a letter of permission and "thereafter"—Ryabov smiled—"everything I needed was given to me." One of the books acquired was Sokolov's, which Ryabov brought to Sverdlovsk. Avdonin took Ryabov to the Four Brothers mine shafts, which, according to Avdonin, made a tremendous impression on the filmmaker. Together, the two men found more objects—buttons, a coin, wires, glass, a bullet—which Avdonin gave to Ryabov. "We treated Ryabov with great respect, as an older person, a well-educated person, a writer," Avdonin remembers.

They went back and forth over the Sokolov and Bykov accounts. Bykov said that there had been remains and that they had been taken quite far from the Four Brothers site. Where had they been taken? Curiously, Nicholas Sokolov, whose book had firmly denied the existence of any remains, provided a clue. In it, there was a picture, taken during his 1919 investigation, of a simple platform or bridge made of fresh logs and railway ties laid over a muddy spot in the Koptyaki road. In the photograph, Sokolov himself is standing beside the bridge. His explanation for its existence was that on the night of July 18, two days after the executions, a truck left Ekaterinburg and went down the Koptyaki road. At 4:30 A.M. (by now it was July 19), this truck got stuck in the mud. The railroad operator at the small workstation where the road crossed the tracks said that men came to him, told him their truck was stuck, and asked for railroad ties to make a bridge across the mud. They made the bridge and the truck left; by 9:00 A.M., it was back in its garage in Ekaterinburg.

Reading Sokolov, Avdonin and Ryabov decided that the investigator had overlooked something important: "From the woods where the truck got stuck, back to the garage, it was half an hour's drive," Avdonin reasoned. "If the truck was stuck and all they had to do was push it out, that is not so complicated—this could have been done by the soldiers in half an hour. So what was it doing there? Something must have been going on there. What was happening in that place for nearly five hours?" Although Sokolov had had his picture taken standing on the bridge, the investigator had never asked himself this question. Therefore, Avdonin and Ryabov decided, it was up to them to look for the spot where a bridge of railroad ties had been placed across the Koptyaki road.

Because Ryabov had to return to Moscow, Avdonin began the search with the help of a friend, a fellow geologist named Michael Kachurov. "We were looking for the bridge," Avdonin said. "There were four low areas in that part of the Koptyaki road near the railway where the mud might have been deep in July 1918, and where they might have had to build a bridge. But, of course, in 1978, when we were looking, the bridge was no longer there. Fifty years had passed since Sokolov took his picture, cars had driven over it, dirt had been added to it, and, with time, it sank into the ground and ceased to exist. Grass grew over it, then the road itself ceased to exist. And then one day, we came to a ravine and Kachurov climbed a tall tree and from his perch called down, 'Sasha, I see the old road and two low places where the bodies might have been buried.'

"We constructed a very simple instrument made of a sharpened steel water pipe to take core samples, a contraption that resembled a large corkscrew. We walked along the path of the old road, and, at intervals in low places, we pounded and screwed this instrument into the ground. If there was nothing there, it went all the way in. If there was a stone in its way, I would move it a little to one side and it would go in right past the stone." When Kachurov made his sighting in the area of the Porosyonk [Pigs'] Meadow, Avdonin began drilling his corkscrew at closer intervals. He recounted, "We hit something soft like wood at a depth of forty centimeters [sixteen inches]. We moved here and there, drilling all around, and discovered an area approximately two meters by three meters [six and a half feet by ten feet] where there was evidence of wood beneath the surface. That is when we wrote to Ryabov that we had found the place."

Geli Ryabov, meanwhile, had made another momentous discovery. With the help of a Urals friend of Avdonin, he had located the eldest son of Yakov Yurovsky, the chief executioner of the Imperial family. In 1978, Alexander Yurovsky, a retired vice admiral in the Soviet Navy, lived in Leningrad. When Ryabov went to see him, the younger Yurovsky did something extraordinary: he gave the filmmaker a copy of his father's report to the Soviet government on the execution of the Romanovs and the disposition of their bodies. The original of this report lay in the secret files of the Central Archive of the October Revolution in Moscow; a copy had gone to the Soviet historian Michael Pokrovsky, who had never been permitted to publish a word. Alexander Yurovsky's reason for giving his own, handwritten copy of this document to Ryabov was that he wanted to repent for "the most horrible page" in his father's life.

Yurovsky's report filled in gaps and corrected errors made by Sokolov and Bykov. This is a synopsis of the account, hidden for sixty years, that Ryabov and Avdonin read in 1978–79:

On the morning of July 17, 1918, after killing the Romanovs and dumping their bodies down the Four Brothers mine shaft, Yurovsky returned to Ekaterinburg to make his report. To his horror, he found the city buzzing with stories describing where the bodies of the tsar's family had been hidden; Ermakov's men, obviously, had been unable to hold their tongues. A new burial site was needed quickly; the White Army was close. Ignoring Ermakov, Yurovsky asked for help from other local officials. He was told that there were very deep mines along the Moscow highway twenty miles away. He went to investigate. His car broke down, and he had to finish the trip on foot, but eventually he found three deep mines filled with water. He decided to bring the bodies there, attach stones to them, and throw them in. If there was time, he would burn the bodies first, then bury whatever remained in the water after disfiguring everything beyond recognition with sulfuric acid.

When Yurovsky finally returned to Ekaterinburg—he started by walking, then commandeered a horse from an unlucky peasant—it was nearly 8:00 P.M. He began assembling the things he needed—more gasoline and sulfuric acid. He and his men did not set out until 12:30 A.M. on July 18. Returning to the Four Brothers, they lighted the original mine shaft with torches. One of Yurovsky's men climbed down and stood in the darkness, icy water up to his chest, surrounded by bodies. A rope was lowered. He tied it around the bodies, one by one, and sent them up.

Yurovsky thought for a while of burying some of the bodies in the earth right by the mine shaft and started digging a pit, but he gave it up when he realized how easily such a grave could be seen. By this time, most of the day had been lost. At 8:00 P.M. on the evening of July 18, the bodies set off in carts for the deep mines. Soon the carts began to break down. Yurovsky halted the procession and went back to town to find a truck. When the truck arrived, the bodies were transferred and the journey resumed. The truck had a hard time, bouncing and slithering through muddy ruts, several times getting stuck in holes filled with water.

"At about 4:30 on the morning of July 19," Yurovsky wrote,

the vehicle got permanently stuck. Since we weren't going to get as far as the deep mines, all we could do was either bury them or burn them. We wanted to burn Alexis and Alexandra Feodorovna, but by mistake instead of her we burned the lady-in-waiting [Demidova] and Alexis. We buried the remains right there under the fire, then shoveled clay on the remains, and made another bonfire on the grave, and then scattered the ashes and the embers in order to cover up completely any trace of digging. Meanwhile, a common grave was dug for the rest. At about seven in the morning, a pit six feet deep and eight feet square was ready. The bodies were put in the hole and the faces and all the bodies generally doused with sulfuric acid, both so they couldn't be recognized and to prevent any stink from them rotting. We scattered it with branches and lime, put boards on top, and drove over it several times—no traces of the hole remained. The secret was kept—the Whites did not find this burial site.

At the end of his report, Yurovsky added the precise location of the secret grave: "Koptyaki, 12 miles from Ekaterinburg to the northwest. The railroad tracks pass 6 miles between Koptyaki and the Upper Isetsk factory. From where the railroad tracks cross [the road] they are buried about 700 feet in the direction of the Isetsk factory."

This was exactly where Avdonin and Kachurov had bored into the old roadbed and found traces of wood beneath the surface.

Confident that they had located the site, Avdonin and Ryabov had to wait until the following spring before continuing their search for the remains. In late May 1979, Avdonin and his wife, Galina, and Ryabov and his wife, Margaret, came back to the area. Using Avdonin's homemade steel-pipe core sampler, they bored deeper into the ground, five feet. All the holes disclosed alluvial, loamy soil, pebbles, and layers of dark brown and greenish clay. Under two of the holes, something was different: the layers were all mixed up, and at the bottom there was a dirty, black, mucousy clay ("black as soot," Ryabov remembered), oily to the touch, with a foul, bituminous smell. They took these samples home for acid testing and found that the soil in these two holes was highly acidic. Yurovsky had written that he had poured acid on the bodies, and Avdonin knew that acid can remain in soil, particularly in clay, which acts as a sealant, for even longer than sixty years. He was certain they had found the grave.

They were impatient. Early on the morning of the following day, May 30, they dug into the site. There were six in the party: Ryabov and Avdonin, their wives, a geologist friend of Avdonin's named Vassiliev, and an army friend of Ryabov's named Pysotsky. (Kachurov was unavailable, and not long afterward, he drowned accidentally in a northern Siberian river.) Throughout the enterprise, Avdonin did his best to impose security. Before the excavation, he introduced no friends or colleagues to Ryabov. Ryabov never met Kachurov and only met Vassiliev the day of the excavation. "I did all of this because I was very much afraid of everything," Avdonin said. "It was a very frightening business. We were scared."

In May near Ekaterinburg, the sun rises near five in the morning. By six that morning, the party, carrying shovels, was in the forest. They were alone except for a few mushroom hunters, wandering about, calling to one another. As soon as Avdonin and his colleagues began to dig, they found the railroad ties, and directly underneath, they saw human bones. In one small area, only eleven square feet, they saw three skulls. All of them were frightened. "I admit that our interference in this pit was barbaric," Ryabov said. "It was horrible. But we did not have the time, we did not have the instruments, and, of course, we were controlled by fear . . . fear that we would be found out. Of course, when we found this, it was even more frightening!" Shaking his head, he said it again: "It was frightening! It was frightening!" Avdonin, also, was afraid: "All my life I had searched for this, or somehow was heading for this. And then, when we first started to lift up the planking, I thought to myself, 'Let me find nothing.' "

Nevertheless, they kept going. "We removed the three skulls," Avdonin said. "We knew that some kind of tests should be done—we didn't know what kind yet. We separated them and lifted them out. Then we closed up the grave, putting everything back the way it was, with the grass on top. We had to do it as quickly as possible; it was six when we started to dig and we were finished by nine or ten."

Back in town, the group was in a state of emotional shock. That evening, some of them went to church and asked the priest to say a *panikhida*, a special service of prayer for the Imperial family and for themselves. (Not wholly trusting the priest, they worked the names Nicholas, Alexandra, Alexis, Olga, Tatiana, Marie, and Anastasia into a much longer list, hoping the priest would assume these were their own aunts, uncles, and cousins.) The service did not greatly calm Avdonin, who, for two months afterward, felt ill.

In the days following, the skulls were cleaned with water and examined. They were gray and black; in areas, etched traces of sulfuric acid were evident. The central facial bones of all three skulls were missing. In the left temple of one of the skulls, there was a large, round hole, as if made by a bullet. The left lower jaw of another skull held an extensive bridge of gold teeth. Ryabov knew that Nicholas II had had bad teeth, and he assumed that this skull had belonged to the tsar. (Later, it turned out to be that of the servant Anna Demidova.) He suggested that one of the other skulls belonged to Alexis, and the third to one of the four daughters, Olga, Tatiana, Marie, or Anastasia.

Facing the question of what to do with the skulls, they decided to divide them up. Avdonin kept the skull presumed to be that of the tsar, and Ryabov remembers how this dialogue proceeded: "Avdonin said that, considering the fact that he, a resident of Ekaterinburg, was the organizer of this expedition, he had the right to keep the emperor's skull with him." Ryabov took the other two back to Moscow, hoping to use his connections with the Interior Ministry to carry out discreet, unofficial testing at the Forensic Service of the Ministry of Health. He was rebuffed. For a year, he kept the skulls in his apartment in Moscow, then, having failed to find any scientist or laboratory which would help him, he brought them back to Ekaterinburg. Avdonin had done nothing with the skull he had kept; it had spent the year hidden under his bed.

In the summer of 1980, Avdonin and Ryabov, frustrated and still afraid of the consequences of their discovery, decided to return the three skulls to the grave. They were placed in a wooden box with a copper icon and returned to the site. The men dug again into the grave. This time, they uncovered a new skull, which they briefly brought to the surface. This skull had teeth made of white metal; Ryabov assumed it must be that of Demidova, whose false teeth might well have been made of inexpensive steel. (Later, he learned that the skull belonged to the empress and that the "cheap, white metal" he had seen was platinum.)

Before returning the box and its three skulls to the earth, Avdonin and Ryabov again discussed at length what they should do with the information they had discovered. They could not tell anyone; it was not a time in Soviet history conducive to interest in—let alone sensational news about—the Romanovs. Three years before, the Ipatiev House had been bulldozed. "We swore an oath that we would never talk about this until circumstances in our country had changed," Avdonin said. "And, if these changes did not happen, we would pass along all of our materials and information to the next generation. We could only leave it to our heirs. Ryabov didn't have any children. That meant there were only my children. Therefore, we decided that this history would pass to the next generation through my oldest son."

In 1982, Leonid Brezhnev died, followed quickly to the grave by his successors Yuri Andropov and Konstantin Chernenko. In 1985, Mikhail Gorbachev became leader of the Soviet Union and gradually began the policies of *glasnost* (openness) and *perestroika* (reform). At the beginning of 1989, Geli Ryabov, believing that the time had come to reveal the historical secrets he and Avdonin were keeping, attempted to contact Gorbachev "to ask for his help on a government level so that all of this could be properly handled." Gorbachev did not reply, but fragments of the story leaked out to the editor of the liberal weekly *Moscow News.* The editor pursued Ryabov. On April 10, 1989, an astonishing interview appeared in that paper. The next day, every major Western newspaper carried the story that, ten years earlier, Soviet filmmaker Geli Ryabov had found the bones of the Imperial family in a swamp near Sverdlovsk.

Ryabov is a short, slender man with a narrow, deeply tanned face, dark brown eyes, white hair, and a white mustache. His manner is nervous; his fingers drum when someone else is talking. Unlike Avdonin, whose stare is hard and voice implacable, Ryabov frequently looks away, speaks softly, and never interrupts. Appearing on television, he told his audience, "I am a typical proletarian. My father was a commissar in the Red Army during the Civil War, and therefore his hands were steeped in blood. My mother was a simple peasant woman. I am now a believer and a monarchist." He said that he had unearthed three skulls and showed photographs of the skulls and of the excavation site. His effort to find them, Ryabov said, had taken three years. "Great efforts were made in 1918 to conceal the identity and location of the bodies," he continued, "because, even then, the moral dubiousness of the execution was obvious." Nevertheless, he said that he was convinced of the authenticity of his findings. "Even for me," Ryabov said, "it was not difficult to identify them." Despite Gorbachev and *glasnost,* he said he was not ready to share his discovery with others, and he did not reveal the exact location of the burial site. "I am prepared to show the remains that I found, as well as the grave itself, to any panel of experts," he told the *Moscow News,* "but only on condition that permission is given for a decent burial befitting human beings and Christians."

The announcement created an international furor. Ryabov was believed and disbelieved, praised and denounced. But one curious aspect of his revelation was that at no point in these interviews, or in a subsequent long article he wrote for *Rodina* (Motherland), did Ryabov mention the name of Alexander Avdonin.

"My reaction was horror," Avdonin said, remembering how he felt when he learned that Ryabov had broken his vow. "It is true that in 1989 change had arrived in our country. And I understood that Ryabov is a writer and couldn't pour out his heart in meaningless articles and letters. Before he gave his interview and published his story, I visited him. He told me that he was writing about this, and he showed it to me. I liked it; I told him it was good. But I also told him that he should hold on to his article for a while and not publish it just yet. We should wait and see which direction our politics would go."

When Ryabov decided to go ahead, did he ask Avdonin's permission? "No," said Avdonin, "and his announcement didn't even mention that other people were involved. To this day I still don't understand why he did that."

Ryabov's response was that Avdonin did not want to be mentioned because his wife was working as an English professor at an MVD academy in Ekaterinburg. "It still was dangerous for him," Ryabov explained. "He didn't want publicity. He thought it was still a bad time to release this information." Ryabov, therefore, in deciding to go ahead, resolved to take all of the risk—and all of the credit.

In one respect, Ryabov did follow advice Avdonin had given him long before. Ryabov's article in *Rodina,* appearing three months after his *Moscow News* interview, indicated the location of the burial site. However, as Avdonin had suggested, his description pinpointed a spot half a mile away from the actual site. One day after copies of this magazine appeared in Sverdlovsk, heavy machinery arrived in the forest, dug up the earth around the false site, and carried away all the soil. "KGB," according to Avdonin.

Avdonin and Ryabov no longer speak to each other. Employing his fame as a finder of the grave, Ryabov wrote to Queen Elizabeth II of England, a relative of the Romanovs, asking that she use her influence to ensure that they were buried in a Christian manner. The queen did not reply. In 1991, when Boris Yeltsin, Russia's new leader, authorized a scientific opening of the burial site, Avdonin met Ryabov for the last time and said, spontaneously, "Come! We are going to exhume them." Ryabov refused. "Maybe his conscience was bothering him," Avdonin says. Ryabov cannot be drawn into criticism of Avdonin. On the contrary, he says, "There can be no question of the priceless role of Alexander Nicholaevich Avdonin in this story. No one has doubts about that. He played a monumental role. He was the one who dug up the remains."

There it might rest. Except that, in the milky darkness of a Siberian summer night, Avdonin blurted out his true feelings: "betrayal, treachery—just like what happened with Ryabov."

CHAPTER 4

.... ✤ ....

A CHARACTER
FROM GOGOL

By the autumn of 1989, the physical disintegration of the Soviet empire was under way. On November 9, the Berlin Wall came down. A few weeks later, Václav Havel became president of Czechoslovakia. Within a year, Lech Walesa was president of Poland. Within two years, Communist governments had collapsed or been overthrown everywhere in Eastern Europe.

On June 12, 1991, the first nationwide election of a political leader in the thousand-year history of Russia took place. Boris Yeltsin, a native of Sverdlovsk, was elected president. When he was inaugurated in the Kremlin on July 10, Yeltsin stripped the ceremony of Communist symbolism. In place of the giant portrait of Lenin that for decades had loomed behind the speakers' platform, he stretched the white, blue, and red banner given to Russia by Peter the Great. The patriarch of the Orthodox Church blessed Yeltsin with the sign of the cross, saying, "By the will of God and the choice of the Russian people, you are bestowed with the highest office in Russia." Mikhail Gorbachev was present too, clinging to office as president of the Soviet

Union and general secretary of the Communist Party. One month later, Gorbachev survived in office only because Yeltsin climbed onto a tank in Moscow and faced down an attempted army-KGB coup. By December 1991, Gorbachev was gone. The Central Committee of the Communist Party was dissolved. Ukraine, Belarus, Kazakhstan, the Baltic states, and other former Soviet republics had proclaimed their independence. In relative peace, seventy-four years of Communist rule in Russia had come to an end.

During these years, turmoil and change affected every part of the Soviet Union, including Sverdlovsk. By 1990, the Communists had been expelled from the City Council. Soon after, the site of the Ipatiev House, now a vacant lot littered with a rubble of crushed bricks and stones, was turned over to the local Orthodox bishop. There was talk of erecting a chapel. The local Union for the Resurrection of Russia, a monarchist group, planted a wooden cross on the site. It was torn down by die-hard Communists. Eventually a six-foot metal cross, decorated with pictures of the tsar, the empress, and the tsarevich, was put in its place. Communists did not lose all their influence in the city once known as the "capital of the Red Urals." The name of the city was changed back to Ekaterinburg, but the name of the region remained Sverdlovsk. The city's main thoroughfare continued to be called Lenin Avenue, and, at a prominent intersection, there remained a statue of Yakov Sverdlov.*

After the new president's election, Ekaterinburg authorities acted quickly to carry out a request from Alexander Avdonin. The regional governor, Edvard Rossel, asked Yeltsin's permission to exhume the Romanov bones. Yeltsin nodded yes. A delegation of senior officials went to see Dr. Ludmilla Koryakova, the leading professor of archeology at the Ural State University, and asked her to help in excavating "an unknown grave from the Soviet period." They refused to be more

---

*The figure perched atop a huge rock and intended to be heroic depicts a small, bespectacled man fiercely angry, wearing a coat too large for him. He is striding into the future, his arm flung out, pointing the way. A pigeon sits on his head. Local monarchists have tried to have the statue removed; failing, they continually scribble graffiti across its base.

specific, but Koryakova guessed what was involved. She was reluctant, mostly on scientific grounds. "There was no time to prepare," she later told the London *Sunday Times.* "There were no tools, no instruments, none of the things you really need for a proper excavation." Nevertheless, under pressure from her superiors at the university, she agreed to help.

On July 11, 1991, the day after Boris Yeltsin's inauguration in Moscow, a convoy of military trucks set out from Ekaterinburg. The trucks carried "two of everything—just like Noah's Ark," Dr. Koryakova said: "two police colonels, two detectives carrying cameras and video equipment, two forensic experts, two epidemiologists, the town procurator and his secretary, and two policemen, each with submachine guns." And, of course, Alexander Avdonin.

Half an hour later, the convoy reached the forest site, a small clearing on the former Koptyaki road about two hundred yards from the Ekaterinburg-Perm railway line. When the exhumation party arrived, they found the site already under guard. A high, temporary fence had been erected, and because of a steady rain, a large tent was stretched over the grave. Inside the tent, powerful klieg lights illuminated the ground. The procurator made a speech about the "responsibility" of everyone present, and the detectives set up their cameras, which filmed, hour after hour, everything that happened. Then everyone took a spade and began to dig.

The pit was only three and a half to four feet deep; beneath that level a layer of rock had prevented a deeper hole. The searchers quickly found the box containing three skulls, which Avdonin and Ryabov had reburied eleven years before. It was intact and unchanged. Digging wider, they encountered more skulls, ribs, leg bones, arm bones, vertebrae. The skeletons lay in disarray, one on top of another, at all angles, as if the bodies had been dumped into the pit at random. The bones were various shades of gray and brown; some had a greenish tinge. The fact that they were not more grievously deteriorated was ascribed to the pit having been dug in clay, which prevented air reaching the bones. The skeleton at the bottom of the pit was the most thoroughly destroyed. Here the explanation seemed to lie in the broken pieces of large ceramic pots with screw-on lids believed to have contained sulfuric acid. Once the pots were placed in the hole and shattered by rifle fire, acid spread across the clay bottom of the pit, consuming the flesh and damaging the bones it encountered.

The pit revealed no traces of clothing; this was consistent with the accounts of both Sokolov and Yurovsky; both had written that all the victims' clothing had been burned before the bodies were thrown down the Four Brothers mine shaft. Fourteen bullets were collected from the grave. Some had been embedded in the bodies; some probably were a result of the firing at the pots of acid.

More terrible was the evidence of what had been inflicted on the human beings to whom these skeletons and bones had once belonged. Some of the victims had been shot while lying down, said Dr. Koryakova ("There are bullet wounds through the temples"), they had been bayoneted, their faces were smashed in by rifle butts, their jaws broken ("the facial parts of the skulls are destroyed"), many other bones were broken, and, finally, they had been "crushed as though a truck drove over them." In the course of her career, Dr. Koryakova has exhumed many prehistoric settlements in western Siberia and unearthed a large number of skeletons. "But never," she told the *Sunday Times*, "so many that were so badly damaged—so violated. I was ill."

The pit had one final, dramatic revelation, which became apparent only after three days of digging and preliminary assembling of the bones: these remains represented only nine skeletons, four male and five female. Two members of the Imperial party (which originally had consisted of two parents, five children, the doctor, and three retainers) were missing. Despite this mystery, on July 17 Governor Rossel announced to the press the discovery of bones which in "great probability" belonged to Tsar Nicholas II, his family and servants. Who was there and who was not, he said, would be left to further analysis by national and international experts.

Two weeks later, Dr. Vladislav Plaksin, the chief medical examiner of the Russian Ministry of Health, was asked to begin the task of validating the bones. Plaksin quickly dispatched his leading forensic anthropologist, Sergei Abramov, to Ekaterinburg. In Russia, it was a time of political crisis; the army and KGB moved just at this moment to overthrow Gorbachev. "Tanks were entering Moscow as we were leaving the city," Abramov recalled. In Ekaterinburg, he found the exhumed remains laid out in separate piles on the floor of the city police firing range. Over three months, he painstakingly identified and pieced together 700 bones and bits of bone. Much was still missing, and Abramov sent a team back to the grave site to sift and pan the dirt and mud. They found another 250 bones and fragments, which Abramov incorporated into the nine skeletons he was assembling. First, he labeled them by number: Body No. 1, Body No. 2, and so on. Thereafter, his task, using cameras, computers, photographs of the victims when they were alive, and space-age mathematics, was to discover whether this was the Imperial family and, if so, to determine which Romanovs were present and which, if any, were absent.

"We had no money, and for that reason any possibility of DNA testing was out of the question," Abramov said in the summer of 1994, looking back on this harrowing chapter of his life. "We decided to determine identity with our own methods. With a video camera, we recorded skulls, front and profile. And then, with the help of a computer program, we matched skull formations to photographs, calculated similarities and probabilities of likeness. Then, in order to compare the people from the grave site with a wider group of people in general, we also taped a control group of 150 other skulls. Unfortunately, the equipment we had at that time was very weak technically, and the program which compared domes—the tops of heads—went very slowly. So we were forced to settle for a control group of only sixty skulls."

"No one, ever in the world, used this system before," Abramov declared. "We invented it. *We!* Here in my department, sitting in the next room, is a brilliant mathematician. They brought him to me from the Institute for Space Studies. I told him what I needed. He said it could be done. And he did it! This method allowed us to calculate the likelihood that this group of skeletons was not unique; that somehow it could have been duplicated.

"The mathematical technique is called combinatorial mathematics. We took four factors: gender, age, race, and height. If we are dealing with a single individual, we prove nothing. With two, we can become a little more certain. With three, we are even more convinced... and so forth. And here we have nine. For each of the nine people, there are these four factors. Each of them adds mathematically to the common statistical kettle. Together, this combination makes an invincible case. How likely is it that these nine skeletons in a single grave could be duplicated in other circumstances? And then we add other evidence, other factors that we learned from superimposition—a wide face, narrow face, a prominent chin, a weak chin. When we added all this up, we realized that the possibility of coming across another group of skeletons with this same combination of factors was 3 multiplied by 10 to the minus 14th degree. This turns out to be 3 incidents in 100 trillion. One hundred trillion people have never lived on the earth.

"Further, when we first did our calculations, we did them using information from only seven of the people in the grave. We did not have the photographs of Kharitonov [the cook] and Trupp [the valet], so we left them out. If you add these two, the odds will be 10 to the minus 18th degree. If we also begin to measure nose lengths, shape of the head... then it will be to the 20th or 30th degree. We are talking astronomical figures, which go far beyond what is necessary. We know beyond doubt that these are the bones of the Romanovs."

But which Romanovs were in the grave? Eleven prisoners were in the cellar; the burial site gave up only nine bodies. Abramov explained how he answered this question. In the process of photo superimposition, he said, it is important that the skull be compared with as many photographs of a person as possible. Seeking a match from many angles, he used the camera and the computer to turn the skull to the angle from which each photograph was taken. He demonstrated: "Like this... and like this... like this... and so forth... frontal... profile... all angles. The more superimpositions we do, the more certain we can be of the result." Abramov and his team began with Nicholas because, he said bitterly, "some idiots already had said that Skull No. 1 belongs not to the woman Demidova but to the tsar." Abramov was not speaking of Ryabov and Avdonin; he was speaking of other Russian scientists who criticized him and his technique, saying that his method was faulty and his results invalid. "These are people," he said, "who try to judge not with knowledge but with authority. When I have to explain our technique to them, it is work for an idiot, time simply wasted. But, because we were attacked, we had to do it.

"So, to refute these idiots," Abramov continued, "we started by comparing two photographs of Nicholas, one frontal, one profile, with Skull No. 1, Demidova's skull. As we expected, there was no match. Then we compared photographs of Nicholas to the other skulls from the grave. With Skull No. 8, we tried three positions; all three were negative. With Skull No. 9, we tried two positions, both were negative. Skull No. 3: three positions, three negative. Skull No. 5: five positions, five negative. Skull No. 6: four positions, four negative. Finally, we compared the photographs to Skull No. 4. We tried in eight positions. We got eight positive results. We knew that No. 4 was the skull of Nicholas II."

Abramov went on to examine and compare the other eight skulls from the burial site. He did not spend much time with Skull No. 2, Botkin's, because it had no teeth. "Everyone else had upper teeth," Abramov explained, "and we knew that Botkin wore dentures. We knew to whom this skull belonged; we didn't need to go further." The remaining seven skulls were examined by superimposition. "We cross-compared all of the skulls with all of the photographs," he said. "That is, on the computer, we put each skull inside the head in each and every one of these photographs. The first time we had seventy-six or seventy-seven cross-references. We searched for differences in age, deformations of the skull, whether the markings on the indentations were exact, whether the inside point measurements matched, even the facial expressions and the position of the head. We considered the thickness of the soft tissue lying over the surface of the skull. We studied how the skull lay inside the face. We checked whether there was too little soft tissue on the chin, whether the nose was in the wrong spot, whether the eyebrows were lying properly. Look, here, we are superimposing Skull No. 4—Nicholas II—and the photo of Kharitonov. You see, there is some similarity, but here the skull sticks out too far. This skull cannot be Kharitonov. In every case, if we could not explain all of these differences, we categorically said that this skull and this photograph are not the same person. It was enough to have just one difference which we could not explain in order to reject a match."

Abramov worked especially hard to identify the remains of the three grand duchesses, who were very close in age and whose physical characteristics, especially given the degraded condition of the skulls, were difficult to distinguish. He compared all the photographs he possessed of these young women with the skulls of three young females, No. 3, No. 5, and No. 6. He compared three photographs of Grand Duchess Tatiana with Skull No. 3 and Skull No. 6. The results were negative. When he compared these photographs with Skull No. 5, the results were positive. Abramov, therefore, identified Skull No. 5 as Tatiana. He had four photographs of Grand Duchess Anastasia. He compared these with Skull No. 3: all were negative. He compared them with Skull No. 5; all negative. But when he compared Anastasia's photographs with Skull No. 6, all the findings were positive. "Here. You see? Olga's skull is wider. Anastasia's is narrower. There is not enough soft tissue here. Now, here is a photo of Anastasia with Skull No. 5, Tatiana. You see? Problems. But here is Anastasia with No. 6. You see, it matches perfectly. This skull, No. 6, is Anastasia."

In Abramov's opinion, the missing daughter was Marie, the third. "Maria [*sic*] has the highest dome (her skull is rounded at the top of the head). Her photographs do not match with the skull of Olga, No. 3. They do not match with No. 6; that is Anastasia. Anastasia's face is narrow, and Maria has a wide one. They do not match with No. 5; that is Tatiana. None of the skulls matches the photographs of Maria. So, Maria is not among these remains. She was not in the grave."

The process of identifying the bones was difficult enough, but for Abramov and his Moscow colleagues, the scientific task was made infinitely worse by two years of bureaucratic infighting. Even after his work was done and he had achieved a considerable success, Abramov became upset when he talked about what happened. Normally he is a pleasant man, looking out with amused eyes over the top of his glasses, running one hand over his small, neatly trimmed gray beard while he holds a cigarette in the other. But on this occasion, sitting in his office across the river from the Kremlin, he spoke in bursts of emotion, sometimes shaking his head, sometimes laughing nervously, sometimes pounding his desk. "I could say that this experience was interesting and complicated," he began. "But, no. It was more than that. It was evil. This research on the tsar's family was the worst experience of my life." From the beginning, he said, the authorities in Ekaterinburg behaved as if the Romanov bones belonged only to them. They were "the owners," he said they told him, and they were determined to treat the murder of the Imperial family as a local matter. Using photography to document work on human remains is an integral part of forensic examination everywhere in the world. Nevertheless, for months Deputy Investigator Volkov of the Sverdlovsk Region Office of the Public Prosecutor refused Abramov permission to take any pictures of what he was doing. "I have written documents forbidding the taking of photographs!" declared Abramov, still angry. "I have written documents stating that at any moment I can be thrown completely off this research project!"

When he arrived in Ekaterinburg, Abramov discovered that the original work of exhuming the bodies had been done incompetently. "I was told that Dr. Koryakova, the archeologist in charge, had left the dig three times to protest the barbaric methods they were using," he said. Abramov saw immediately that many of the bones were missing. His first request to the local authorities to go back and dig into the grave was refused. Eventually, he succeeded, and collected another 250 bones or bone fragments.

Abramov next asked permission to take the remains back to Moscow, where the process of examination and testing would have been facilitated. Ekaterinburg said no. He appealed to the Russian Parliament. The Parliament said no. At that point, no one in the central government of the Russian Federation, from Boris Yeltsin down, wished to confront and overrule the government of the Sverdlovsk Region.

Abramov's work, therefore, had to be done in Ekaterinburg. He had no money for expenses. The budget for his office is decided a year ahead of time, and no project of this magnitude had been expected. Therefore, during the autumn of 1991, Abramov repeatedly had to travel to Ekaterinburg, live in a hotel, eat his meals, and pay these expenses partially out of his own pocket. Avdonin—whom Abramov calls "a good man"—promised to help from his foundation, Obretenye, but then Avdonin found that he, too, had no money. The local forensic people had no time to assist Abramov during working hours—"they had their hands full dealing with current murders," he said. Some were willing to work overtime on Saturdays and Sundays, but they wished to be paid and Abramov was unable to pay them.

In December, Abramov told Investigator Volkov that for financial reasons he could not continue. Volkov suggested that this Russian government forensic scientist find commercial sponsors. Abramov started looking. He found a television company, Rus, from the city of Vladimir, which agreed to pay some of his expenses if they were allowed to film the bones. Another sponsor, a charity called the Fund for the Potential of Russia, was willing to pay for work and travel in return for being acknowledged everywhere as sponsor of this research. Abramov was pleased; while he had these sponsors, he traveled to Ekaterinburg three times in the spring of 1992 and even was able to bring some of his technicians from Moscow.

The television people were invaluable to Abramov, not only because they provided money but because they brought cameras. "We did not even have a camera in Ekaterinburg, and our superimposition work required cameras." Later, it was said that it was impossible to identify these skulls by superimposition because Abramov did not properly photograph his work during their reconstruction. "It is true," he admitted, "that there are no photographs of the work I did in the fall of 1991. The reason is that I was not permitted to take photographs. Only in May 1992, when we had help from these television people, were photographs taken.

"But"—Abramov's face darkened with disgust—"once they had the film, the television people spat at us. They went out and tried to sell these films. And then"—he threw his arms up in the air; he was a character from Gogol, caught in a maze of bureaucratic villainy and deceit—"the government of Ekaterinburg demanded that all films and tapes of the remains must be left in Ekaterinburg. Further, the authorities demanded that everything written down on a piece of paper must be left behind in the city. And then, these same Ekaterinburg people turned on me and said, 'Abramov deceitfully has brought in a television company, which, despite the ban of the Ekaterinburg government, has taken and is selling this film.'"

In the summer of 1992, still shuttling between Moscow and Ekaterinburg and trying to complete his work, Abramov encountered an apparently disinterested angel, Baron Eduard von Falz-Fein, a wealthy Russian emigre in his middle eighties, now living in Liechtenstein. Falz-Fein had heard about Abramov's superimpositions and, when in Moscow, came to his office to see them. "When he found out that I had people working for nothing," Abramov remembered, "that we did not have enough diskettes, enough of this or enough of that, he silently reached into his pocket, peeled off ten hundred-dollar bills, and gave them to me. I immediately told my superiors. Their eyes lit up...the biologists wanted serum, everybody wanted something. But I said no, this is only for the research on the Imperial family. The first thing I did was pay the people who were working for me. I paid them in dollars. My brilliant mathematician who came to us from the space rocket program had worked here, doing only this, for a year without pay. He was the first one I paid out of the money Baron Falz-Fein gave me."

By the summer of 1992, Sergei Abramov and his colleagues were convinced that they had found Nicholas, Alexandra, Olga, Tatiana, Anastasia, Dr. Botkin, Demidova, Kharitonov, and Trupp. Alexander Blokhin, deputy vice governor of the Sverdlovsk Region, had backed them publicly, holding a press conference on June 22 to announce that "computer modeling, comparing ancient photos of the tsar and the empress, has definitely proved that the remains found were *their* remains." Everyone knew that the tsarevich was missing. And Russian experts accepted Abramov's finding that the ninth skeleton he had examined belonged to the youngest of the tsar's daughters, Grand Duchess Anastasia. The missing daughter, everyone believed, was Marie.

CHAPTER 5

......................❖......................

SECRETARY

BAKER

In February 1992, U.S. Secretary of State James A. Baker III, in his last year of office, was barnstorming around the former Soviet Union. During his three years of working for President Bush, the Soviet Union had splintered into a plethora of independent states, all of them interested in attracting American investment capital and technological know-how. Baker, accordingly, was warmly welcomed in Moldavia, Armenia, Azerbaijan, Turkmenistan, Tajikistan, Uzbekistan—and, of course, in Russia. On February 14, his blue and white Air Force 707 touched down at Ekaterinburg, his last stop before Moscow. In fact, visiting Ekaterinburg itself was not the primary reason for this stop. Baker was on his way to a secret nuclear research center called Chelyabinsk 70, one hundred miles to the south. The very fact that Baker was coming measured the distance recently traveled by the two superpowers. For decades, Chelyabinsk 70 had been considered so secret that the entire small city was encircled by high barbed-wire fences and watchtowers. For miles around, the country-side had been kept empty of population. The purpose of Baker's visit was to see how the scientists who had been making nuclear weapons now were using their technology to make artificial diamonds; this was being offered to the Americans as a reassuring example of Russia's ability to convert former war-making capability to peaceful purposes. Accordingly, Baker, his staff, and a group of American reporters made the trip to Chelyabinsk 70, the secretary addressed the scientists, and then the Americans returned to Ekaterinburg for the night.

The following morning was what the State Department calls "downtime"; that is, there was nowhere official to go and nothing official to do. President Yeltsin, whom Baker was scheduled to see in Moscow, was not returning to the Russian capital until the afternoon and did not want Baker to arrive before he did. As it happened, Margaret Tutwiler, Baker's principal spokesperson, had been looking forward to a morning free in Ekaterinburg. For years, Tutwiler had been interested in the Romanovs, and she had read widely on the subject. She knew that the Ipatiev House had been destroyed, but she hoped, nevertheless, to be able to go and see the site. Before arriving in the city, she had mentioned this to Secretary Baker.

After returning from Chelyabinsk 70 the previous evening, Baker had eaten dinner with Governor Edvard Rossel in Rossel's small family apartment. Baker, himself a hunter, had admired Rossel's hunting rifle and the large moose head mounted on the wall. He had listened to Rossel's description of the attractive business opportunities awaiting Americans in this part of the Urals. Then, as he had promised Margaret Tutwiler he would, the secretary had asked about seeing the site of the Ipatiev House. Yes, of course, Rossel had responded, and as you are interested in the Romanovs, why not also come and see their bones? Baker had asked if he might bring another person.

In the morning, Baker and Tutwiler accompanied Rossel to the Ipatiev site. "There was snow on the ground, red and white carnations lay at the foot of the concrete cross, and people were coming and lighting candles," Tutwiler remembered two years later. Baker went up to the cross, leaned over, and touched it with a gloved hand. Then the party drove to the two-story morgue where the bones were kept. Alexander Avdonin was there, and Rossel introduced him. The visitors watched a demonstration of computer superimposition and then looked at the skeletal remains. At one point, Baker picked up one of Nicholas II's bones. The singular nature of the situation was not lost on him. Early in 1994, sitting in his Washington law office, he recalled his feelings: "There was a real sense of history in that room. When we—the Bush administration—came into office, we were still confronted with a threat to our very existence from the Soviet Union and its ability to destroy the United States in a nuclear war. I remember how chary we were of the Soviets even as late as May and June of 1989. So, a scant three years later, here was an American secretary of state, standing there in what had been one of the most closed cities of the Soviet Union, just back from the nuclear site at Chelyabinsk, looking at the bones of the tsar. It was a striking example of how far things had come."

Tutwiler remembered another moment from that unusual day. In the morgue, she and Secretary Baker were told that the tsar's son and one of his daughters were missing from the skeletons laid on tables before them. "Is it Anastasia?" Tutwiler asked. Someone—she does not know which of the Russians present—answered decisively, "Anastasia is in this room!"

While Baker was still in the morgue, Rossel asked a favor. He said that scientists in Ekaterinburg were certain the bones belonged to the Romanovs, but they knew that in order to have this finding accepted in the West, they needed the endorsement of Western forensic experts. "Do you have anyone who could assist us?" Rossel asked. Baker replied that, when he returned to Washington, he would see what he could do. The American reporters accompanying the secretary wrote down this statement, and the following day it appeared in many newspapers.

Baker was as good as his word. Passing through Moscow, he instructed the U.S. Embassy to establish direct contact with the Ekaterinburg authorities. Returning to Washington, he told the assistant secretary of state for European affairs, "See what we can do to help." Tutwiler remained involved, and cables stressing that "the secretary is very interested in this" flowed from her office. The two primary U.S. government forensic and pathological laboratories, the Armed Forces Institute of Pathology based at Walter Reed Army Medical Center, and the FBI, were asked to participate. The AFIP had extensive experience in identifying bones unearthed after many years. Samples of the bones and teeth of American servicemen killed in Vietnam that could not be identified in Hawaii by standard anthropological, dental, and radiological methods were sent to AFIP for DNA analysis. Similarly, the FBI laboratory stands behind federal, state, and local police authorities as an ultimate resource for identifying criminals, victims, and missing persons. With the agreement of the secretary of defense and the director of the FBI, both laboratories agreed to help.

A joint team, led by Dr. Richard Froede, then the armed forces medical examiner and a past president of the American Academy of Forensic Sciences, was assembled. Dr. Froede was a forensic pathologist; that is, he dealt with remains when they were dead bodies. His assistant for the trip was Dr. Bill Rodriguez, a forensic anthropologist who deals with remains when they have become bones. Dr. Alan Robilliard of the FBI also was coming; his specialty, like that of Moscow's Dr. Abramov, is computer graphic reconstruction. In all, eight American specialists, all employees of the U.S. government, made up the team. The costs were to be borne by the government as a contribution to good relations with Russia. (In fact, the salaries of the team members were already part of the federal budget; the additional expenses were primarily travel.)

The team met several times in Washington and began assembling materials and equipment. Glass-plate X-ray photographs of the tsar and the empress for radiographic comparison were acquired. Hand-held X-ray machines, special laser scanning equipment, and computer graphic equipment, designed to work from different power sources in the field, were collected. There was a sense of urgency about these preparations; the Russians had stressed that they wanted the team in place by May. The team was ready on deadline: the equipment was crated, the scientists had their passports, Russian visas, typhoid and diphtheria shots, and airplane tickets. Then suddenly, two days before departure, the trip was canceled. A cable from the American Embassy in Moscow said that the authorities in Ekaterinburg preferred a different American team, led by Dr. William Maples, a forensic anthropologist from the University of Florida.

Members of the AFIP-FBI team were shocked and disappointed—some still are angry. "I'm not saying anything against Bill Maples, because he's an excellent man," one of the proposed leaders of the team said of the episode. "But this was an offer to the Russians by Secretary Baker, and we were the U.S. government team. From the point of view of forensic investigation, we are probably the best the U.S. has. We could have offered much more, particularly in the way of DNA analysis, because Maples couldn't do that, and it ended up being done by the British. We have one of the few labs in the world capable of doing mitochondrial DNA, so we could have done it here, in house. We're a huge pathology lab with state-of-the-art equipment both here and at the FBI. Being a U.S. government team, we thought we could really represent the United States. Nobody ever said 'thank you' or 'we're sorry.' It was a sore subject around here for quite a while."

CHAPTER 6

·········· ❖ ··········

CURIOUS
ABOUT DEATH

The Gainesville campus of the University of Florida sprawls over several square miles of lush central Florida landscape. Divided into a grid of streets, it is so large that students sometimes need buses to travel from one class to the next. Some of these blocks are empty, others almost so. On one of these flat, mostly empty plots, a grove of tall bamboo trees breaks the horizon. A bumpy, rutted driveway turns off the concrete street, leads past an impromptu vegetable garden, and arrives at a high wire fence crowned with rolls of coiled barbed wire. Behind the fence, nestled under the bamboo trees, is a windowless, light green, all-metal building with a number of ventilator pipes on the roof. This is the C. A. Pound Human Identification Laboratory, the creation and workshop of Dr. William Maples.

The building is not large. The door opens on a small secretarial office; behind this is Dr. Maples' office. There is a small conference room and a bathroom. And there is the laboratory which Dr. Maples himself designed on a Macintosh computer. No one enters this room without his permission. The door lock has pins coming from three directions, and neither the university police nor the university locksmith possesses one of its unique keys. There is no possibility of entry through the roof. The building has an elaborate, highly sensitive alarm system. In the four and a half years of the Pound Laboratory's existence, the alarm has never gone off.

Few people would wish to enter this room. On the tops of work tables there are human skulls, skeletons, and parts of skeletons awaiting examination. Along the back wall are shelves filled with carefully labeled cardboard boxes containing numerous other human bones. There are computers, X-ray machines, X-ray drive processors, and a video camera; there is a workbench with a drill press, a small anvil, screwdrivers, wrenches, and diamond blade saws; there are refrigerators and freezers. Along one side wall, there are three large stainless-steel vats, each closed by a transparent plastic odor hood, which is connected to one of the ventilating shafts on the roof. In these vats, Dr. Maples and his assistants "macerate remains."

"Macerate?"

"That's a euphemism for 'boil the meat off the bones.' "

Dr. Maples is a forensic anthropologist; he deals with bones. If the bones come to him still encased in flesh, he must remove the flesh before he can begin to work. He places the body in one of his vats, fills the vat with boiling water, and tends the contents until he has a skeleton. Actually, most of this work is done by his graduate and undergraduate students, who rotate observing the vats, switching every hour or two.

"It takes a lot of attention to make sure that the soft tissue comes off as quickly as it can," Maples explained. "We have to make sure that the bone isn't softened by being in the water too long and also that the water doesn't boil dry and burn the bone. The hoods protect against splash—we worry about hepatitis B, AIDS, and tuberculosis—and, at least partially, against odor. Yes, it's a very distasteful task, but I can only recall one or two students who have been unable to handle it."

Maples' office next door is a relatively cheerful place. It is true that there are eighteen human skulls on top of three large file cabinets, but the cabinets are painted a sprightly orange. Maples' desk lies under an untidy mountain of documents, correspondence, photographs, and X rays. But William Maples himself, a balding man in a blue blazer, gray flannel trousers, and wire-rimmed glasses, is almost exaggeratedly neat. His voice is low, flat, and Texan, reflecting his childhood. His speech, like his methodology, is controlled and precise. Dr. Maples almost always knows exactly what his next word or act is going to be and why he is going to say or do it.

"All my life I have been curious about death," he said. In college at the University of Texas, where he was majoring in English and anthropology, he paid for his education by riding in an ambulance owned by a funeral home. Night after night, he hurtled at 105 miles an hour toward accident scenes in order to be there first and get the business. He saw "terrible things," but before he was twenty he had learned to eat a chili-and-cheese hamburger in an autopsy room after a watching an autopsy. At twenty-four, he and his wife began four years of trapping baboons in Kenya for research. When one old baboon bit deep into Maples' arm, tearing an artery, Maples himself had a brush with death. In 1968, Maples arrived in Gainesville with his Ph.D. and became an assistant professor of anthropology. After six years, he moved out of active teaching to the Anthropology Department of the Florida Museum of Natural History.

"My field is the human skeleton, its changes through life, its changes across many lifetimes, and its variations around the world," Dr. Maples said. By examining the different bones of a skeleton, Maples usually can quickly tell the sex, the age, the height, and the weight of the owner of the skeleton in life. This special knowledge has made him enormously valuable as an expert consultant to local and state police trying determine the identity of a victim, what happened to the victim at the scene of a crime, and who was responsible. From 1972, when he began with a single case, his caseload has grown to two to three hundred a year. Among them was serial killer Ted Bundy, who murdered at least thirty-six young women before he was caught, tried, and executed—in Florida. Twice a year, Maples visits the U.S. Army Central Identification Laboratory in Honolulu to assist with difficult cases of military remains brought back from Vietnam.

For most of this consulting work, Dr. Maples' fee is two hundred dollars an hour. He also receives a partial salary from the University of Florida. Together, this income still does not fully support the work of his laboratory, and he has turned for help to outside donors. The C. A. Pound Laboratory was paid for by Gainesville native Cicero Addison Pound, Jr., a man now in his seventies, who, as an early naval aviator, participated in the search for Amelia Earhart. Pound became wealthy in real estate and contributed money to build Maples' laboratory. Maples also has a generous benefactor in retired Gainesville lawyer William Goza, whose Wentworth Foundation gives to the university and specifically to projects involving William Maples.

Goza's financial support has made possible a number of Maples' forensic investigations. These are historical cases, in which there is no client other than history and the primary motive is the sheer satisfaction of discovering truth and solving a mystery. (It is also true, of course, that success in these high-profile cases confers valuable prestige. It is extremely useful to a prosecutor when he can stand up before a jury and say to his expert witness, "Are you the same Dr. Maples who...?") Maples has been involved in four of these historical cases. In 1984, he proved that mummified remains thought to be those of Francisco Pizarro, the Spanish conquistador assassinated in Lima in 1541, and thereafter venerated for over four centuries in a magnificent marble and bronze sarcophagus in Lima Cathedral, actually belonged to someone else. Further, he proved that another set of ancient bones, buried beneath two layers of wooden planking in the cathedral crypt, were those of Pizarro. In 1988, Maples examined the skeleton of John Merrick, the nineteenth-century Elephant Man, restored to fame in our time by Broadway and Hollywood. (Just before Maples appeared, pop star Michael Jackson reportedly had offered to buy Merrick's skeleton from the Royal London College of Medicine Museum for one million dollars.) Maples' effort was to establish how much of the grotesquely abnormal growth that disfigured Merrick was the result of soft tissue tumors and how much was attributable to changes in the structure of his bones. He found that Merrick was afflicted by both. In 1991, he exhumed the skeleton of Zachary Taylor and proved that this former president of the United States had not been poisoned, as was often alleged, but had probably died of an intestinal infection. And, in 1992, Dr. Maples became involved with the Romanov bones.

William Maples first encountered the Russian Imperial family years ago by reading two books. As a boy in Dallas in the 1940s, he read Richard Halliburton's *Seven League Boots*, which contained Halliburton's "deathbed" interview with the executioner Ermakov. Much later, he read *Nicholas and Alexandra*. In February 1992, he was in New Orleans attending the annual meeting of the American Academy of Forensic Sciences when he read in a newspaper that Secretary of State Baker had been asked for American assistance in identifying a group of skeletal remains exhumed from a grave in Siberia. Maples walked over to Dr. Richard Froede, the armed forces medical examiner, and asked whether Baker had been in touch with Froede about providing help. Dr. Froede said no, he hadn't heard anything. "I decided right then that we would make an attempt," Maples said. "While the meeting was still going on, I organized what I think was an extremely powerful team. It consisted of Dr. Michael Baden, a forensic pathologist, Dr. Lowell Levine, a forensic dentist, Dr. William Hamilton, our local Gainesville medical examiner, and Cathryn Oakes, a hair and fiber specialist with the New York State Police. I was to serve as the forensic anthropologist and team leader."

Returning to Gainesville, Maples drafted a letter for the president of the University of Florida, John Lombardi, to sign and send to Alexander Avdonin in Ekaterinburg. The letter presented the credentials of Maples' team and said that the members would be willing to travel at their own expense; in fact, the funds would come from Bill Goza's foundation. Further, Lombardi declared that he intended to organize a scientific conference in America to discuss the findings. "It would be necessary for several members of your team to come to this conference," he told Avdonin. "Funds raised by Dr. Maples would... provide the required transportation costs for your representatives." April arrived, and Maples still had received no reply. Then, indirectly, he learned that Avdonin was waiting for him to telephone. Maples did so immediately, and the following day a faxed invitation arrived in Gainesville, signed jointly by Alexander Blokhin, deputy vice governor of the Sverdlovsk Region, and Avdonin. The Florida team was asked to come in mid-July, to spend several days examining the remains, and then to participate in an international conference on the subject of the bones.

Told that Dr. Froede and Dr. Rodriguez of the AFIP-FBI team continue to be upset about their sudden dismissal from the project, Maples said, "We learned only later that Secretary Baker had asked Dick Froede. I'm certain that when I spoke to Dick in New Orleans, he had not been contacted. After all, Baker was still in Russia. Anyway, when I asked Dick, he said no." Maples admitted that, in America as in Russia, there is fierce competition among scientists. "I'm not a particularly competitive individual," he said, "but if no one else was going to do something like this—something I was interested in for years—then I was eager to do it." In Maples' opinion the AFIP-FBI project was hampered by lack of funds and by the fact that a highly respected forensic anthropologist, Douglas Ubelaker of the Smithsonian Institution, dropped off the government team. The Russians, he felt, weighed the caliber of the two teams and chose his.

Dr. Maples did, indeed, have a powerful team. Dr. Michael Baden, the forensic pathologist, was a former chief medical examiner of New York City. He had been the chairman of the forensic panel established by the Congressional Select Committee on Assassinations to review the murders of John F. Kennedy and Martin Luther King, Jr. He was then codirector of the New York State Police Forensic Sciences Unit. Dr. Lowell Levine, his codirector with the New York State Police unit, had had an equally celebrated career. He too had worked with the congressional select committee on the Kennedy and King assassinations. At the request of the State Department, he had gone to Argentina and identified the remains of many of "the disappeared"—men and women who mysteriously vanished under the Argentine military dictatorship. A few years later in Brazil, Levine was instrumental in identifying the teeth and skull of Josef Mengele, the doctor from Auschwitz. Cathryn Oakes, one of the nation's leading hair and fiber specialists, was also with the New York State Police Crime Laboratory.

On July 25, 1992, Maples and his team arrived in Ekaterinburg and checked into the Hotel October, formerly used only by high Communist officials. They paid a full rate in Western dollars; the local authorities provided them only with a car and a driver. Early the following morning, they arrived at the branch of the Ekaterinburg morgue where the Romanov bones were kept. They met Nikolai Nevolin, director of the morgue, Alexander Avdonin, Galina Avdonina, who speaks good English, and others. Nevolin told them, "Go down and do what you want." The morgue, according to Maples, was similar in design to an American morgue in a city of comparable size: the autopsy rooms and body storage area on the first floor, offices on the second. And something else was familiar. "It was the odor," Maples said, "a typical morgue odor." On the second floor, at the end of a long hall, there was an iron gate. The gate opened into a small anteroom, and from there, opening another locked door, they walked into the room with the bones.

The room is eighteen by sixteen feet, about the size of an average American living room. It is a corner room and has two windows, both covered by drawn shades which permit light to enter. The walls are painted a glossy medium green. In the center of the room is a large table, which holds a computer and a microscope. Against the walls on all four sides of the room are metal tables. The bones are laid on these tables in skeletal form, that is, not connected but with the skull at the top, then the vertebrae forming the spinal column, the ribs on either side of the vertebrae, the arm bones outside the ribs, and the pelvic, leg, ankle, and foot bones at the bottom. Maples was horrified to see that some of the long bones of the thigh and arm had been cut in half; this could only make it more difficult for him to estimate height. When he arrived, the tables were not covered, so that anyone in the room could pick up a bone, as Secretary of State Baker had done five months before. Nor is there any temperature control in the room; when Maples and his team were there in midsummer, the room was warm, and they quickly removed their jackets.

Maples opened his camera bag and took out one of his cameras. "Nyet," said one of the Russians with them in the room. "You cannot take any photographs." Stolidly, Maples put his camera away and, with Baden, Levine, and Oakes, spent three hours examining the bones. To Maples, the identities of the skeletons were quickly obvious. "That is Demidova," he said. "That is Botkin. That is one of the daughters, probably Olga. That is another daughter, probably Tatiana. That's the third daughter, probably Marie. That is Nicholas. That is Alexandra. And these two are the male servants."

At midday, Maples and his team packed their bags and walked down the hall to Nevolin's office. "We're finished and we're leaving now," Maples said. "You're going to lunch?" Nevolin asked. "No," said Maples, "we're finished. We've done as much as we can, and we're going home." Nevolin was shocked. "But you can't go," he protested. Maples explained, "We have to document what we do, and unless we are allowed to do this, we cannot do any more. I've never done a forensic case where I've been unable to document what needed to be done. And unless you give permission for us to photo-document this case, we're finished. I've reached my conclusions." Maples' voice was flat, but he was clearly angry. "You were so angry you were shaking," Galina Avdonina told him later.

Nevolin needed time. "Go to lunch, and when you return, we'll discuss this and have some answers for you," he said. The American team went back to the hotel, had a long Russian lunch, then returned to the morgue. Nevolin greeted them by saying, "Take all the pictures you want." ("Obviously," Maples said later, "he called Blokhin and Blokhin said, 'Let them do what they want.' So we stayed for the rest of the week and documented everything. But in the first two or three hours we had the findings. We knew that we were dealing with the remains of the Imperial family, and we knew which one was which.")

The nine skeletons lying on the morgue tables were labeled only by number. Maples—who at this point had no knowledge of Dr. Abramov's previous findings—continued to use this labeling system. Five of the skeletons were female, four male. All of the males were mature; there was no adolescent boy. Of the five females, three were young women, only recently grown to maturity. All of the faces had been badly fractured. All of the female skeletons had dental work. One of the males apparently had used an upper plate.

The easiest body to identify—labeled by the Russians as Body No. 7—was that of a middle-aged woman whose ribs showed possible signs of damage from bayonet thrusts. What immediately caught the eye and the attention of Dr. Levine was the elaborate and beautiful dental work in this skull. Two crowns in the lower jaw were made of platinum. Elsewhere in this mouth, there were elegant porcelain crowns and finely wrought gold fillings. On display was a kind of dentistry developed in the United States at the end of the nineteenth century and subsequently practiced in Germany, Alexandra's homeland. Seeing this work, Levine and Maples pronounced this skull and these remains as belonging to the Empress Alexandra.

Identifying Nicholas II also was not difficult. The remains labeled Body No. 4 belonged to a fairly short, middle-aged man. The hip bones showed the signs of wear and deformation produced by years riding on horseback, a characteristic activity of Russian tsars. The skull had the wide, sloping forehead, jutting brow, and broad, flat palate possessed by Nicholas. The teeth were extraordinarily bad. The lower jaw showed the devastating inroads of periodontal disease, and there were no fillings in any of the remaining teeth. In the skull, there was no middle to the face; everything below the eye sockets and above the jaw had been obliterated.

Holding Nicholas II's skull in his hands, Maples had an eerie experience: "We were passing the skull around among ourselves, when we heard something rattling dully inside the braincase. Training a flashlight on the base of the skull, peering in through the aperture where the spinal column would have been anchored, we descried a small, shrunken object about the size of a small pear, rolling to and fro. It was the desiccated brain of Tsar Nicholas II."

The American team had little difficulty with the other four adults. Body No. 1 was identified by its pelvis as a fully mature female. The skull held a basically prefabricated gold bridge of poor workmanship on the lower left jaw; this was identified as belonging to the maid, Demidova.

Body No. 2 was the skeleton of a large, mature man with a distinctive flat, sloping forehead. Unique among the remains, this body still had a portion of the torso intact, held together by adipocere, a grayish white, waxy substance that forms when fatty tissue combines with water after death. From this mass, the Russians had recovered one bullet from the pelvic area and one from a vertebra. The skull had a gunshot wound from a bullet that had entered the left forehead. There were a few teeth in the lower jaw, no teeth at all in the upper jaw. Knowing that Dr. Botkin's dental plate had been found over seventy years before by Sokolov at the Four Brothers helped Maples and Levine to identify these remains as his.

Body No. 8 and Body No. 9 were identified as the remains of, respectively, Kharitonov, the forty-eight-year-old cook, and Trupp, the sixty-one-year-old valet. The skeleton of Kharitonov was the most fragmentary of all the nine; having been the first to be flung to the bottom of the pit, his body had lain deepest in the pool of acid. The body of Trupp had rested directly beneath that of the tsar. As decomposition proceeded, some of the bones became commingled. Today, Maples believes, short of performing a DNA test on each fragment, it will be impossible to determine whether certain of these bones belonged to the tsar or to his valet.

The remaining three skeletons, Bodies No. 3, No. 5, and No. 6, were those of three young adult or near-adult females, all of whom shared with one another and with Body No. 7 (Empress Alexandra) an uncommon protruding bone structure in the back of the head. This feature, called wormian bones and found in only 5 or 6 percent of the population, strongly suggested a sibling relationship between the three younger women, and a mother-daughter relationship between the three of them and Body No. 7. The three young women also all had numerous fillings and similar dental work, suggesting that they were treated by the same dentist.

The oldest of these young women, Body No. 3, was in her early twenties when she died. Although half of her middle face and her lower jaw were missing, the shape of the head, with its unusually prominent forehead, was similar to that of Grand Duchess Olga. This woman was fully grown; Olga had been twenty-two years and eight months old when she was killed. The leg bones had been cut, but by extrapolating from the lengths of her arm bones, Maples estimated her height at just under five feet, five inches. Dr. Levine found fully developed roots to the third molars or wisdom teeth, further supporting Maples' opinion that she was a mature adult. Gunshot wounds showed that a bullet had entered under her left jaw and exited through the front of her skull. "Such a trajectory," Maples observed, "could come from a gun placed under the chin and fired up, or from firing at a body already on the floor."

The next of the daughters—the remains labeled Body No. 5—had been a woman "in her late teens or early twenties," Maples decided. "Dr. Levine and I agreed that she was the youngest of the five women whose skeletons lay before us." They concluded this from the fact that the root tips of her third molars were not completely developed. "Her sacrum, in the back of her pelvis, was not completely developed. Her limb bones showed that growth had only recently ended. Her back showed evidence of immaturity, but it was nevertheless the back of a woman at least eighteen years old. We estimated her height at five feet, seven and a half inches." Although half of the middle face was missing, Maples concluded that this skeleton belonged to Grand Duchess Marie, whose nineteenth birthday had occurred five weeks before she died.

The third of these young females, whose remains were labeled Body No. 6, had been shot in the back of the head, the bullet entering her skull from the left rear and exiting from her right temple. She had been fully grown, and her dental and skeletal development placed her in age between Bodies No. 3 and No. 5. The root tips of her molars were still incomplete, which was consistent with a woman of age nineteen to twenty-one, but not a woman of seventeen. Maples put her height at just over five feet, five and a half inches; he found no evidence of recent continuing growth. Her sacrum and pelvic rim were mature, which made her at least eighteen. Her collarbone was mature, making her at least twenty. Grand Duchess Tatiana had been twenty-one years and two months old at the time of the executions. Maples therefore assigned Body No. 3 to Olga, Body No. 5 to Marie, and Body No. 6 to Tatiana.

Dr. Maples was convinced that none of these three skeletons was young enough to have belonged to Anastasia, who had been seventeen years and one month old on the night of the murders. One reason was height. Numerous photographs of Anastasia standing next to her sisters taken up until a year before her death showed that she was shorter than Olga and much shorter than Tatiana and Marie. In September 1917, ten months before the murders, Empress Alexandra wrote in her diary: "Anastasia is very fat, like Marie used to be—big, thick-waisted, tiny feet—I hope she grows more." Could Anastasia have undergone a growth spurt of more than two inches during her final year? It is possible, says Maples, but highly unlikely.

A second reason was the development of the third molars of the three daughters whose remains are present. Dr. Levine, who examined the teeth in every skull, firmly supports Maples' findings. "He did it anthropologically, I did it dentally; then, independently, we wrote down our estimates of the ages," said Levine. "We came up with the same numbers."

Finally, and for Maples most significantly, there was the condition of the vertebrae of the three youngest skeletons in Ekaterinburg. In his opinion, none displayed the characteristics of a seventeen-year-old female. Later, in his laboratory, Maples explained that human beings grow when their bones lengthen at the ends. Soft, cartilagelike material forms at these ends and gradually hardens into bone, making the overall bone—and the human being—larger or taller. In the vertebrae—the column of roundish bones making up the spine—the bones grow larger (and the human being taller) when cartilage forms and hardens on the edges of the upper and lower rims. "In an older person," Maples explained, "or in portions of the back of a younger person, we have a completed ring around the top and bottom edge of the vertebrae. But when this person still is incomplete in this part of the vertebrae, it gives me a clue that we're dealing with a young individual."

Death, of course, arrests the process which transforms cartilage into bone, and in the skeletal bones of young people, the cartilage turns to a yellowish, waxy substance which tends to crumble and flake off. In his laboratory, Maples has several skeletons of adolescents; he used them to make his point: "This person's vertebrae have the ring, but you see it is in the process of uniting and has flaked off here.... It is almost complete here, but you see is still open there.... Here, this one has virtually flaked off all around.... On this, it is present on the base, completely united with just a little scar on front, but the sides still show the opening." Maples applied this knowledge and experience to the vertebrae he saw in Ekaterinburg: "Females age more quickly than males in the same age-group," he said. "In a seventeen-year-old female, you expect to see incomplete vertebrae like this. None of the three skeletons in Ekaterinburg had any incomplete or even partially complete rings. This condition simply is not seen with a seventeen-year-old woman. I've never seen it. Since that time, I had a graduate student do a master's thesis on it, and not in one seventeen-year-old female did we find any complete vertebrae in the back."

Dr. Maples was well aware of the contradiction between his findings and those of Dr. Abramov. "I believe that Anastasia is missing, and he believes that the missing daughter is Marie," he said. "I won't change my mind and he won't change his." Why was Maples so certain that Abramov was wrong? His answers were blunt: he faulted Abramov's technique in attempting to reconstruct with glue the damaged faces in Ekaterinburg. This job was done so poorly, he continued, that any effort to superimpose photographs and skulls could not possibly produce accurate knowledge. Reconstructing damaged faces from fragments of bone can be done, Maples said, but it has to be done with exquisite care. "I frequently reconstruct faces by gluing pieces of bone together," he declared. "And for this reason I know that even when all the pieces of bone are there, a slight variation in the angle at which two pieces are glued together may result in several millimeters or even half a centimeter difference in where the bone is set. Then, when you try to piece another fragment in, it doesn't fit. You've got a gap. It's a half a centimeter too big or too small for the next fragment. You can't get any of the rest to fit, all because one little angle was wrong earlier in the process.

"In the case of the Romanovs, whole portions of the face—the whole of the right or left side of the face in some of the daughters— were missing." When Maples at one point discussed this with Abramov and asked the Russian scientist, "What happens if you have landmarks that are missing?" Abramov's answer was "We estimate." This was unacceptable to Maples. "The Russians had labored manfully over Body No. 6, attempting to restore its facial bones with generous dollops of glue stretched over wide gaps," he said. "They were forced to estimate over and over again while assembling these fragments, almost none of which was touching another. It was a remarkable and ingenious exercise, but it was too fanciful for me to buy. Seeing what they had done reinforced my conviction that Anastasia was not in that room."

Nor did Dr. Maples accept Dr. Abramov's technique of computerized superimposition. "I do video superimposition," he said, "but in my video superimposition setup we put the photograph under one video camera, we put the skull under another video camera, and we superimpose the images on a single monitor. I can change the position of the skull, I can change the size of the skull, I can move a skull, I can change its overall size in relation to the photograph, I can change its position relative to the face, but I can't change proportion. It's not within the system for me to be able to manipulate data. I do this using only cameras. If you use cameras and add a computer into the system, the computer can manipulate data and make things fit. And, in fact, Abramov's whole system is designed to start with the skull that he digitalizes in three dimensions by only a few points. Then he manipulates that skull by the computer until it fits the photograph."

Actually, before coming to Ekaterinburg, Maples had planned to return bringing his own superimposition photographs and equipment. But "because of the damage to the faces, I decided during my first visit that there wasn't any use doing superimposition even to establish that it was the Imperial family, let alone discriminating between the three sisters," he continued. "And then I learned that Abramov was basing his identification of which of the four sisters was missing upon the reconstructed faces. When that disagreed totally with the age findings that I had made with the skeletons and Lowell had made with the teeth, I simply could not accept the presence of Anastasia."

On the larger issue, Maples agreed absolutely with Abramov that these are the Romanovs. The nine skeletons fit the requirements of age, sex, height, and weight of nine of the prisoners in the Ipatiev House. "If you were to go out at random and try to assemble another group of people to fit exactly these historical and physical descriptions, you would have to do remarkable research and then go out and find and kill nine identical people," said Maples. He regards this as so unlikely as to be impossible.

What happened to the two missing bodies? Maples' long experience with violent death tells him that all eleven prisoners were killed. Given the ferocity of the attack on the family, he cannot believe that anyone was allowed to escape alive from the Ipatiev cellar. For further explanation, he looks to the Yurovsky account, which he accepts as truthful. Yurovsky described the burning of two bodies. One was the tsarevich, the other a female body which Yurovsky at first thought belonged to Alexandra, then decided must be that of Demidova. This female body, Maples believes, belonged to Anastasia. But how could Yurovsky have mistaken the body of a seventeen-year-old girl for that of a mature woman, whether forty-six like the empress, or forty like the chambermaid?

The answer, Maples believes, lies in the changes wrought in the appearance of human bodies by decomposition. The Imperial family was killed in mid-July, when the daily temperature averaged seventy degrees Fahrenheit. Their faces had been crushed by repeated blows from rifle butts. Their hair, soaked with blood, would have dried into a black, caked, impenetrable mass. As the corpses, stripped of clothing, lay on the ground, the sex of the victims would have been obvious, but beyond that the naked bodies would have bloated to unrecognizability. Maples sometimes sees the bodies of adolescent girls, which, a few days after death, have ballooned to resemble obese middle-aged women.

There is more to the process of decomposition. In the open air, flies easily find their way to recent death. They lay eggs in eyes, nostrils, and—as in these victims—in the bloody flesh of mutilated faces and mangled bodies. Within two days in these temperatures, the eggs would have hatched into maggots. No more need be said except that Maples understands why Yurovsky might not have been sure which female body he burned.

In April 1993, Dr. William Hamilton, the Gainesville medical examiner, accompanied Maples on Maples' second trip to Ekaterinburg. Later I asked them, based on their experience, what occurs in the mind of an executioner who is shooting, bayoneting, and crushing the faces of helpless people. Hamilton was first to answer: "I think it's fairly typical of this kind of assassination. You depersonalize the victim and make him or her into a symbol, something other than an individual human being. You are killing the regime, the tsar, getting rid of the whole hated past and creating a new world order. Serial killers do the same thing. Commonly, they compartmentalize and completely dehumanize their victims and then can commit atrocities impossible for an ordinary person to imagine." Maples agreed. "Once the decision was made to kill, under the circumstances you had that night in the Ipatiev House, I suspect that most of the participants wanted to make sure that it was done completely," he said. "People don't die the way you would like them to when you shoot them with handguns. They continue to live, they continue to moan, they convulse. And so, after emptying your handguns, you tend to use other means. And the rifle butts and bayonets were close at hand. That's why I'm certain there were no survivors."

CHAPTER 7

THE
EKATERINBURG
CONFERENCE

M aples and his team did not return directly home after their three days with the Romanov bones. Instead, they remained in Ekaterinburg for a two-day conference organized by the government of the Sverdlovsk Region, "The Last Page of the History of the Imperial Family: The Results of Studies of the Ekaterinburg Tragedy." About a hundred people attended, and twenty papers were presented, mostly by scientists from different parts of Russia and the former Soviet Union. The governor of the Sverdlovsk Region, Edvard Rossel, opened the conference. Alexander Avdonin described how he and Geli Ryabov had found the bones. Professor Krukov of Moscow denounced the "rude violations of archaeological and forensic norms" involved in the exhumation of the bones. Nikolai Nevolin analyzed the condition of the bones taken from the grave. Professor Popov from St. Petersburg described the damage done to the bones by pistol bullets. Dr. Svetlana Gurtovaya of Dr. Plaksin's office in the Ministry of Health described finding pubic hair from Bodies No. 5 and No. 7 and "objects resembling hair" from Body No. 4. All of these objects, she reported, "turned out to be extremely fragile and breakable and if they were touched would turn practically to powder." Dr. Abramov described his identification of the family using computer-assisted superimposition. Dr. Filipchuk from Kiev explained his determination of age, sex, and height obtained by examination of the skulls, long tubular bones, and pelvises of the victims.* Victor Zvyagin from Moscow insisted that Body No. 1 (whom both Abramov and Maples had identified as the maid, Demidova) was a male; Filipchuk gently corrected Zvyagin, saying, "According to our data, this skeleton belongs to a large female...there is absolutely no doubt that the pelvis of this skeleton is that of a female."† Dr. Pavel Ivanov of the Molecular Biology Institute of Moscow spoke of the further information that might be obtained from DNA analysis of the bones, possibly in England.

Some of the speakers were not scientists. One discussed the uniforms worn by Nicholas II as a reflection of his personality. A monarchist from the Russian Nobility Society in Moscow presented himself as the representative of "Their Imperial Highnesses, the Grand Duchess Maria Vladimirovna and the widowed Grand Duchess Leonida Georgievna." Even Baron Falz-Fein, the Liechtenstein millionaire, was allowed to speak. He talked exclusively about himself, mentioned that the estate where he was born, "Askanya Nova, had been the largest in Russia," and said that his devotion to Russian history and culture was enthusiastic and everlasting. The American team was not on the original program, but, at the end of the conference, Maples was invited to present its findings.

---

*Filipchuk's findings regarding the younger grand duchesses were more compatible with Maples' than with Abramov's. He believed that Body No. 5 was the tallest of the daughters and had been killed at the age of twenty. This was the skeleton which Maples had identified as Marie and Abramov as Tatiana. Filipchuk declared that Body No. 6 was the next tallest of the daughters and had died somewhere between the ages of twenty and twenty-four. Maples had identified No. 6 as Tatiana, Abramov as Anastasia.

†This public rejection of Zvyagin's research may have given some personal satisfaction to Abramov, who was in the audience. Zvyagin had been foremost in Abramov's mind when he denounced the "idiots" who had criticized his work in Ekaterinburg and patronized him the preceding autumn, winter, and spring.

In the press conference that ended the program, Maples was asked, "What is the level of Russian forensic science medical expertise if you were able to accomplish in three days what took our people an entire year?" His answer was diplomatic: "Don't forget, they spent a great deal of time in putting all the skeletons in order, reconstructing broken faces and skulls. After this, I and my colleagues only had to come and look." Nevertheless, although they did not speak Russian, the Americans understood enough to be surprised by the apparent lack of coordination among the Russian scientists present. Everyone, it seemed, specialized in a different part of the body and applied a different technique. An expert from Saratov specialized solely in human wrists; he determined everything about skeletal remains, including age, by examining the small bones of the wrist. The best way to determine the age of a skeleton, says Michael Baden, is to examine the skull, the teeth, the vertebrae, and the pelvis. "But"—Baden shrugged—"if you only know about the anthropology of the wrist, you do everything using the wrist."

Some of the Russians seemed to be hoarding their research, guarding what each thought was unique information. Maples and his colleagues were accustomed to Western scientific conferences, whose basic purpose is to share and disseminate new knowledge. Before a conference, Maples said later, Western scientists often prepare abstracts which are purposefully vague because the authors have not completed the research. But by the time of the meeting, a paper is expected to present results, analysis, and conclusions. In this respect, the behavior of the Moscow serologist, Gurtovaya, whose paper was on blood typing from hair samples, particularly fascinated Maples. She told the conference that she had tested bone and hair from the burial site for A, B, and O blood types, but at the conclusion she did not announce what she had found. Maples, sitting in the audience next to an English-speaking Russian art historian, leaned over to his neighbor and said, "Ask her if they were able to blood-type the remains." The Russian asked the question, saying that it came from the American sitting next to him. "The speaker's answer," Maples said, "was 'Da.' Nothing more. I said, 'Ask her if she got results from hair or from bone.' She said, 'Both.' I said, 'Ask her if the results were the same with the hair and the bone.' He asked her, and she said, 'Da.' So I said, 'Ask her what blood type it was.' And she said, 'Oh, we must keep our own little secrets.' " This reminded Maples of a quotation: " 'In Russia everything is a secret, but there is no secrecy.' In fact," he said, "within fifteen minutes, somebody told me what her results were: A positive."

Cathryn Oakes, the hair and fiber specialist on Maples' team, had an even more frustrating experience with Gurtovaya. Oakes made the trip from America because she had been told that there was human hair in the burial pit. Accordingly, when she arrived in Ekaterinburg, she asked, "May I look at the hair?" "Oh, that's in Moscow," she was told. But, her informer continued, Gurtovaya, the Moscow expert, would be in Ekaterinburg at the conference a few days later and would be bringing the hair with her. When Gurtovaya arrived, Oakes introduced herself and asked, "May I look at the hair?" "Oh, yes," Gurtovaya replied. But she did not supply any hair. At their next encounter, Gurtovaya told Oakes that "the hair wasn't any good." Even now, Oakes does not know what to believe: "She did not appear to have the hair with her. Or perhaps she did and simply didn't want to show it to me. In any case, I never got to see or do anything." In the subsequent visits to Russia and Ekaterinburg by Dr. Maples and his team, Cathryn Oakes refused to participate.

Maples did not know it when he arrived, but this compartmentalization of knowledge among the Russians extended to having kept secret from Plaksin and Abramov the fact that he and his American colleagues were going to be at the conference. "They didn't know we were there until they walked in the door," Cathryn Oakes remembered. "And they were not pleased." "They were shocked," agreed Lowell Levine. "There was a tug-of-war going on between Moscow and Ekaterinburg," Maples explained. "The forensic people in Moscow wanted the remains sent to Moscow. The Ekaterinburg people wanted to keep the remains there. At some point in this struggle, Ekaterinburg realized that they were going to be outgunned. If they were going to maintain control, they had to have their own forensic team. But there were no forensic scientists of that caliber in Ekaterinburg. That's when they made their request to Secretary Baker. As a result, we arrived, and we—without realizing it—became the Ekaterinburg team."

It was in this atmosphere of mutual shock, misunderstanding, and only partly concealed hostility that William Maples, who believed that the missing grand duchess was Anastasia, first met Sergei Abramov, who believed that the missing daughter was Marie.

"Professor Maples' participation at the conference in Ekaterinburg was arranged solely by the government of Ekaterinburg," Abramov said later. "We found out by sheer accident. It was strange. He was allowed to photograph the bones, but we—Russian experts—had not been allowed to do this. I don't have anything against Dr. Maples. I respect him greatly. But his role in all this has been puzzling to us. If he is doing the research independently from us, then why are we needed? And if he is doing the research together with us, then why is he hidden from us? We never stood side by side at the bones."

During the conference, after Maples announced his conclusion that Anastasia was the missing daughter, Abramov came up to him and advised him not to pass this opinion around when he returned to America. "I did this to protect him," Abramov explained. "He had spent three days with the bones. We had spent a year with them. For his sake, I would not have liked it to turn out that we were right and he was wrong." Unbeknownst to Abramov, of course, Maples already planned to tell the press conference at the end of the meeting in Ekaterinburg that he believed the missing grand duchess was Anastasia.

One year later, in July 1993, Maples came back to Ekaterinburg to be filmed examining the bones by *Nova,* the PBS television science program. On his way home, he stopped briefly in Moscow and for the first time called on Abramov in his office. "Dr. Maples was exhausted," Abramov said. "He had gotten up at 4:00 A.M. in Ekaterinburg to fly to Moscow. He had his television people with him; they were taking pictures of us shaking hands and being friendly." Maples explained to Abramov that his technique of examining and measuring bones proved to him that none of the young female skeletons could be a seventeen-year-old. "Then it turned out," Abramov said, "that he and I were not measuring the same bones. We measured the hip and the femur; he measured the bones of the forearm, the ulna, and the radius, which are a much less accurate indication of height. 'But,' Maples said to me, 'you sawed the femur in half.' I said, 'No, we did not do that. Someone else did. But we measured the femur before it was cut. And, frankly, we did not expect any other experts would be coming.' "

During that conversation, Abramov mentioned to Maples a problem regarding these forearm bones about which Maples already was concerned: "These bones easily could have been mixed up between the bodies. They were not brought out of the ground with the most scrupulous care. And once they were on the tables in the morgue, anybody could pick them up and, by mistake, put them down in another place. Professor Popov was there—without us. Professor Zvyagin was there—without us. And now Professor Maples has been there—without us."

Toward the end of this meeting, Maples, wishing to be conciliatory, said to Abramov that although his own results were different, if Abramov could prove absolutely that Anastasia was among the skeletons, "I will be happy for you." Abramov, responding agreeably, asked Maples whether he knew of any other renowned Western scientist who, using superimposition, could help solve the problem. Maples supplied a name, Professor Richard Helmer of the Institute of Legal Medicine in Bonn, Germany, who was the president of the Craniofacial Identification Group of the International Association of Forensic Sciences. Abramov, who knew Helmer's reputation and had read his monographs, immediately invited him to Moscow. A commercial company provided expenses, and, in early September 1993, Helmer spent five days in Moscow going over Abramov's technique and results. He told Abramov that his was the best superimposition program he had ever seen—and that he had seen all the superimposition programs in existence. Further, he said he now believed Abramov's results and agreed that Anastasia was one of the skeletons in Ekaterinburg.

After that meeting, Abramov continued to propose solving the problem by having both Helmer and Maples come to Ekaterinburg to work with him at the bones. He would also invite Dr. Filipchuk from Kiev. In the absence of any such joint investigation, Abramov rests on his findings, buttressed by Professor Helmer. And by the fact that Dr. Maples gave him Professor Helmer's name.

❖

"The fact of the matter is that with the methods which now exist and based on the comparative material we now have, I do not believe it is possible to determine who is missing, Marie or Anastasia."

The speaker was Nikolai Nevolin, director of the Sverdlovsk Region Bureau of Forensic Medicine, responsible for the Ekaterinburg morgue in which the bones have rested for four years. He lives in a multistory apartment building almost next door to the morgue, and it was there we went to look for him because we were late. We sat under the rustling poplars in the light of the setting sun, watching children play in the courtyard while Avdonin went inside to find him. Soon, Nevolin emerged, a powerfully built, soft-spoken man in his forties. He was wearing a black and orange American T-shirt, a gift of Lowell Levine. He is a forensic anthropologist whose routine work deals with the violent crimes and death which contemporary Siberians inflict upon each other. But he had grown familiar with these special bones. He had worked at the side of Abramov and at the side of Maples, and he had carefully studied the techniques of both. In his opinion, both were wrong.

"Maples speaks of pinpointing age to such a degree that he can say that none of the skeletons belonged to a seventeen-year-old woman," Nevolin said. "Yes, you can talk about averages. But a professional knows that from bones you cannot tell precisely the growth or age of an individual adolescent. Teeth are a better yardstick. Forensic dentists, studying growth, say they can estimate age within plus or minus two and a half years. That is reasonable. I would accept that."

Nevolin was neither defensive nor vehement in his criticism. He knew that both Maples and Abramov had reputations greater than his. But he was gently firm. He did not accept Maples' contention that he can establish age by the degree of growth on the upper and lower edges of the vertebrae. "I don't say that the calcification of the vertebrae which Dr. Maples is talking about does not occur; of course, it always takes place. But the process is not fixed to any particular age, such as sixteen or seventeen years old. Medical science does not know such a thing. What exist are intervals—let's say fourteen to nineteen years old—when the growth process occurs. I think that Dr. Maples may have been misled by the fact that these bones have been in the ground for more than seventy years. The surface of the bones has been somewhat destroyed; they are very different from recent bones, which he—and we—usually work with in our laboratories.

"Finally, I have to say that determination of age by vertebrae has never been considered reliable, either here or abroad. The most reliable methods of determining age are the degree of wearing of the teeth, the knitting of seams on the skull, and, most reliable method of all, Hanson's method—investigating the structure of the upper portions of the long tubular bones. These are the basic methods that allow us most precisely to determine age. Vertebrae are not involved in this. Americans, Europeans, Russians—everybody is the same. And if someone attempts to differentiate these remains by height, that won't work either. You cannot blame the difficulty on the fact that the bone has been sawed through.... Even if it were whole, it would be impossible to determine exact height. So if a person, judging by height, says that this is this victim and this is that victim, then I think, mildly speaking, this person is not quite telling the truth."

Nevolin turned to Abramov's results, achieved with superimposition. "This is slightly better," he said. "Because here we use the method of elimination. We take a photograph of the person taken as close as possible to the moment of death. We have the image of the skull. They are placed on top of each other. If the image of the skull fits into the image of the face of the person in the photograph, we can say that the skull *can* belong to the person shown in the photograph. It works better in a negative sense. If the skull does not fit within the image of the photograph, we can say that this skull did not belong to the person in the photograph. So each skull is fitted into each photograph. It will not fit into some of them; it may fit into one of them. One must not accept this as a categorical method, especially in this case. The method still is not very reliable, and second, in this case, practically all of the facial parts of the skulls have been destroyed and some of the cranial parts of the skulls are damaged by bullets."

Nevolin's personal conclusion was offered with a wry smile: "Russian scientists believe one way, American scientists believe another. I believe in a third way. I believe that the argument regarding Marie and Anastasia cannot now be conclusively solved. They were too close in age and were not so very different in height so that forensic experts here or abroad could determine their identity." The ultimate solution, he insists, must be found the time-honored way: by locating the medical records and comparing teeth, bridges, crowns, fillings, broken bones, and any other skeletal abnormalities to written records and, if possible, X rays. Like Lowell Levine, Nevolin maintains that the medical records of the Imperial family must be somewhere in the archives. "I cannot believe that the medical records of the Romanovs have been lost," Nevolin said. "They exist somewhere. Such documents do not get lost. But so much has happened in our country that only the Lord God knows where these documents have ended up. I believe that they will be found. If they are, there will be no more questions. We will know who was who."

· · · · · · · · · · · · · · ❖ · · · · · · · · · · · · · ·

CHAPTER 8

AT THE
FRONTIERS OF
KNOWLEDGE

The seventeenth paper presented at the July 1992 conference in Ekaterinburg was given by a cheerful, dark-haired, forty-one-year-old molecular biologist, Dr. Pavel Ivanov, of the Englehardt Institute of Molecular Biology of the Russian Academy of Sciences in Moscow. Ivanov's subject was DNA testing. He told the conference that, at the end of 1991, Russian Chief Medical Examiner Vladislav Plaksin had asked him to look into the possibility of using this new technique to help identify the bones found by Alexander Avdonin and Geli Ryabov. Ivanov knew that this work could not be done in Russia. No one "in Russia had the experience of working with bone materials," he explained to the conference, nor did Russia possess the necessary technology. Nevertheless, while in London in December 1991, he had visited what he called the "Central Criminal Research Center" of the British Home Office at Aldermaston in Berkshire and begun negotiations for a joint British-Russian study of the bones.

Early in July 1992, just two weeks before this conference, an agreement had been reached between the Russian Ministry of Health and the British Home Office. A joint effort would take place at Aldermaston involving Dr. Peter Gill, director of the Molecular Research Center of the Home Office Forensic Science Service, Sir Alec Jeffreys of Leicester University, founder of the DNA fingerprinting technique, and Dr. Erika Hagelberg of Cambridge University, a specialist on molecular genetic analysis of bone remains. The Russian scientist would be Ivanov himself. All expenses except travel would be borne by the British Forensic Science Service, and travel costs (essentially Ivanov's airfare to and from Britain) would be paid by the Sverdlovsk regional government, which had approved the arrangement. The tests in England, Ivanov told his audience, would enable the researchers to determine whether, among the nine exhumed skeletons, a family group existed. Further, if enough uncontaminated DNA could be extracted from the remains, and if living persons descended from blood relations of the Imperial family could be persuaded to donate samples for comparative purposes, it would be possible to prove whether or not the family group found in the grave was that of Tsar Nicholas II.

The fact that the bones were going to England because DNA technology was not available in their own country was embarrassing for Russian scientists. "We were working on molecular genetic testing at one time," said Nikolai Nevolin with a wry smile. "Academician Vavilov began using this method. Then Mr. Stalin shot his entire team. As a result, we began lagging behind."

When Stalin died in 1953, Pavel Ivanov was two years old. Twenty years later, in the era of Brezhnev, Ivanov was on his way to acquiring a degree in molecular biology at Moscow State University—"the best we have in Russia, very well regarded in Europe." He began as a pure research scientist, working on the international human genome project at the Institute of Molecular Biology. In 1987, his group, trying to read the genetic codes which create human beings, discovered a technique of DNA fingerprinting similar, but not identical, to work first done by Alec Jeffreys in England. Ivanov, still a basic scientist, began to explore and develop this technique. His work came to the attention of "everyday, working" organizations, such as the forensic crime laboratory and the KGB. "They expressed interest in practical applications of my work and suggested that I establish a forensic DNA laboratory," he explained. "I agreed because forensic science was very interesting for me and because, with the level of crime so high in Moscow, I thought I might be able to do something to help. I did not work for the KGB; I have never been a Communist. But I understood the potential of these techniques for combating crime. Since then, I have had two jobs. I have kept my position as a pure scientist at the Institute of Molecular Biology and I have also become the DNA adviser to the chief medical examiner of Russia, Dr. Plaksin. Later, when the Romanov case arose, I became the principal Russian DNA investigator by appointment of the Russian state procurator general."

Ivanov worked in both places in order to earn money. His wife, an assistant professor of biology, had a small salary; he helped his mother, a retired economist with a miserably inadequate pension; and he had two children. Despite his workload, he considered himself fortunate. He traveled far more widely than most Russian scientists, attending conferences as far afield as Australia and Dubai. He had worked at the FBI DNA laboratory in Washington, D.C., and had traveled back and forth across the United States. In the mid-1990s, his work on the Romanov bones had made him Russia's best-known molecular biologist. During the summer of 1994, he drove his Volvo from Moscow to Ulm on the Danube in southern Germany in order to perform DNA tests on the remains of a recently deceased Russian emigre who claimed to have been the Tsarevich Alexis. During a long evening in a German restaurant, he talked about his involvement with the Romanov bones:

"I was the one who decided we should go to England when Plaksin asked for my recommendation," Ivanov said. "The FBI laboratory in Washington and the AFIP both do excellent DNA work, but I chose Peter Gill because I knew him and because the British Forensic Science Service had the highest level of expertise in this particular sort of investigation—that is, using mitochondrial DNA. Also, of course, I already had considered asking Prince Philip, the Duke of Edinburgh, to help us. And I knew that he would be much more likely to help if the work was being done in England. But we had to find money. For a Russian scientist today, it is always a question of money. There are no political barriers, but there are financial barriers. You can't go where you want."

On September 15, 1992, Pavel Ivanov boarded a jet in Moscow. With him in a British Airways travel bag, carefully wrapped and sealed in polyethylene, he carried pieces of the femurs of each of the nine skeletons lying on tables in the Ekaterinburg morgue. At Heathrow, Ivanov was met by Nigel McCrery, a BBC television producer who had been active in the negotiations to bring the bones to England.* McCrery, feeling that it was "inappropriate to carry the Russian Imperial family in the boot of my Volvo," had hired a Bentley limousine from Co-operative Funeral Services. In style, therefore, Ivanov, McCrery, and the Romanov remains were driven to Peter Gill's house in the woods near Aldermaston, where the three men took photographs to memorialize the occasion. In the morning, Gill and Ivanov carried the bones through the high barbed-wire fences and security checkpoints of Britain's huge Ministry of Defence atomic-research facility at Aldermaston. Inside the complex and off to one side, the Forensic Science Service had been given a small building to use as a research laboratory. For the next ten months, the two men and a team of others would attempt to compare and match the DNA of the Ekaterinburg skeletons with one another and with that of living relatives of the murdered Russian Imperial family.

---

*McCrery, a florid, enthusiastic man who was a policeman before he went to Cambridge to study Russian history, takes considerable credit for engineering the British-Russian effort. Hearing about the discovery of the bones, he says, he rang up Avdonin in Ekaterinburg. Avdonin put him on to Pavel Ivanov. Ivanov told him that the best place in the world for DNA testing was Aldermaston and gave him the name of Peter Gill. McCrery telephoned Gill, who, he says, was "quite excited, but not sure the Home Office would approve. Well, Kenneth Clark, [then] the home secretary, lives around the corner from me and I've known him for years. He is my M.P. So I contacted him and pointed out how prestigious it would be for the Forensic Science Service to be involved. 'Will you give permission?' And Clark said, 'It's a wonderful idea.' So then I rang Ivanov back and Ivanov said, 'How do I get there? I don't have any money.' So I said, 'I'll pay for it.' Actually, somebody in Russia paid for Ivanov's trip, but I got in touch

✤

If the Central Crime Laboratory of the U.S. Federal Bureau of Investigation were to be turned into a private business, instructed to develop a "commercial, customer-focused, cost-conscious approach," and told to break even or make a profit by charging fees and offering its services to all who walk in the door, this would approximate what happened recently to Britain's equivalent of the FBI lab, the Home Office Forensic Science Service. For fifty years, beginning in the 1930s, the Forensic Science Service functioned as a source of expert investigative assistance to provincial and local police departments in England and Wales. Experts from FSS scrutinized evidence in cases of murder, rape, arson, burglary, drug use, poisoning, and forgery. They visited crime scenes, examined bodies, fingerprints, weapons, bullets, stains, alcohol levels, handwriting samples, and old typewriters. The beneficiaries of this specialized knowledge were the Crown prosecutors, on whose behalf the FSS provided expert testimony in court. The people of Britain paid for these services by paying taxes.

In April 1991, the FSS was overtaken by Thatcherism. Its six hundred scientists, technicians, and other staffers, working at six laboratories scattered around the country, suddenly were transformed into scientific guns for hire. The FSS became a business, required to make its own way in the world by charging fees for services. The door was opened to everyone—"widening the customer base" was the terminology used. Defense attorneys, foreign governments, insurance adjusters, regional health authorities, and private citizens were invited in. The transformation was "turbulent," admitted FSS Director General Janet Thompson. To most scientists, "the world of business still seemed radical." In 1991–92, police case work dropped 18 percent and a deficit of £1.1 million was posted. But the following year, matters improved. The police came back and paid the required fees. The

---

with Applied Biosystems, which makes gene scanners and other machines they use in DNA work, and asked them whether they would pay Ivanov's expenses in England. They said yes, and they came up with three to five thousand pounds for him to live on for ten months. So he came and brought the bones."

FSS made a profit equal to its earlier loss. Most spectacularly, in the summer of that year, the service and its leading molecular biologist, Dr. Peter Gill, made headline news, not only in Britain but around the world.

Dr. Gill, the head of Biological Services (Research) of the Forensic Science Service, is a slightly built man in his early forties, about five feet nine, with a pale face, uncombed hair, a brown mustache, and watchful eyes behind thick spectacles. He owns a dark blue suit, which he wears for press conferences, but in and around his laboratory his typical dress is a tattered sweater, shapeless corduroys, and elderly loafers. Born in Essex, Gill did an undergraduate degree in zoology at Bristol University, received a doctorate in genetics from Liverpool University, and did a five-year postdoctoral fellowship in genetics at Nottingham University. In 1982, he joined the Forensic Science Service Research Laboratory at Aldermaston to work on forensic applications of conventional blood typing methods. In 1985, against strong opposition in the service, he began to study the utility of DNA profiling in forensic science. Aware of the significance of Alec Jeffreys's work, he briefly joined Jeffreys's laboratory and, that same year, coauthored with Jeffreys the first scientific paper which demonstrated that DNA profiling could be used in forensic science. The methods described in this paper are now routinely used around the world. Gill himself has published over seventy papers in the scientific literature.

Although he is shy and speaks cautiously with strangers, there is one point on which Dr. Gill is quietly emphatic: his laboratory is the best of its kind in the world—"We have retained our world lead" is his way of putting it. In his opinion, therefore, it was entirely understandable that Pavel Ivanov had wished to bring the Russian bones to Aldermaston. "Ivanov asked me a long time ago whether we'd be interested in carrying out these tests," Gill said. "When he asked, I had to go through the Home Office. They considered all the political ramifications, and eventually we got the go-ahead."

The political ramifications existed on many levels. The most obvious was the current relationship between John Major's Conservative government in Britain and Boris Yeltsin's presidency of Russia. Both parties were interested in bringing to fruition a long-suspended diplomatic project: a visit to Russia by the queen. No British monarch had visited Russia since 1908, when King Edward VII and Queen Alexandra came by yacht to Tallinn (then Reval) to visit Tsar Nicholas II and Empress Alexandra.* Mikhail Gorbachev and Boris Yeltsin both had invited the queen to come, and Her Majesty and the British Foreign Office wanted the visit to take place.

But first there was some unfinished historical and family business. The Russian Imperial family and the British Royal family were closely related. King George V, Elizabeth II's grandfather, was Nicholas II's first cousin. Indeed, so close was the physical resemblance between the cousins that at George's wedding, Nicholas often was mistaken for the groom. King George also was a first cousin of Empress Alexandra. In the spring of 1917, after the tsar had abdicated and while Alexander Kerensky and the Provisional Russian government were trying to provide for the safety of the Imperial family by sending them to political asylum abroad, King George V at first welcomed a proposal that Britain bring his Russian cousins to safety by ship. Then the king—fearing that the former tsar's unpopularity in Britain would tarnish the British monarchy—reversed himself and insisted that they not be brought. George V's act helped doom Nicholas, his wife, and his five children. When the British door slammed shut, Kerensky sent the family to Siberia, hoping to put them out of reach of the Bolsheviks. They still were there when, seven months after Kerensky's fall, Lenin's long arm reached out.

This catastrophe led to many recriminations. Members of the Russian Imperial family who escaped, aristocratic emigres, and numerous White Russians abroad bitterly condemned King George and his family and descendants. For three quarters of a century, many Russians have regarded England with deep suspicion and resentment. The British Royal family is aware of this hostility. Over the years,

---

*In fact, the security men of both monarchs were so concerned about the possibility of terrorism that King Edward never actually set foot on the soil of the Russian Empire. All meetings were held on the two yachts.

palace officials have attempted to bury the king's role in the Romanov tragedy; official biographers of George V were advised that they should "omit things and incidents which were discreditable." In 1992, the possibility that the Romanov bones might come to Britain to be verified by British scientists with the help of British Royal persons offered an opportunity to put some of these passionate feelings to rest.

According to a Forensic Science Service spokesperson who stays close to Dr. Gill specifically to answer nonscientific questions, the decision to bring the bones to Aldermaston was made on a relatively low level; that is, by Janet Thompson, the FSS director general. "Of course," said the spokesperson, "with the high profile that came with this project, we put it before the home secretary. He could have objected if he had wanted to." The spokesperson does not know whether Kenneth Clark discussed the project with the foreign secretary or the prime minister. Or whether anyone thought to consult the Royal family. If this was not done, however, Dr. Thompson and Secretary Clark were assuming historical and diplomatic responsibilities far beyond the normal range of their professional and political assignments.

There was one area in which Thompson—no doubt supported by Clark—did make a decision on her own. This was the decision to ignore the new Thatcherite decree that the FSS was to charge for services and attempt to make a profit. The service spent a large sum of money on the Romanov project. "We did all nine of them, the whole lot," said Peter Gill. "It managed to be expensive." "It was very expensive," chimed in the spokesperson, adding that no figure is available. The sum can be roughly estimated. A year later, the FSS negotiated with a private citizen to perform DNA testing on an unknown woman and a possible relative. These tests were to be performed on preserved tissue and recently drawn blood, both sources from which DNA is far easier to obtain than from old, long-buried bones. For this work, the FSS demanded a five-thousand-pound down payment, plus another five thousand pounds placed in escrow in an English bank. All of this money was spent. The Romanov project involved typing and comparing bone fragments from nine people in Russia, plus blood samples from at least three relatives alive today. Even using the same expense figures for much more difficult tests, this would mean that twelve

DNA profiles would cost sixty thousand pounds (over $100,000). Dr. Alka Mansukhani, an American molecular biologist routinely doing DNA extraction and sequencing at New York University Medical Center, believes that, if overhead was included, the figure probably is accurate.

The Home Office and FSS accountants funded these costs as pure research.

An adult human body is a cohesive mass of 80 trillion cells, yet in all this amplitude and diversity, there is an extraordinary sameness: each one of these cells contains all the genetic information needed to produce a complete and unique human being. This hereditary knowledge is carried in the chromosomes; in a normal person, forty-six in each cell nucleus, twenty-three from the mother, twenty-three from the father. Chromosomes are made up of molecules of DNA (deoxyribonucleic acid), which use their own chemical structure to store genetic information and commands. The DNA molecules are created from four basic chemical building blocks called bases, and the sequence in which these bases occur provides the information necessary to commence and control the building of a human body. For simplicity's sake, molecular biologists describe the four bases by their initial letters, A, G, C, and T (adenine, guanine, cytosine, and thymine). The bases appear in pairs bonded with hydrogen; A bonds with T; G bonds with C; these combinations are known as base pairs. In 1953, James Watson and Francis Crick discovered the detailed, overall molecular structure of DNA. They found long, tightly coiled strands, each resembling a ladder twisted into the form of a spiral staircase. The A, C, G, and T base pairs formed the rungs; the sides of the ladder, to which the rungs were attached, were made up of alternating molecules of sugar and phosphate. Watson and Crick named their discovery the double helix.

The unique structure of every individual human body is dictated by the different combinations of these four letters in base pairs in the DNA. For example, at some point in the strand, one individual will read A, C, G, T, C, C, T. Another person, in the same part of the strand, will display a different sequence, say A, T, T, C, A, G, C. Whatever the base pair sequence, each cell in a human body contains the same DNA sequence, storing the same information and commands. But, to avoid massive confusion, nature activates only that part of the command system necessary for the function of that particular cell.

Each cell with its set of forty-six chromosomes contains approximately 3.3 billion DNA base pairs, strung together in clusters of spiraling double helixes. If one magnified this structure to a humanly visible five characters (A, G, T, C, T) per half inch, it would require a strip of paper 162 miles long to write the entire base sequence of a single chromosome. Approximately 99.9 percent of the 3.3 billion base pairs found in a single cell appear in the same sequence in all human beings; they ensure that all humans possess similar characteristics: two eyes, two ears, one nose, ten toes, blood, saliva, stomach acid, and so on. However, in the remaining 0.1 percent (that is, 3.3 million base pairs), the sequence of these base pairs differs from one person to another. It is the fact that individuals vary at this basic molecular level that now permits scientists to determine which human being was the source of this or that sample of bone or tissue, blood, semen, or saliva.

In the early 1980s, Dr. Alec Jeffreys, working at Leicester University, first recognized the enormous potential of the DNA variable in human beings to resolve questions of identity. He identified regions within hypervariable areas and used radioactive isotopes, called probes, to create an image on film of the DNA strands extracted from individuals. These visible symbols appear strikingly similar to the bar codes which are printed on packages and cans at every supermarket. The DNA patterns—Jeffreys called them "DNA fingerprints"— could then be used to compare one person's DNA with that of another. Because children would derive half of their DNA base pairs from their mother and half from their father, family relationships could be established or refuted. In 1983, a boy was refused entry into England because an immigration officer doubted that he was the son of a Ghanaian woman who had rights to settlement in the United Kingdom. Jeffreys's new DNA technique was employed and proved that the boy was the woman's son. The chance of this match occurring at random was one in ten million.

Nicholas II, painted by Serov.

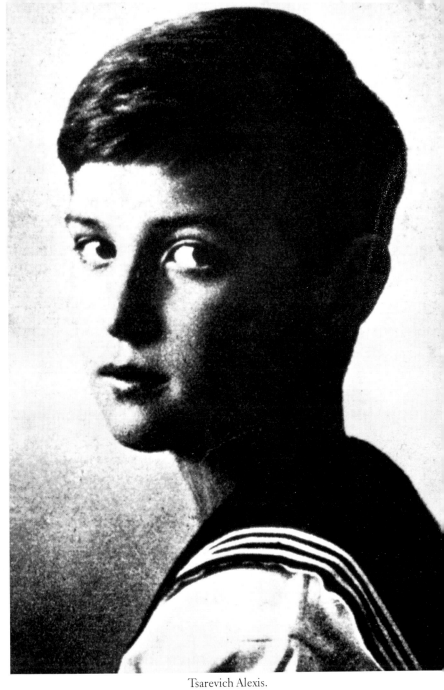

Tsarevich Alexis.

Facing: Empress Alexandra.

Grand Duchess Tatiana. *(Bettmann archive)*

Facing: Grand Duchess Olga. *(Bettmann archive)*

Grand Duchess Anastasia. *(Bettmann archive)*

Facing: Grand Duchess Marie. *(Bettmann archive)*

The Ipatiev House. Nicholas, Alexandra, and Alexis occupied the main-floor corner room, with two windows facing the front and two windows on the side. The four daughters were next to them in the side room, with a single window. The cellar room where the prisoners were massacred is directly below the daughters' room, behind the small central window on the side of the house.

The Ipatiev House surrounded by a palisade and guards, 1918.

The Ipatiev House being demolished, July 27, 1977.

The Ipatiev House cellar room, with wallpaper and plaster destroyed by the fusillade of bullets.

Dr. Eugene Botkin, who died with the family.

Above: Yakov Yurovsky, "the dark man," who was the chief executioner.

Right: Nicholas Sokolov, the White investigator.

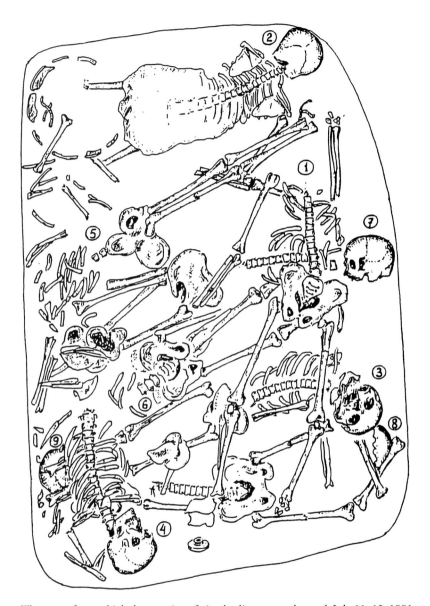

The grave from which the remains of nine bodies were exhumed, July 11–13, 1991:

Body No. 1: Demidova; Body No. 2: Botkin; Body No. 3: Olga; Body No. 4: Nicholas; Body No. 5: Maples believes this is Marie; Abramov believes it is Tatiana; Body No.6: Maples believes this is Tatiana; Abramov thinks it is Anastasia; Body No. 7: Alexandra; Body No. 8: Kharitonov; Body No. 9: Trupp

Three additional skulls were found in the wooden box into which Avdonin and Ryabov had placed them in 1980.

Alexander Avdonin.

Within less than a decade, DNA typing has become the most powerful forensic science tool since the nineteenth-century discovery that the fingerprints of no two persons are the same. Comparisons of DNA now routinely solve paternity cases. Murderers are identified by samples of blood, hair, other tissues, or fluids, liquid or dried. Samples of DNA from bones and teeth have helped resolve long-standing mysteries involving missing persons and unidentified bodies. DNA is remarkably stable: it has been extracted and identified from a three-thousand-year-old Egyptian mummy, from a seven-thousand-year-old mammoth, from the dried saliva remaining on a licked postage stamp. And, properly handled and identified, it is unerring. No prosecutor or defense attorney, no historian, no churchman of any faith, no believer in any political ideology, can disprove the essential message of DNA: that every human being is distinct from every other. DNA evidence, declared one American district attorney, is "like the finger of God pointing at someone and saying, 'You are the one!' "

Because of the age and deteriorated condition of the Romanov bones, Dr. Gill and Dr. Ivanov faced a task radically more difficult than in any previous DNA typing examination. In a sterile environment, they began by grinding away one millimeter of the contaminated outer surfaces of the bones with sand wheels attached to a high-speed electric drill. The remaining bone was frozen in liquid nitrogen, then pulverized to a fine powder and dissolved in various solutions, then centrifuged to release a microscopic quantity of DNA. So paltry and degraded, in fact, were the sample yields that Gill and Ivanov applied an even more recently developed technique called PCR (polymerase chain reaction), in which selected relevant sections of base pair strands are chemically duplicated over and over in a test tube to provide sufficient quantities of DNA material for scientists to study.

Using nuclear DNA, the Aldermaston team first turned to determining the sex of each of the skeletons. A gene on the X chromosome (females have two X's) is six base pairs longer than the similar gene on the Y (males have one X and one Y) chromosome. Using PCR, the scientists could obtain sufficient material to measure and determine this six-base-pair difference. The result was a confirmation of the anthropological findings of Abramov and Maples: there were four males and five females. Next, still using nuclear DNA and studying base pair sequences, Gill and Ivanov tested all nine for a family relationship. Short tandem repeat (called STR) sequences are natural base pair repetitions in certain hypervariable regions of a chromosome—say, T, A, T, T—occurring over and over again. Within a family, these sequences and the number of repetitions tend to be constant; a different sequence or different number of repetitions in each individual sample would indicate that no family group was present. Again, the results were what was to be expected if the bones had come from the Imperial party. In Gill's words: "Skeletons 3 through 7 exhibited patterns which would be expected in a family group where 4 and 7 were the parents of children 3, 5, and 6." The other four adults were excluded as possible parents. Further, Gill's report continued, "If these remains are the Romanovs then... test data indicated that one of the daughters and the Tsarevich Alexis were missing from the grave." Other tests established paternity. STR DNA patterns from Body No. 4 were found in No. 3, No. 5, and No. 6; thus, the adult male presumed to be Nicholas was confirmed to be the father of the three young women. This was as far as Gill and Ivanov could go using the small quantity of degraded nuclear DNA available. They had established a party of four males and five females. They had established a family: a father, a mother, their three daughters. But to identify these men and women—to give them names—they had to try another tack.

Fortunately, a second form of DNA is available in human cells. Called mitochondrial DNA, it appears plentifully in units outside the nucleus which function as power stations for the cell. Mitochondrial DNA is inherited independently of nuclear DNA, and whereas nuclear DNA is inherited half from the mother, half from the father, mitochondrial DNA is inherited exclusively from the mother. From mother to daughter, it is transmitted intact, "passing from generation to generation unchanging, like a time machine," said Gill. "The same genetic code would be shared by mother, grandmother, great-grandmother, great-great-grandmother, and so on." At all points in this chain, sons possess mitochondrial DNA received from their mothers, but sons cannot pass this mitochondrial DNA along to their daughters or sons. Thus, as a tool for establishing identity, mitochondrial DNA can be used to identify a woman anywhere in a vertical chain of women descended from one another. And it can identify a son of one of these women. But it cannot continue through the male line; with sons the chain is broken.

Gill and Ivanov extracted mitochondrial DNA from the nine bone samples brought from Russia. The extracts were amplified to workable quantities by using PCR. To their delight, the quality of the DNA sequences obtained, said Gill, was "generally comparable to that produced from fresh blood samples." Focusing on two different stretches of the DNA sequence normally hypervariable between different humans, and deriving between 634 and 782 base pair letters for each of the nine subjects, the scientists achieved DNA profiles for all nine of the bone samples they possessed.

Next, they needed contemporary DNA to make comparisons. The search for living relatives began. People at the FSS and the Home Office drew books from libraries and pored over genealogical trees. Someone drew up a list of names of people who would be scientifically suitable and might be approached. In the case of the Empress Alexandra, finding a genetically useful living relative was easy. Alexandra's older sister, Princess Victoria of Battenberg, had a daughter, who became Princess Alice of Greece. Princess Alice, in turn, produced four daughters and a son. In 1993, only one of these daughters, Princess Sophie of Hanover, was living. The son was Prince Philip, who became Duke of Edinburgh and the consort of Queen Elizabeth II of England. Prince Philip, Empress Alexandra's grandnephew, was perfectly suited for a mitochondrial DNA comparison with bone material of the murdered Russian empress. Accordingly, Dr. Thompson, director of the FSS, wrote to Buckingham Palace and asked whether the prince would be willing to help. Philip agreed, and a test tube filled with his blood soon made its way to Aldermaston. The testing was done in those parts of the mitochondrial DNA sequence where the greatest variety between family groups occurs. By November, Gill and Ivanov had results: the match was perfect; the sequence of DNA base pairs between the mother, the three young women, and Prince Philip was identical. Gill and Ivanov knew that they had located the remains of Alexandra Feodorovna and three of her four daughters.

Confirming the presence of Tsar Nicholas II was far more difficult. The search for DNA material to compare with that extracted from the femur of Body No. 4 was widespread, prolonged, and, in several instances, controversial. The first attempts were made by Pavel Ivanov. It occurred to him that Nicholas II's younger brother Grand Duke George, who died in 1899 of tuberculosis at the age of twenty-eight, was buried in the mausoleum of the Romanovs, the Cathedral of St. Peter and St. Paul in St. Petersburg. Comparison of DNA between brothers would nicely suffice. From England, Ivanov contacted Anatoly Sobchak, the mayor of St. Petersburg, and Vladimir Soloviev, who would become the investigator assigned to the Romanov case. "They protested that it would be too expensive," Ivanov recalled. " 'The tombs in the fortress are made of Italian marble.... You must break it.... Who will pay for this?' And so on." For eight months, Ivanov persisted, and, at one point, Mstislav Rostropovich, the cellist and conductor, who is a friend of Sobchak, seemed about to pay for the exhumation of Grand Duke George.

Before this happened, however, Rostropovich told Ivanov that he was about to set out on a visit to Japan. Ivanov, still in England, remembered that in 1892 Nicholas II as tsarevich had visited Japan. In Otsu, the heir to the Russian throne suddenly had been attacked by a sword-wielding Japanese. The blow, aimed at his head, glanced off his forehead, bringing a gush of blood but failing to bite deep. The wound was bound with a handkerchief. For one hundred years, a museum in Otsu had kept the blood-soaked handkerchief in a small box. For DNA comparison purposes, nothing could provide more accurate positive identity than achieving a match between bone material of unknown origin and blood from a known person. Ivanov was eager to go to Japan, but, as always, "there was no money. The English said, Why should we pay for this? The Russians said, We have no money." Eventually, Rostropovich arranged for Ivanov's trip. "It was the money we were going to use to dig up George," Ivanov said. "So, instead of George, we did Japan."

The Japanese were not anxious to give up or even to disturb the handkerchief, but Rostropovich spoke to his friend the emperor of Japan, and the emperor spoke to the relevant authorities. When Ivanov arrived he was permitted to remove and take with him a strip of the handkerchief three inches long and one eighth of an inch wide. Unfortunately, back in Gill's laboratory in England, Ivanov ran into difficulties. "The handkerchief had been handled by too many people," he said. "Cells slough off from fingers. There was a lot of blood on the handkerchief, but who knows how much of it was Nicholas's? And there was a lot of dust and dirt. It would be impossible to say that any result you got from that handkerchief was reliable. There were too many other possible contaminants."

Having failed with both George and Japan, Ivanov came up with a third possible source of DNA for comparison to the piece of the presumed tsar's femur at Aldermaston. In 1916, Nicholas II's younger sister Grand Duchess Olga married Colonel Nicholas Kulikovsky, a commoner. With Kulikovsky, Olga had two sons, Tikhon, born in 1917, and Guri, born in 1919. In 1948, Olga and her family moved to Canada, where Kulikovsky bought a farm and raised cattle and pigs. Guri Kulikovsky died, but in 1992, when Gill and Ivanov began their work together, Tikhon, at seventy-five, was living in retirement in Toronto. He was, by that time, Tsar Nicholas II's only living nephew and, as such, the best available source for comparative mitochondrial DNA. If the femur from Body No. 4 had belonged to Nicholas II, it should match perfectly with DNA from Tikhon Kulikovsky.

Mr. Kulikovsky, however, refused to cooperate. When Ivanov wrote to him, explaining the purposes of the investigation and asking for a blood sample, he received no reply. Ivanov tried again through Bishop Basil Rodzianko of the Orthodox Church in America, and, finally, through Metropolitan Vitaly, the head of the Russian Orthodox Church Abroad. Ultimately, Kulikovsky replied to Ivanov. "He told me he believed this whole bones business was a hoax," Ivanov recalled. "He said, 'How can you, a Russian man, be working in England, which was so cruel to the tsar and to the Russian monarchy?' He said, 'For political reasons, I will never give you a sample of my blood or hair or anything.'" Ivanov was disappointed, but he did not give up. "At that time, it was critical," Ivanov said. "He was the closest relative. I spent a lot of my own money talking with him and his wife by telephone, assuring them that I was not a KGB agent. And they replied, 'Then probably the only reason for your investigation is to prove that Tikhon Nicholaevich is not of royal blood.' " Ivanov gave up. "Okay, so we forgot about this Tikhon," he said. "And after we published our work, some people wrote that our analysis was not accurate because we didn't use the blood of Tikhon Kulikovsky. The fact is that his blood is no longer necessary. We found two other relatives. They gave us their blood, and we had everything we needed for our research."

To locate the other two relatives, the Aldermaston genealogists looked again at the family tree. Because the chain of similar mitochondrial DNA is repeated indefinitely down through generations of females, they focused on the women closest by blood to Tsar Nicholas II. Beginning with his mother, Dowager Empress Marie, they found an unbroken line of five generations of mothers and daughters leading to a contemporary descendant willing to help. The tsar's sister Grand Duchess Xenia had one daughter, Princess Irina. This Irina married Prince Felix Yussoupov, famous for having murdered Rasputin. Irina and Felix produced one child, a daughter, also named Irina. This second Irina married Count Nicholas Sheremetyev, with whom she had one child, a daughter, Xenia. Upon her marriage, young Countess Xenia Sheremetyeva became Xenia Sfiris. Now in her early fifties, Mrs. Sfiris lives in Athens and Paris, and it was in Athens that she received the FSS's appeal for help. An exuberant, warmhearted woman, she agreed immediately. Following instructions, she pricked her finger, let some blood run into a paper handkerchief, where it dried, put the handkerchief in an envelope, and took it to the British Embassy. From there, it went, via diplomatic pouch, to Aldermaston.

The other donor of DNA material given to identify Nicholas II was found on what must seem an infinitely remote branch of the massive European royal family tree. Nevertheless, although the line stretched back over six generations, the connection was as reliable and productive as it was in the case of Mrs. Sfiris. James George Alexander Bannerman Carnegie, third Duke of Fife, Earl Macduff, and Lord

Carnegie, is a sixty-six-year-old Scottish nobleman and farmer who descends from a common female ancestor of Tsar Nicholas II. She was Louise of Hesse-Cassel, a German princess who married King Christian IX of Denmark. One of her daughters became Empress Marie Feodorovna of Russia, the mother of Nicholas II. Another, older daughter, Alexandra, married the Prince of Wales, later King Edward VII. Queen Alexandra's daughter Louise married the first Duke of Fife. In 1929, Louise's daughter Maud produced James, who, in 1959, succeeded to the title. The duke was willing to donate blood but, not wishing to incur publicity, made it a condition that he remain anonymous. Inevitably, in the course of time and with an investigation of this significance, knowledge leaked out.

As Gill and Ivanov expected, Xenia Sfiris's mitochondrial DNA matched perfectly with that of the Duke of Fife. But when the matching 782 base pair letters lengths of the Greek woman and the Scottish peer were compared to the same section in the mitochondrial DNA extracted from the presumed tsar, there was a mismatch. A single letter was different. At a position numbered 16169, Xenia Sfiris and the Duke of Fife had a T; in this position Nicholas had a C. The other 781 pairs were in identical sequence. To check their data, Gill and Ivanov did a second mitochondrial DNA extraction from the bone believed to be the tsar's. They cloned the DNA in this region after amplifying it with PCR and then transformed the product into *E. coli* bacteria. When fresh sequencing of these new clones was performed, seven of the clones were found to have a T at position 16169, thus matching Mrs. Sfiris and the Duke of Fife. But twenty-eight clones still presented the single spelling mistake, a mismatching C. The Aldermaston scientists concluded that Tsar Nicholas II had possessed two forms of mitochondrial DNA, one of which matched his relatives exactly; the other, at a single point, did not. This rare condition is known as heteroplasmy.

This single mismatched base pair letter caused great anxiety at Aldermaston. In their paper, the two scientists presented their interpretation of what they had found: "We consider... that the mitochondrial DNA extracted from the tsar was genetically heteroplasmic. This complicates the interpretation because the strength of the evidence depends upon whether we accept a priori that a mutation has occurred in the tsar. The probability of a single mutation was calculated to be approximately one in three hundred per generation, but this estimate does not take account of the incidence of heteroplasmy (much of which may be undetected)."

Gill understood that this one-letter mismatch raised questions about the validity of his findings. He believed that a mutation did occur, although he admitted that the odds against a mutation in any given generation were long. "A mutation is thought to occur [in a family] about once in three hundred generations," he said. But he insisted that he is talking primarily about a heteroplasmy, which he found, not a mutation, which he could not prove but which is the probable cause of that heteroplasmy. "Heteroplasmy is different from a mutation in nuclear DNA; it means that there are two types of mitochondrial DNA in the same person. What we did was demonstrate that there are two types of mitochondrial DNA in the tsar. One of these types differed by just one base; the other was identical to the relatives'. That's pretty good evidence that there has been a real mutation. Bear in mind that we're working right at the frontiers of knowledge. The actual incidence of this type of phenomenon is not really known, and we suspect that it is much more common than originally had been anticipated."

In July 1993, after ten months of work, Gill and Ivanov were ready to announce their results to the world. The Forensic Science Service convened a press conference and, on July 10, a large hall at the bleakly modern Home Office building in Queen Anne's Gate was filled with reporters, photographers, and television cameramen. Dr. Janet Thompson, the director general of the FSS, presided. Aware that questions might be asked as to who had borne the cost of this research, she began by expressing hope that "the FSS will soon be able to put the techniques used, once validated, into practice in criminal casework to the benefit of the criminal justice system as a whole."

Gill explained what he and his colleagues had done. He described how the sex of the specimens had been determined, how the family relationship between five skeletons had been established, how Prince Philip's blood had made certain the identity of Alexandra Feodorovna and her daughters, and how the heteroplasmy found in the tsar's DNA had complicated the effort to make an absolute statement about Nicholas. Nevertheless, the Aldermaston team announced that, given the DNA evidence and adding it to the anthropological and historical evidence provided by others, they were 98.5 percent certain that these were the Romanovs. This percentage, Gill said, was based on the most conservative interpretation of the DNA evidence. A more generous interpretation would increase the probability to 99 percent. Pavel Ivanov took a broader view of what had been done. "We are very close to the last part of this mystery, to one of the great mysteries of the twentieth century, one of the great mysteries of my country, of Russia," he said.

The press conference produced headlines: RIDDLE OF ROMANOV REMAINS IS SOLVED (*Financial Times*), DNA TESTS IDENTIFY TSAR'S SKELETON (*The Times*), TSAR NICHOLAS'S BONES IDENTIFIED (*The Washington Post*). Tass told Russian readers that "British scientists" were "almost without any doubt" that the remains found in Siberia were those of Tsar Nicholas II and his family. Seven months later, in February 1994, Peter Gill, Pavel Ivanov, and others put their findings in print in their own words, publishing a description of their work in *Nature Genetics*, the authoritative journal of their profession. Their findings and article have never been challenged or even mildly criticized, in print or orally, by another DNA scientist.

CHAPTER 9

❖

DR. MAPLES
VERSUS DR. GILL

W illiam Maples, after his examination of the bones and his presentation of his findings at the Ekaterinburg conference in July 1992, was unwilling to let go of the Romanov inquiry. In his talk at the conference, he recommended that there be further archaeological exploration of the burial site and more extensive photo documentation and DNA testing of the remains. Apparently, he intended to do—or at least to supervise—most of this himself. In April 1993, Maples, Dr. William Hamilton, and Mrs. Maples returned to Siberia, assisted by two airline tickets provided by the television program *Unsolved Mysteries*. In Ekaterinburg, Maples rephotographed the skeletal remains more carefully than he had been able to do on his previous trip. He also removed one tooth from each of the skulls, except that of Dr. Botkin, which had few teeth to spare, and that of Kharitonov, where only the top of the skull was available. From Botkin and Kharitonov, he took leg bone fragments. The teeth, he believed, would be far more suitable for accurately identifying the Imperial family by DNA testing than the pieces of femurs taken to Britain by

Pavel Ivanov. Along with these teeth, Maples carried away from Ekaterinburg a decree from the Sverdlovsk regional prosecutor authoriz-
ing him to export the bones, oversee DNA tests, and report the results
back to the Sverdlovsk authorities. Curiously, no one bothered to tell
Dr. Vladislav Plaksin, the chief medical examiner of the Russian government, or Pavel Ivanov, then in his seventh month working with
Peter Gill at Aldermaston.

Returning to Florida, Maples held the Russian teeth in his laboratory for six weeks, then "transferred custody" to Lowell Levine, who
carried them to California and, in June 1993, gave them to Dr. Mary-
Claire King, who held two professorships at the University of California, Berkeley, one in epidemiology in the School of Public Health,
the other in genetics in the Department of Molecular and Cell Biology. According to Maples, Dr. King "is the foremost forensic genetics
scientist in the United States and one of the most highly regarded scientists in this field anywhere in the world." She drafted the report
prepared for the National Academy of Sciences on the use of DNA
for forensic identification purposes. She has worked with a United
Nations team in Argentina to identify kidnapped children and re-
unite them with their families. She has assisted the United Nations in
El Salvador to try to identify the remains of victims of a mass murder
in the village of El Mozote. Doctors Maples, Levine, and Baden knew
her because she had worked with them on the remains of American
servicemen brought back from Vietnam. By 1993, Maples said, she
had more experience with mitochondrial DNA than the British
Forensic Science Service. And she had a far larger database. According to Maples, Dr. King's database held mitochondrial DNA information on one thousand people; Peter Gill and Aldermaston had only
about three hundred. "In this field," said Dr. Maples, "there simply
isn't anyone to compare with Dr. King." Michael Baden and Lowell
Levine agreed.

Maples and his colleagues had a secondary regard for Peter Gill,
and, until they met him at the Ekaterinburg conference in 1992, they
had never heard of Pavel Ivanov. Unable to understand Russian, they
were not sure what Ivanov had told the meeting about his arrangements to test the bones in England. Nevertheless, Ivanov was friendly

and tried to be helpful. Their return to Moscow that summer was disagreeable for the American team: a dog ran up and down the aisle of
the Aeroflot plane; at the domestic airport in Moscow, people shoved
and shouted at them. Dr. Ivanov, whose English is fluent, appeared
and confidently steered the Americans to safety. The following day,
wearing his FBI Academy T-shirt, he showed them through Red
Square. He explained what he was doing, that he had been in touch
with Gill and was making arrangements to do DNA tests in England.
The Americans attempted to change his plans. "We offered him the
chance to come and work in an American laboratory," said Baden,
"but he went to England because he could get there quicker and they
would pay his way." "The best thing for Ivanov," Levine said, "was that
he personally was going to take the bones to England and he was
going to get to stay there."

William Maples met Peter Gill for the first time and Pavel Ivanov
again in July 1993, soon after Gill's press conference announcing
identification of the Romanov bones. Maples was in England, returning to America from his third visit to Ekaterinburg, where he had
been filmed by *Nova* examining and describing the remains. From
London, Maples and his wife drove to Aldermaston, where they took
Peter Gill and Pavel Ivanov to lunch. The luncheon conversation was
polite, this ambience being achieved by both sides ignoring feelings of
mutual grievance. Maples was annoyed that Gill had just announced
that he was 98.5 percent sure that the bones he had tested belonged to
the Romanovs; this event had occurred just as Dr. Maples was arriving
in Russia to be filmed by *Nova*. Ivanov was indignant that Maples, with
the permission of the Sverdlovsk authorities, had initiated a second
round of DNA tests at Dr. King's laboratory in California without his
being informed and while his own tests with Gill were still under way.
There was no discussion at lunch about the heteroplasmy which Gill
had discovered in Tsar Nicholas II, or the possibility that it had been
caused by a mutation. The scientists did talk briefly about the Aldermaston finding that the three young females had the same mitochondrial DNA as one of the older females and therefore undoubtedly
were mother and daughters.

Until their meeting at lunch in July 1993, Peter Gill had been only
dimly aware of William Maples. Within six months, this situation

radically changed as Maples became the source of a vigorous attack on Gill's findings, his administrative procedures, even his competence as a scientist.

Dr. Maples, believing that Ekaterinburg, not Moscow, possessed the primary authority to dispose of the Romanov bones, began by suggesting that the Aldermaston tests were illegal under Russian law. In fact, when Pavel Ivanov carried the Romanov bones to England, he did so on behalf of the Russian Ministry of Health and on the specific instructions of the chief medical examiner of the Russian government, Vladislav Plaksin. And earlier, at the July 1992 conference in Ekaterinburg, when Ivanov had announced his forthcoming mission to England, none of the Russians present, including those from Ekaterinburg, had objected. Nevertheless, Dr. Maples thought there had been wrongdoing. "I have no idea what permission was given Ivanov, officially or unofficially," he said. "Ivanov got the samples somehow, but I don't know how official it was for him to take them to England for DNA purposes. They had bone samples in Moscow for blood typing, serology, and they probably used those samples for the DNA tests. Whether they asked the people in Ekaterinburg for permission to send them out of the country, I don't know."

Dr. Levine supported Maples' belief that Ekaterinburg, not Moscow, was the legal proprietor of the bones and therefore had the sole right to arrange for DNA testing. "My impression is that the person in whose jurisdiction the remains were found has the legal responsibility to identify them and sign a death certificate," he said. "Right now, he has nine homicides that occurred in his district of Sverdlovsk and that's all. He's the person who should have all the evidence coming back to him."

Levine had a further complaint. He argued that even if he was wrong about proprietorship and the Aldermaston tests were legal under Russian law, Gill's announcement of his findings at a press conference in London constituted improper scientific procedure. "His report should have gone back to whoever it was who commissioned this work," Levine declared. "If it was Plaksin, then the report should have gone back to Moscow, to the Ministry of Health, to be released there.

Look, if you give me a piece of evidence to analyze for you, my scientific report goes to you. It doesn't go to *The New York Times, The Washington Post, Time, Newsweek,* and CNN. Then I would expect you, the donor of the evidence, to release the results. That's the way we did it with Mengele. We gave our report to the Brazilians. Then they arranged a joint news conference. What Gill did was to shoot before he should have. How could he release a report that says, 'I did DNA studies and this is the tsar; I'm 98.5 percent certain of it'? That's ridiculous. He should have sent his report back to Moscow to be correlated with all the other evidence. And when he released it, he only should have said, 'I did DNA studies and these are my findings.' The fact is that the way Gill did this in London was a PR thing, a glory grab."

More serious charges by the Americans struck at the scientific competence of the Aldermaston team. To begin with, Maples questioned whether Gill and Ivanov even used the right bones for their study. "Ivanov brought long bone samples to England for their DNA sources," Maples said. "And I personally know that in the Ekaterinburg morgue, the long bones may not be on the correct table. That's why I used teeth drawn directly from the skulls. There is no problem mixing up the skulls, and my teeth came directly from the sockets of Nicholas, Alexandra, the three daughters, and from one of the male servants. Botkin's skull had only a few teeth left in the lower jaw so I used a long bone sample for him."

The most critical of Maples' charges against Peter Gill and Pavel Ivanov were leveled against the Aldermaston finding of heteroplasmy in Tsar Nicholas II's mitochondrial DNA, and Gill and Ivanov's statement that they were 98.5 percent certain that they had identified the bones of the Romanovs. This attack appeared in print in November 1993, when William Maples prepared and signed an affidavit to be used in a court case in Virginia. In this affidavit, he wrote:

> I…am familiar with the mitochondrial DNA research into Romanov remains from Ekaterinburg being conducted at the Aldermaston Laboratory in Britain.
>
> … Because Aldermaston is relying on bones from varying parts of the human anatomy, they cannot be certain that they have re-

ceived samples from each of the human remains at Ekaterinburg, as I can.

...A press release [provided by the Home Office at Dr. Gill's press conference]...indicates that the Aldermaston Laboratory has had difficulty identifying the remains of Tsar Nicholas II...

...The evidence of heteroplasmy interpreted by Aldermaston more likely is the result of contaminated samples.

...Aldermaston's public statements that they found different mitochondrial DNA (heteroplasmy) in the remains of the Tsar means that they have been unsuccessful in determining the true mitochondrial DNA for Tsar Nicholas II. For this reason, Aldermaston's public statements do not show that they have definitively identified the remains of Tsar Nicholas II.

Two months later, in conversation, Maples amplified his criticism of Gill and Ivanov: "They were claiming heteroplasmy in the DNA of Tsar Nicholas, and that, more than likely, is just some contamination of the DNA. It's called shadow banding and is frequently seen. No one, in most circles, interprets that as heteroplasmy. So I would assume that the DNA letter code which Gill said was off, probably wasn't."

"And Gill just got it wrong?"

"That's correct."

Baden and Levine shared Maples' opinion. "That's silly," Baden said about Gill's figure of 98.5 percent certainty. "With DNA, it's either 100 percent or it isn't." Levine agreed, more colorfully. "Ninety-eight point five percent doesn't make any sense. That figure would never be allowed in a courtroom in this country.* You know, if you really think about it, 98.5 percent means that three of the next two hundred elderly men you come across could be the tsar."

---

*Dr. Walter Rowe of George Washington University in Washington, D.C., is a professor of forensics who works closely with DNA identification teams at the Armed Forces Institute of Pathology, the FBI, and Cellmark Diagnostics in Bethesda, Maryland, the largest commercial DNA identification laboratory in the United States. Frequently, on behalf of one or another of these organizations, he gives courtroom testimony. He admires William Maples' work in

✤

Peter Gill was surprised by Maples' attack. When he read the statements in Maples' affidavit, he did not understand why this respected forensic anthropologist had ventured so far outside the field in which he is an acknowledged expert. Assuming a normal regard for scientific accuracy and professional courtesy, he did not understand how Maples could condemn him solely on the basis of a press release and newspaper stories; when Maples signed his affidavit in November 1993, publication of Gill's paper in *Nature Genetics* was still three months away.

Nevertheless, even before his paper was published, Gill responded vigorously to the two main points of the American attack: that the heteroplasmy found in Tsar Nicholas's mitochondrial DNA was caused by contamination, and that the 98.5 percent probability assigned the Aldermaston findings was insufficient, unscientific, or "silly."

"The possibility of contamination of our sample is highly unlikely," Gill said, deliberately choosing his words to avoid emotion. "We tested two different kinds of DNA, mitochondrial and genomic [nuclear]. Yes, we managed to extract nuclear DNA from these samples; they are probably the oldest samples from which this kind of DNA ever has been extracted. Then we tested this genomic DNA for STR, short tandem repeat, to confirm the tsar's paternity. It was very difficult, much more difficult than the work with mitochondrial

---

forensic anthropology and has great respect for Peter Gill's reputation in DNA testing. Rowe's quarrel on the matter of the Romanov bones is with Dr. Lowell Levine's assertion that 98.5 percent probability "wouldn't stand up in court."

"Well, I'd tell Dr. Levine that it stands up in court all the time," said Dr. Rowe. "We go to court many times with a lot less certainty than that. I'm sure Dr. Levine is knowledgeable about some aspects of forensic science, but I don't think he's quite as knowledgeable as he'd like to believe. I notice he's often given to making statements that are frankly contrary to my personal experience in court. Most chemists [Rowe's Ph.D. is in chemistry] are happy to operate at a 95 percent confidence level on most things they do, so why does 98.5 percent bother anybody?"

DNA. But it was crucial in showing that this was a family; that the father's DNA was present in the daughters. This is the first major historical investigation in which both STR and mitochondrial DNA have been used as investigative tools. We spelled this out in detail in our *Nature Genetics* paper. No, STR was not mentioned in the press release. I don't think people realized that we did STRs."

This bears directly on Maples' charge of contamination because, as Gill explained, "The nuclear DNA we used came from the same bone segments as the mitochondrial DNA. If there was contamination, you would have seen it in the tsar's nuclear as well as his mitochondrial DNA. We didn't see anything like that." Dr. Gill paused, smiled slightly, and said, "This knocks the contamination theory on the head quite nicely."

In addition, Gill continued, Aldermaston verified its findings with a number of backup tests. "We duplicated our findings several times ourselves, obtaining identical results from two different bones, each extracted in duplicate at different times." Further, as a precaution against precisely the kind of laboratory contamination of which they were accused, Gill and Ivanov sent samples of bone from each of the nine remains to Dr. Erika Hagelberg of Cambridge University. Hagelberg is a specialist in the use of polymerase chain reaction techniques to investigate DNA in ancient, archeologically recovered bones. She used it, for example, to extract DNA from a leg bone of salted pig meat recovered from Henry VIII's warship *Mary Rose,* which capsized in 1545. Several years after Lowell Levine and other specialists identified the remains of Josef Mengele by forensic means, a German court, insufficiently satisfied, asked Alec Jeffreys to verify the finding by DNA testing. Jeffreys chose Hagelberg to assist him. Now in 1993, independently and without knowing the results of the Aldermaston tests, she extracted, amplified, and sequenced DNA from the nine remains in her laboratory. Her results were consistent with Aldermaston's.

Dr. Gill was equally secure about his use of the figure 98.5 percent to describe his degree of certainty that these were the Romanovs. "We had an upper [most likely] and lower [least likely] boundary figure," he explained. "The lower boundary is based on what we call the likelihood ratio. That's the probability of the evidence if this is the tsar and his family, divided by the probability if it is an unknown family. You end up with a likelihood ratio. When we worked out this lower boundary probability, assuming that a mutation did take place, we arrived at a likelihood ratio of seventy to one. That is, it is seventy times more likely that this is the tsar and his family than that it is an unknown family. A likely ratio of seventy to one is equivalent to a probability of 98.5 percent. [When you divide seventy by seventy-one, the result is .9859.] On the other hand, when we worked out the probability assuming that a mutation did *not* take place—which you can argue that we were entitled to do because we did find a sequence in which the tsar's mitochondrial DNA was identical to his relatives'—then the likelihood is in the thousands, many thousands. It would be at least 99.9 percent. We were very cautious. We took the lower boundary. That's why we said 98.5 percent."

The certainty of the identification can be reinforced beyond 98.5 percent when adding in all the other evidence available, Gill continued. "We are one hundred percent sure about the women. We have the mother of three daughters; we have the father of the same three daughters. The mother is a relative of Prince Philip. Beyond DNA, you have the anthropological evidence. Before we had any DNA results, Dr. Helmer [and Dr. Abramov] estimated that the odds that this was the tsar's family were ten to one. It is fair to multiply those odds by the odds given by the DNA evidence. So if we ended up with seventy to one on the DNA evidence and ten to one on the anthropological evidence, you multiply the two together and you get a probability of seven hundred to one that these are the tsar's remains." In sum, Gill declared, the figure of 98.5 percent was the most cautious available.

In February 1994, Peter Gill and his laboratory had been moved from Aldermaston to new, larger quarters in Birmingham. By then, he was aware that Dr. Maples was working with Mary-Claire King and that Dr. King was doing DNA testing on the teeth and bone samples which Maples had brought from Ekaterinburg.

What did Gill think of Maples?

"I have no comment to make," Peter Gill replied. "It is my understanding that he does not do DNA testing."

What does he know of Mary-Claire King, and how does he feel about her doing further DNA tests on the Romanovs?

"Why not? I met her briefly on one occasion. She's got a pretty good reputation in this field. In principle, scientists don't have any problem with people repeating their results, just to make sure. So, if anyone wants to look at our results again, they're welcome. There's a lot of effort involved, especially if they want to do it with short tandem repeats. That would be very difficult for another laboratory because not many laboratories have the necessary skill to do it. Maybe one or two. Remember, also, that Dr. Hagelberg already has repeated and independently verified our tests in her laboratory. So Mary-Claire King's would be the third laboratory to do this."

Pavel Ivanov, as Gill's principal colleague in the Aldermaston testing and as the only Russian scientist involved, deeply resented Maples' criticism. A part of Ivanov's indignation was directed at Maples and a part at the Ekaterinburg authorities, who, as Ivanov sees it, abetted Maples' illegal—or at least improper—removal of the Romanov teeth from Russia.

"Maples was never officially invited by the Russian government," Ivanov said. "He was invited by the local authorities. There is great jealousy there. It is not a good story, not good at all. It is very much Russia. You know"—Ivanov grew angrier as he spoke—"this is an official investigation. It is a criminal case. This is under the jurisdiction of Russian law. Then Maples arrives, and the local authorities write the law by themselves, for themselves. They just took some bone samples and teeth and gave them to Maples. And he put them in his pocket and carried them through the border. I am a Russian scientist and must have official permission from the general prosecutor to take bone samples to England. But, for Maples, it is different. Plaksin doesn't know. Nobody knows.

"It was a sad story. For me and for Russia. Because, before I went to England, the English said, 'Yes, we will pay for Dr. Ivanov's visit. We will pay for all of the analysis.' It was very expensive. And the only request they made to Dr. Plaksin, our chief coordinator, was that there not be any competition, that no one be allowed to perform parallel tests until we had a result. Plaksin said, 'Yes, I agree. Dr. Ivanov will be our official representative according to Russian law. He will come to England, and, until you give your opinion, we will never recheck you.' Then the British learned from their own channels that Maples had taken samples from Russia to perform tests in Mary-Claire King's laboratory. The British didn't know or care who gave Maples these samples. I called Plaksin and said, 'Why? Why? I am in Britain in a terrible situation. The British authorities have said to me, 'We know that some samples have gone to America. Why?' And I had to tell them truthfully, 'I don't know anything about this.' There was an official inquiry from England to Plaksin. Plaksin was very uncomfortable because he had to say, 'I don't know why this was done. It is beyond my control. It is over my head.' This seemed very strange to the British, because he is the chief forensic expert of Russia. The reason is that this is Russia. But the British are not Russian, and they do not understand.

"I thought that I might find out from Maples what was happening, so I called and asked him. He said, 'I'm sorry, but they have asked me not to talk about this until Mary-Claire King has done her analysis.' I wrote two letters to Mary-Claire King asking for her results for discussion. She did not answer. Later, in the autumn of 1993, when I was in Arizona, I telephoned Maples again and asked him to arrange a meeting with Mary-Claire King. There was no answer, so I had no possibility of seeing her. But Maples did tell me, 'You know, it is not so interesting. She has done her analysis and confirmed your result.' I thought that this was a very strange comment for a scientist to make. If she used one method and we used another and we both got the same results, that is very interesting."

Ivanov is furious that Maples ascribed the heteroplasmy found in the tsar's mitochondrial DNA to laboratory contamination. "It is very strange that Maples should say this, because he is not a specialist in this field. He doesn't know these things. Our article in *Nature Genetics* was reviewed by specialists. He should have waited to read it before he attacked our work." Ivanov is particularly unhappy that Maples' attack followed soon after their lunch in Aldermaston. "He came to us, we had a good conversation, and we explained our methods to him. Then he made his announcement that we had contaminated the bones. He understood nothing. It is the same as if I said, 'Maples made a mistake because he doesn't know his cartilage.' "

Did Ivanov believe that this kind of competition was normal between scientists when a high-visibility, high-prestige case was involved? "Not to such an extent," he replied. "Of course, everyone would like to be first. But not to such an extent. Maples is a bad example. I can't speak of Dr. King. I never reached her."

The strangest part of the story of William Maples, Mary-Claire King, and the teeth that went to California for DNA testing is that no report has ever been released. In November 1993, when Maples signed his Virginia court affidavit, he declared that Dr. King and her associates had been working for five months extracting and sequencing mitochondrial DNA. In her research, Maples told the court, Dr. King had found no heteroplasmy in the tsar's mitochondrial DNA (as Gill and Ivanov had done), and therefore she "needed no speculation about rare genetic conditions [a mutation] to establish family relationships to a very high degree of scientific certainty." King was in the process of preparing her report, Maples declared, which had to go to the Sverdlovsk government before she or he could make a general announcement.

In December 1993, Dr. Levine said that King would "put out a final report within the next month." In January 1994, Dr. Maples said that he expected to receive King's report "within a month or two." In February, Maples anticipated an imminent press conference in Berkeley. In the middle of April, Levine said, "Yes, we are hoping." At the end of that month, Maples revealed that Dr. King herself had not done the DNA testing; he said it had been performed in her laboratory by her associate, Dr. Charles Ginther. Ginther, Maples was told, had written a report in technical language decipherable only by an expert. Dr. King was not pleased with the report and therefore was holding it until such time as she herself was able to write it in a form suitable for the Sverdlovsk authorities and for general release. In fact, at this point, Maples was "totally upset" with King. He had just been invited back to Moscow to testify before a Russian government commission, and he was eager to take her findings with him. "I am sending her a fax," he said, "telling her that her report is desperately needed because, if we can't produce the results now, it will seriously damage our entire credibility."

Dr. Maples' fax produced no result, and, in June 1994, one year after Dr. King had received the teeth and bone fragments, she still had not released her report. Maples' trip to Moscow was postponed; he continued calling her and receiving no reply. Ultimately, King did return his call and told him that her findings were ready and that, if he wished, she would accompany him to Moscow to testify before the Russian government commission. At that point, however, Maples' Moscow invitation had evaporated.

In June 1994, although Maples had not seen King's final report, he did pass along startling information: "Dr. King and Dr. Gill," he said, "both have difficulty in the same area of Tsar Nicholas's mitochondrial DNA." King, Maples reported, still needed to resolve whether this difficulty "is a problem of contamination or whether the tsar had an unusual genetic anomaly (that is, a heteroplasmy) or whether there was a mutation." The possibility of heteroplasmy and a mutation, of course, was precisely what Peter Gill and Pavel Ivanov had reported eleven months before and what William Maples and his American colleagues had vehemently attacked.

CHAPTER 10

EKATERINBURG CONFRONTS ITS PAST

Peter the Great, tall, visionary, and impatient, founded two of the preeminent cities of modern Russia. One was St. Petersburg, which he named after his patron saint; its purpose was to give Russia access to the sea. The other was Ekaterinburg, named after his wife, Ekaterina (Catherine), who became his successor and Russia's first sovereign empress. This town in the Urals, just thirty miles east of the border between Europe and Asia, was constructed because of the region's immense mineral wealth. The first ore brought out of the ground was iron; in the eighteenth century, four fifths of the iron produced in Russia was mined and smelted here. Later, the earth also yielded coal, gold, silver, and other metals in such profusion that the town became rich, famous, and proud.

In the 1990s, the city of 1.4 million is one of the preeminent industrial centers of modern Russia. The massive, belching defense factories that long epitomized Soviet power are being converted to production of civilian goods. Heavy machinery, electrical equipment, metallurgical and chemical plants encircle the city. Civic pride continues strong. In June 1991, 91 percent of the city's voters cast ballots for their native son, Boris Yeltsin. At the time of the August 1991 coup, Sverdlovsk was chosen as the alternative headquarters of the Russian government should the president be forced to leave Moscow. On September 4, 1991, the city changed its name from Sverdlovsk back to Ekaterinburg.

Unhappily, all these good things—wealth, fame, civic pride—continue to be shadowed by a single grim event. During this same momentous summer of 1991, the exhumation of the Romanovs occurred. When this happened and the world turned to look, the city was forced to confront the fact that it is and always will be famous throughout the world not for its minerals or its industry but for what happened there on the night of July 16–17, 1918.

People in Ekaterinburg developed a variety of reactions to this most famous event in their city's history. Some were defensive: "Sure, we knew this story, but why publicize it?" said the city's last Communist Party chief. "Don't people have more important things to think about?" Others are curious, uneasy, anxious to understand and to come to terms. "As someone raised in an environment of hostility to the monarchy, I was taught that the shooting of Nicholas II was the people's revenge for years of oppression," recalled the chief architect of the city government. "But reprisals against the children? This I could never understand." A twenty-seven-year-old computer assembler brought his four-year-old son to the site of the Ipatiev House. "I had no idea what happened here," he said. "I only learned the truth a few years ago. Now I bring my son here and tell him about our history. It's good we're finally learning the truth about these things. The killing of the tsar was a great tragedy for our country, and we should know all the details." "We must remember," a metallurgist agreed. "We must not allow a barbarian act like this to happen again."

Recently, it has become a tradition for newly married couples to visit the tall white cross erected on the site of the bulldozed Ipatiev House. They kneel, leave flowers, and are photographed. "We wanted our picture taken in front of the cross," said a newly married twenty-five-year-old gold miner. "We hope for good luck, but we also came because it makes us feel more Russian. It's part of the revival of real Russia that is taking place today." Another group of visitors, most of them older, look to the cross for something more than luck; they are sick, believe in miracles, and hope to be healed. "They say this is a holy place," said Lilya Subbotina, a fifty-two-year-old elementary school teacher whose headaches and high blood pressure have not responded to medical treatments. "I've heard about people who came here with sickness and went away completely healed. I'm hoping that happens to me too." Drawn by these stories, afflicted people walk up to the cross, lean over the flowers, and reverently press one hand against it. "When you touch the cross, you feel an explosion of positive energy," said a fifty-nine-year-old pilgrim from Vladivostok who traveled three thousand miles hoping to halt a progressive weakness in his legs. "After three days in this sacred place, my legs are strong again. God blessed this cross because our tsar was murdered here."

The Russian Orthodox Church, crippled by seventy-five years of compromise with an atheistic state, is still struggling to find a way to deal with the execution of the Romanovs. If the family died as martyrs, then they must be canonized as saints—as, in fact, they were in 1981 by the Orthodox Church Abroad. Even if Nicholas and his family are not deemed to merit martyrdom and canonization and are considered simply victims of political assassination, the church would seem to be obliged to take some notice of their violent deaths. (The Russian Orthodox Church did not consider the 1881 assassination of Tsar Alexander II in St. Petersburg a martyrdom, but nevertheless it constructed the Cathedral of the Blood on the assassination site to perpetuate Alexander's memory.)

Even before the exhumation of the skeletons in Ekaterinburg, the local archbishop wished to construct a memorial church on the site of the Ipatiev House. "This is the place where the suffering of the Russian people began," said Archbishop Melkhisedek. The church, he explained, would be called the Cathedral on Spilled Blood and "would symbolize society's penance and cleansing of the lawlessness and wholesale repressions inflicted during the years of Bolshevism." A competition to design the church was announced in 1990, and architects from everywhere in Russia were invited to submit drawings. In October 1992, Konstantin Yefremov, a Siberian architect, won the contest with a design for a tall white stone-and-glass church combining old Russian and modern design, a bell tower, and, nearby, a hotel for pilgrims and tourists. Unfortunately, there was no money available to the archbishop from his own diocese, or from the city of Ekaterinburg, or from the patriarch who is the religious chief of the Orthodox Church in Moscow, or from the Russian Orthodox Church Abroad. In April 1995, two and a half years after a design was chosen, the memorial cathedral remains only a drawing.

In another sense, however, money has been much on the minds of some citizens of Ekaterinburg. From the time the bones were exhumed, hope stirred in the city that they might prove a bonanza. "We think these remains will be very valuable," said a local police official. "There is talk of a reward. At least, people think they will have some value for tourists." In a curious but not uncommon mingling of Communist and capitalistic perspectives, a college student said, "Today we take pride in the fact that the tsar was killed in our city. We hope something good will come out of this tragedy."

A disagreeable manifestation of Ekaterinburg huckstering of the Imperial remains took place at the time of the scientific conference in July 1992. The conference organizers first attempted to charge foreign journalists a thousand dollars apiece for "accreditation" to the press briefing after the conference. The foreign reporters refused and, after a brief standoff, were admitted anyhow. Next, the reporters were asked to pay ten thousand dollars apiece to see and photograph the bones. Some paid, but far less than the demanded sum. Behind this commercial enterprise was a Swiss-Soviet firm called Interural, commissioned by the Ekaterinburg authorities to handle publishing and picture rights to the remains. Its motive, Interural told the London *Sunday Times,* was a noble one. "We are doing it out of love," said Vladimir Agentov, a director of the company, explaining that the profits would be used to help build the church on the site of the Ipatiev House. "We had a proposal from an American newspaper," Agentov said, "whereby they would buy the copyright in everything connected with the remains and then give us a share in the syndication rights. How much do you think that might be worth?"

The key to all of these civic hopes lies in Ekaterinburg somehow keeping the remains permanently in the city. Historical precedent would call for them to be entombed in St. Petersburg in the Cathedral of St. Peter and St. Paul, the traditional resting place of the Romanov tsars. Nevertheless, early in 1995, Ekaterinburg still hoped that precedent could be overturned. This attitude troubled and sometimes outraged other Russians. "Today, as before [their death], Ekaterinburg doesn't want to give up the Romanovs," said Edvard Radzinsky, the Russian playwright and author of *The Last Tsar.* "In Ekaterinburg, they have a crazy dream, to create the Romanov grave as part of a tourist complex. It is fantastic, terrible, awful. The Romanovs, who were executed by Ekaterinburg people, would have to lie in the same ground and make profits for Ekaterinburg people."

CHAPTER 11

INVESTIGATOR
SOLOVIEV

The struggle between Moscow and Ekaterinburg for control of the Romanov bones began as the remains were exhumed. Indeed, from the moment in 1989 when Geli Ryabov revealed what he and Alexander Avdonin had discovered, Ekaterinburg regarded the bones as belonging to it. The exhumation in 1991 was ordered by the Sverdlovsk regional governor, Edvard Rossel, and his deputy, Alexander Blokhin. The actual digging was supervised by Deputy Investigator Volkov of the Sverdlovsk Region Office of the Public Prosecutor. With the bones laid out in the morgue, Volkov began the investigation into their identity. It was Volkov who forbade Moscow forensic expert Sergei Abramov from taking pictures of the skeletons and who, once pictures had been taken, demanded that all film and written notes be left behind in Ekaterinburg. It was Rossel who asked Secretary of State Baker for American scientific help.

Throughout this period, the Russian government never accepted the argument that the murder of a Russian emperor and the discovery of his bones was a local issue. But at the time of these events, the government's political position was weak. President Yeltsin survived one coup attempt by Old Guard Communists and another by the leader of the elected Parliament and his own vice president. During this battle for survival in Moscow, the only central government officials concerned with the Romanov investigation were in the relatively low-level Chief Medical Examiner's Office in the Ministry of Health. In addition, the Ekaterinburg authorities were certain that what they were doing had the unofficial support of their native son, President Yeltsin.

This belief was publicly articulated by Sverdlovsk Deputy Governor Blokhin at the July 1992 conference in Ekaterinburg. His statement came in response to a pointed question from Vladimir Soloviev of the Office of the Public Prosecutor of Russia, who was present as an observer. During the press conference, Soloviev asked: "At present, the Sverdlovsk administration has decided to appropriate the remains of the Imperial family. This discovery belongs to Russia. Has the question of burying the remains been posed to the Russian government?" Blokhin calmly replied that the regional government did not consider what it had done as "appropriation." Sverdlovsk Region had not officially asked the Russian government for permission, but—he said to Soloviev—"you, apparently, are informed that prior to starting any investigative or exhumation work, the head of the administration phoned the Russian president Boris Nicholaevich [Yeltsin] and reported to him the fact that such work was being contemplated by the region." Soloviev was rebuffed but not defeated. To him, it continued to seem absurd that a provincial capital should attempt to seize and profit from a significant event in Russian history. Besides, he had observed and been disgusted by the fledgling efforts to market the bones that had accompanied the 1992 scientific conference.

In August 1993, the Ekaterinburg monopoly abruptly ended, and the Office of the Public Prosecutor of Russia assumed control of the Romanov investigation. Vladimir Soloviev was assigned as chief investigating official. A Russian government commission was appointed to sit in Moscow.* Its assignment was to receive from the Russian pub-

---

*The appointees made up what Americans call a blue ribbon commission. Its twenty-two permanent members represented a wide spectrum of Russian

lic prosecutor all available evidence as to the validity of the bones, weigh this evidence, and then inform the government of its conclusions. If the commission ruled that the remains were legitimate, it was to make further recommendations as to where, when, and by what ritual they should be buried.

The commission worked on an ad hoc basis. There were no regularly scheduled meetings; members were summoned when there was new evidence to receive and discuss. Few members attended regularly. Edvard Rossel, still nominally on the commission, never came. Veniamin Alekseyev appeared only rarely. From Ekaterinburg, that left only Alexander Avdonin, who came to every meeting at his own expense. Sometimes, people were invited to join and then not informed about meetings. Bishop Basil Rodzianko, who is eighty and is respected throughout Russia for his twenty-five years of religious radio broadcasts from London and Washington, D.C., was officially asked by Anatoly Sobchak, said that he would be happy to come to a meeting, and then never heard from anyone again.

Vladimir Soloviev, although not a member of the commission, quietly became the pivotal figure in its work. He was the representative of the Public Prosecutor's Office assigned to provide the commission with evidence. His task was to track down scientists, historians, and archivists, locate documents, authorize tests, and gather results. He attended most of the commission's meetings in order to answer questions or to receive requests for additional infor-

---

political, scientific, historical, and cultural institutions. The chairman was Yuri Yarov, vice premier of Russia, and meetings were held in Yarov's office in the Moscow White House. The vice chairman was Anatoly Sobchak, mayor of Russia's second largest city, St. Petersburg. The Russian Orthodox Church was represented by Metropolitan Euvenaly. The commission also included the deputy minister of foreign affairs, the deputy minister of culture, the deputy minister of health, and Vladislav Plaksin, the chief medical examiner. Also, a historian, a painter, the president of Moscow's Nobility Society, and the playwright-biographer Edvard Radzinsky. From Ekaterinburg, three members originally were listed: Edvard Rossel, the former governor, Veniamin Alekseyev, director of the Institute of History and Archeology in Ekaterinburg, and Alexander Avdonin.

mation. He had been given broad powers. When, in the summer of 1994, Alexander Avdonin asked on my behalf whether I could see the remains in Ekaterinburg, the first answer of the local authorities was no. Soon, a fax arrived from Soloviev in Moscow instructing that I was to be shown "everything."

Vladimir Nicholaevich Soloviev is a short, balding, barrel-chested man with light brown eyes and a brown beard finely trimmed in exactly the style of the beard of Nicholas II. In his deep voice, Soloviev said that when as part of his work he visited the Imperial palaces at Tsarskoe Selo outside St. Petersburg to examine the uniforms, dresses, helmets, and hats worn by the Imperial family, he found that the tsar's measurements and his own were identical. Out of curiosity, he tried on one of Nicholas's now-faded military tunics. It fit perfectly. Soloviev's own day-to-day uniform was a simple brown semi-military shirt with epaulets but no insignia.

Vladimir Soloviev was born in 1950, the son of a lawyer, in the Stavropolsk region of the Russian Caucasus, near the resort towns of Pyatigorsk and Kislovodsk—"Lermontov places," he called them. He finished high school at eighteen, did odd jobs for a year, spent two years in the army, then entered the Moscow University Department of Law. When he graduated in 1976, he was sent to Taldom, a town sixty miles from Moscow, where he worked in the Prokuratura (Office of the Public Prosecutor) as one of two regional investigators. His primary duty was investigating murders, which, he recalled, "unfortunately, at that time, were quite numerous... peasants burning bodies in a stove inside a small hut... that kind of thing." Transferred after two years to the Office of the Public Prosecutor of the Moscow Region, he worked in a branch overseeing the work of the militia, then moved on to the Moscow Region Transportation Prokuratura, where he investigated cases of violence connected with transportation: airplane crashes, train accidents and, again, "many murders, aboard trains, for example, or near railroad tracks." Next, Soloviev returned to Moscow University as supervisor in charge of the laboratory of the Criminology Department, training students in criminological procedures. In 1990, he transferred to the Office of the General Procurator of Russia, where his title became procurator criminologist of the Office of the General Procurator of the Russian Federation. Here, too, his specialty was murder. Throughout his career, Soloviev had nothing to do with the KGB. "The Office of the Public Prosecutor does not get involved with political matters," he said. "The two organizations have different purposes."

Soloviev always has been interested in history and archeology. When Geli Ryabov first announced that he had found the Romanov remains in Siberia, Soloviev didn't totally believe him, but he was interested. Once the remains were exhumed, Soloviev—because of his familiarity with the major government archive (formerly the Central Archive of the October Revolution, recently renamed the State Archive of the Russian Federation)—was asked to assist Sverdlovsk Deputy Investigator Volkov. In the archives, Soloviev located much useful material: four volumes of Sokolov's work, photographs of Kharitonov and Trupp, materials on Yurovsky and on Grand Duke George Alexandrovich (Nicholas II's younger brother). In doing this work, Soloviev found his interest in the Imperial family sharpened. In August 1993, his superiors handed him responsibility for conducting the Romanov investigation on behalf of the Russian government.

When Soloviev assumed control, he immediately designated the investigation of the Romanov murders and the validation of the bones as a criminal case. This definition gave him greater powers. Now he could compel testimony; no Russian could refuse to answer his questions, and the people interrogated were accountable for their replies. Turning the matter into a criminal case also broadly extended the scope of Soloviev's investigation. In addition to establishing the specific facts of the murder, he now was required to answer the question of responsibility: essentially, if these were murders, who were the murderers? "The criminal case was resurrected in order to determine whether a murder was committed in Ekaterinburg or a legal execution by a sentence of a lawful government," Soloviev explained. "If a man commits a crime for which he receives a lawful death sentence, then the executioners carrying out this sentence are not committing a crime. So, I must determine whether it was legal for the Ural Soviet in 1918 to pronounce the death penalty on the tsar and his family." In this context, Soloviev had further questions: "Who was Yurovsky? Who was Sverdlov? Who was Lenin? Legally, how were they connected to these executions? Were they criminals or were they respectable people?"

Soloviev was aware that questions of this nature transformed his criminal investigation into a probing of the highest and most sensitive political and historical issues. "Yes," he said, "I have much more to do than simply establish the identity of a skull or several skulls. That is difficult enough, but the real questions are about something else. Beneath the surface, there is a gigantic iceberg."

Agreeing that these questions have great political and historical impact, Soloviev nodded and smiled ruefully. "Yes, but my bosses, thank the Lord, do not yet know this," he said. "I am leading the investigation, and now, thank God, no one is stopping me from doing my job. Actually, it interests the Office of the Public Prosecutor very little. My bosses have other, more pressing problems. Their heads hurt because in Russia we have finally caught up with and surpassed America in the murder rate."

Soloviev began as any criminal investigator anywhere in the world would begin: by retrieving and examining the weapons said to have been used in the killings. He took the pistols, which had been given to museums, and had ballistic experts fire them to see whether the newly fired bullets had characteristics similar to those of the bullets found in the grave. Unfortunately, the bullets from the grave were badly corroded, and the tiny details studied to establish identification had been obliterated. In addition, Soloviev had noted grimly, these particular pistols had been fired many times over many years and any unique characteristics of their barrels had disappeared. Nevertheless, he said, "While there was no proof that these bullets *were* fired from these guns, there also was no contradiction. These bullets *could* have been fired from these pistols."

Next, Soloviev tried to provide the commission with final verification of the identities of the skeletal remains. Although he, personally, accepts the universal verdict of Russian, English, German, and American scientists that these are the Romanovs, he discovered that some senior officials of the Russian Orthodox Church—both the Patriarchal Church in Russia and the Russian Orthodox Church Abroad—still had doubts. Both churches continued to be bothered by the heteroplasmy found by Gill and Ivanov in Nicholas II's DNA. Subsequently, Soloviev and the Russian government commission were told unofficially that Dr. King and Dr. Ginther in Berkeley, using the teeth brought to America by Dr. Maples, had confirmed the findings of Gill and Ivanov in England, including the heteroplasmy. But, officially, the commission has received no report from Berkeley. Therefore, the Patriarchal Russian Orthodox Church, which is considering the canonization of the Imperial family, insisted on further testing and hinted that it would withdraw its representative, Metropolitan Euvenaly, from the government commission unless its request was granted. The commission relented. Investigator Soloviev thereupon reactivated Pavel Ivanov's earlier proposal that the remains of Nicholas II's younger brother Grand Duke George be exhumed from the Cathedral of St. Peter and St. Paul in St. Petersburg and the DNA of the two brothers be compared.

George's exhumation took place between July 6 and July 13, 1994. There was difficulty lifting the marble plate over the coffin, but once that was done, the body inside was found undisturbed. The upper part of the body was still dressed in superbly preserved clothing; the lower part lay in six inches of water (a reminder that St. Petersburg was built on a swamp where water is never far beneath the surface of the ground). The scientists removed a piece of the top of the grand duke's skull and a part of a leg bone for DNA testing. Originally, Soloviev had intended to send these fragments to Dr. Gill in England, but when word of this plan leaked out, there was, in Soloviev's words, "a lot of yelling and screaming in our Russian newspapers that Gill had falsified something." The result was a protracted series of negotiations with the U.S. Armed Forces Institute of Pathology, which eventually agreed to perform the tests without charge. "So, now we can say that we are handing this examination over to people who are totally independent of us," Soloviev said. "Although our specialist Dr. Ivanov will be there, too."

Pavel Ivanov arrived at the gleaming new Armed Forces Institute of Pathology DNA laboratory in Rockville, Maryland, on June 5, 1995, bringing with him a section of the femur of Grand Duke George. His mission was to reinforce the certainty that Body No. 4 in the Ekaterinburg morgue belonged to Nicholas II. "In Peter Gill's laboratory two years ago, we obtained a probability of 98.5 percent," Ivanov explained. "Now, in this new laboratory, using new approaches and more advanced technology, we may be able to go to 99.5 percent or 99.7 percent. In order to make it easier for our Russian government commission to make its decision, we want to get as close as possible to 100 percent."

Ivanov also brought with him from Moscow two other potentially useful pieces of evidence. One was the bloodstained handkerchief originally obtained in Japan and from which no usable DNA could be extracted in Gill's laboratory. In the AFIP laboratories, with their special air locks and air-purifying systems designed to reduce laboratory contamination to a minimum, and with the latest equipment for enhancing degraded DNA, Ivanov intended to try again. He also brought with him a strand of Nicholas II's hair, cut when the tsar was a child of three, preserved in a locket in a St. Petersburg palace, discovered there by Soloviev and given by him to Ivanov. "There is no follicle attached and cut hair has very little DNA," Ivanov said, "but AFIP has enormously powerful amplification equipment. We will do our best."

These DNA tests—on Nicholas II's brother, Nicholas II's blood, and Nicholas II's hair—were to be completed in the autumn of 1995.

❖

The whereabouts of the remains of the two children missing from the grave also baffled the investigator and the commission. Avdonin, attending every meeting, continually urged on his fellow members, "If we could find these two bodies, then everything would be clear, everything would be concluded, the story would be complete."

Soloviev agreed. "Unless we find them," the investigator said—and here he supplied a Russian proverb: "In the depths of every soul exists a snake"—"then in the hearts of the scientists and all of us connected with the investigation, there always will be doubt."

The task of finding the missing bodies was immensely complicated when, in the spring of 1993—that is, before the Moscow public prosecutor had taken control of the investigation—an Ekaterinburg academic, Professor V. V. Alekseyev of the Urals Institute of History and Archeology, descended with tractors and agricultural plows on the area around the open grave site. A bitter enemy of Avdonin, Alekseyev hoped to locate the missing bodies in time to present his findings to the July 1993 conference in Ekaterinburg. Alekseyev found nothing, but when he left, the earth was churned into large, rough furrows. Dr. William Maples, arriving in Ekaterinburg that summer, was incensed by what Alekseyev had done. Maples had arranged to bring to Ekaterinburg a sensitive, mobile machine the size of a lawn mower which sends sound waves into the ground and records any disturbance in the normal pattern of the upper layers of the earth. Maples had seen this used to locate buried bodies in America, and he thought it had promise for finding the missing Romanov children. When he saw what Alekseyev had done, his face darkened. "There's no hope now," he said. "It's absolutely ruined!"

Soloviev admits that hope of finding the two bodies is growing dim. "Too much time has passed," he said. "The soil has been moved. A cable has been laid through the area." Nevertheless, he believes that a faint chance still exists. "Yurovsky says that two bodies were burned," he said. "Sokolov found a place where there were fires. He found bones and congealed fat. Sokolov believed that all the bodies were burned on this spot. Sokolov also wrote that, in his day, no methods existed to establish whether these were human or animal bones. Now, these methods exist. If only we could find these bones."

Ryabov, like Soloviev, believed in Yurovsky's note and, therefore, that the remains of two bodies were buried under a bonfire. If they were there, and still are there, they can be found, but the search would cost, by Ryabov's estimate, somewhere between $5 million and $20 million. Even then, Soloviev worried that the bones, being near the surface, might be in much worse condition than the remains found in the protective clay of the mass grave. The missing bones might be there, he feared, but still not have survived.

⚜

In his effort to locate the two missing bodies or, at least, to determine what had happened to them, Soloviev would dearly love to get his hands on one collection of evidence which so far has been denied to him. This is the contents of the box brought from Ekaterinburg to Europe in 1920 by Investigator Nicholas Sokolov in the wake of the White Army defeat in Siberia.

Fleeing the victorious Bolsheviks, Sokolov traveled across Siberia, clinging to this box, whose contents he referred to as the "Great National Sacred Relics." From Vladivostok, he and his wife sailed for Europe with a White officer, Colonel Cyril Naryshkine, and Naryshkine's wife aboard the French ship *André le Bon*. During the voyage, the box traveled eight thousand miles under Mme. Naryshkina's shipboard bunk. The connection between Sokolov and the Naryshkines was long-standing. Before the First World War, Sokolov had been a magistrate in the town of Penza, west of Moscow, where he became a friend of General Sergei Rozanov, commander of the local army regiment. Frequently, Rozanov and Sokolov hunted together on Rozanov's estate. When the Russian Civil War began, Rozanov became chief of staff to Admiral Kolchak, the White "Supreme Ruler" in Siberia. When Ekaterinburg fell to the Whites, Rozanov and his future son-in-law Naryshkine were the first two White officers to rush to the Ipatiev House, break through the surrounding palisade, and enter the deserted mansion. A few months later, Nicholas Sokolov appeared at Kolchak's headquarters, having made his way through the Bolshevik lines on foot. It was on Rozanov's recommendation that Sokolov was appointed to investigate the circumstances surrounding the disappearance of the Romanovs.

When the *André le Bon* arrived in Venice, Sokolov and Naryshkine went together to the French Riviera to present the box to Nicholas II's cousin Grand Duke Nicholas Nicholaevich, former commander in chief of the Russian Imperial Army, whom most Russians in emigration regarded as the most suitable successor to the Russian throne. To Sokolov's dismay, the grand duke, not wishing to offend the Dowager Empress Marie, who still believed her son and his family were alive, refused to accept the box. Sokolov and Rozanov then traveled to England and attempted to present the box to Nicholas II's first cousin King George V. The king also did not want it. Eventually, Sokolov gave the box for safekeeping to the Russian Orthodox Church Abroad.

For many years, the Church Abroad has guarded the box. Until the exhumation of the bones near Ekaterinburg, the box was believed to contain the only surviving relics of the vanished Imperial family. Still deeply suspicious of the Russian government, bitterly antagonistic to the Moscow Patriarchal Church, whose patriarch and senior clergy they accuse of being former agents of the KGB, the metropolitan and bishops of the Church Abroad refuse to release the box to anyone for examination and testing of its contents. Even the location of the box is a secret, although everyone knows that it is kept in the Russian Orthodox Church of St. Job in Memory of the Martyred Tsar Nicholas II and His Family in Brussels. The contents of the box have been described by witnesses, but the church will not endorse their reports.

What makes the church's refusal to permit examination of the box particularly frustrating is reports as to what it contains. Prince Alexis Scherbatow, the octogenarian president of the Russian Nobility Association in America, visited Brussels in the summer of 1994 and, thanks to family connections with important members of the clergy, was told that the box contained the scooped-up remnants of a fire in which bodies were consumed: "little pieces of bone, a lot of earth full of blood, two little bottles of [congealed] fat from the bodies, and several bullets." And—Prince Scherbatow was unwilling to say who told him this or how anyone would know—but he added, "Yes, yes, absolutely. It was from two bodies."

Nevertheless, in April 1995, the Church Abroad continued to adamantly refuse to release the box. Neither Soloviev nor any qualified Western investigator may examine its contents to help determine what happened to the two missing children. Soloviev can do nothing but wait. "If someday this box appears," he said, "I think many questions will be solved. If there are whole bones, then a scientist like Maples might be able to tell whether they came from a young woman or a fourteen-year-old boy. A DNA test could match the bones with the DNA of the mother and daughters already found. DNA cannot tell which of the daughters it is, but we would know that this was the fourth daughter. We would not know which was which, but all four would be accounted for."

In the West as well as in Russia, the findings of Avdonin and Ryabov, and the investigative efforts of Soloviev, were aggressively challenged. The Russian emigre community contains men and women who have spent a lifetime hating the doctrines, personalities, and administrative paraphernalia of the Communist state. Their hostility goes deeper than ideology; members of their families were slaughtered in one of the Red Terrors; their possessions were stripped away and redesignated as property of the state. For seventy-five years, they watched Soviet historians lie about the past and Soviet politicians, newspapers, radio, and television lie about the present. During this time, they developed suspicions not easily eradicated. Therefore, in 1989, when Geli Ryabov announced to the world that he had located the bones of the Imperial family, many Russians in emigration were skeptical. One group, calling itself the Expert Commission of Russians Abroad, appointed itself to monitor everything said and done inside Russia in connection with the remains. The chairman of this group was a Connecticut engineer named Peter Koltypin. The vice chairman was Prince Alexis Scherbatow. The secretary was a former CIA officer named Eugene Magerovsky. In the collective view of this commission, Ryabov's story was bogus and the discovery of the remains in the grave a clever hoax arranged by a still-active KGB.

Alexander Avdonin first encountered Koltypin and Scherbatow in March 1992 in St. Petersburg at the burial of Grand Duke Vladimir, the pretender to the Russian throne. Avdonin, by then, was well known among Russian emigres for his role in the discovery of the grave in Ekaterinburg. After the service, people wanted to ask him questions, and he suggested gathering so he could speak to everyone simultaneously. He spoke for an hour, after which most of the audience applauded. Then he was questioned by Koltypin and Scherbatow. "I understood that they did not believe me, not for one minute," Avdonin says. "What they were really saying with their provocative questions was that the murder of the tsar had been thoroughly investigated by Sokolov and that they deemed his investigation sufficient. They believed that the heads were cut off and taken away and the rest of the bodies burned. They believed that everything I was telling them had been set up by the KGB." When Avdonin told them that Russian and Ukrainian scientists were testing the remains, Koltypin and Scherbatow declared that no one would believe these scientists. When Avdonin said that American scientists had been invited to participate, Koltypin and Scherbatow laughed: "So you have sold yourself to the Americans." "Then," Avdonin proposed, "*you* choose competent people and send them to us." "No," Koltypin said, "you will still cheat." "In that case"—Avdonin shrugged—"we will never be able to prove the truth to you." "No, there is one way," Koltypin said. "It is DNA. But you in Russia don't know how to do it." Avdonin asked who did know. "In England," Koltypin replied.

The next meeting between Avdonin and the emigre Expert Commission took place in February 1993, in Nyack, New York. Avdonin and his wife had flown to Boston as guests of William Maples so that Avdonin could present a paper on finding the Romanovs at the annual meeting of the American Academy of Forensic Sciences. Avdonin gave another talk in Nyack and afterward retreated into a library for private discussions. Koltypin and Scherbatow were there, joined this time by Magerovsky. As in St. Petersburg, the emigres attacked Avdonin. "I may be an old White Russian so-and-so," Magerovsky told him, "but I just don't believe you." "I don't like Avdonin," Scherbatow said later. "He was lying. He's a real, old Communist."

The attack from outside Russia became formal on December 25, 1993, when the Expert Commission of Russians Abroad wrote to Yuri Yarov, deputy premier of Russia and chairman of the Russian government commission examining evidence on the Romanov remains. The emigre commissioners began by warning Yarov to beware of information coming from anyone ever connected with "the Communist

Party, the KGB, or the Procurator's Office [i.e., Soloviev]." They declared that "some facts of Geli Ryabov's biography are rather doubtful...he was connected with the KGB...his getting acquainted with A. N. Avdonin causes suspicion." The Expert Commission rejected the authenticity of the Yurovsky note, declaring that "it is a known fact that the head of the last emperor was brought to Moscow." Therefore, the commission hypothesized, if it was Nicholas II's skull that Ryabov found in the Ekaterinburg grave, the skull must have been put there later "under someone else's direction." Finally, the emigre commissioners announced, "We suppose the other bones were put there in 1979 so that it was possible to fake the recovery of the remains in July 1991."

Vladimir Soloviev read the emigre letter and vigorously refuted the charges against Ryabov and Avdonin. "There is talk, especially abroad, that this grave was not the grave of the tsar's family; that this burial was 'fixed' or arranged by the KGB or the Cheka or one of the other 'organs' of olden days," he said. "They say that Ryabov was and is an agent of the KGB. The fact is that we now have access to the KGB files, and I have officially checked this allegation against both Avdonin and Ryabov. Prior to 1989, there are no documents on either man in the KGB records. Once Ryabov published his interview and article in *Moscow News* and *Rodina*, surveillance on both Ryabov and Avdonin was established. And the KGB began trying to find out where the grave site was. In fact, there was a thick file on previous KGB efforts to find this grave. So, all of the rumors that this discovery was an action of the KGB or other special organs is ridiculous. I give you my word of honor, knowing those times and those circumstances, that if this grave site had been known to either the KGB or the Party, it would have existed for exactly the amount of time necessary to gather up a crowd of soldiers and get them to that site."

In dealing with their attack, Soloviev has tried to understand the emigre point of view. "You know, people have stereotypes," he said. "As they get older, it is difficult to change them. For many years, they had no reason to trust what was said here. But now, the investigations we have done and the conclusions we have produced in this case would be sufficient for any other criminal case. There would be no doubts of any kind, not in the courtroom, not from anyone. But in this case, we must do five or six times more than has already been done. So there will be no doubts. They [Koltypin, Scherbatow, and Magerovsky] do not believe anything we say. In their view, I am a scoundrel, Ryabov and Avdonin are scoundrels, everyone is a scoundrel. Only Koltypin knows the truth. He should come here himself and see everything. But he has not done that."

Soloviev was talking about the absence of any serious research by the emigre Expert Commission. "When I come into the archives," he said, "I see the list of documents pulled and I see the names of those who have looked at them. There is the signature of Avdonin, there is Geli Ryabov, there is a third, a fourth, a fifth, and so on. With this circle of people, I can have discussions. These are people who have actually familiarized themselves with firsthand sources and are able to say something meaningful. Whereas, the others do not want to see anything, do not want to learn anything, do not want to know anything."

The emigres, Soloviev believed, attacked him because they had pinned all of their faith on Sokolov's findings of seventy-five years ago. "It is often written," Soloviev said, "that I am leading the investigation without knowing Sokolov's material, am not interested in it, and do not accept Sokolov as a prominent investigator. This is not true. The fact is that Sokolov made a mistake, but this mistake could have been made by any investigator in his place. His mistake was to believe that the corpses were totally burned and destroyed. At that time, the evidence supported that theory. Now, we have more evidence. However, in my opinion, this was Sokolov's only mistake."

One charge made by Koltypin's Expert Commission was true: it was that not every Russian archive had been completely opened. Soloviev admitted this, saying that he had been given access to all the archives "except the Presidential Archive," the archive of the Politburo. Naturally, this restriction inflamed the suspicions of Russian emigres that important facts still were being hidden. One able to help in this matter was Edvard Radzinsky, who was a member of the government commission and, independently, was writing a biography of Stalin. "It is true that Soloviev can't get permission to work in the

Presidential Archive," Radzinsky said, "but I have permission. The chief of administration of the Office of the President personally permitted me to work there on materials concerning Stalin. When I became a member of the government commission, I asked to expand my research to the Romanovs. Now I have a special pass to check all papers regarding the Imperial family in the Presidential Archive. Everyone agrees that it makes sense for me to do this work."

Radzinsky believed, based on his experience, that the reason no materials on the Romanovs were turning up was not that they had been deliberately concealed or withheld but that they were unfindable. The Presidential Archive, he explained, was still active; it contained secret diplomatic documents not only of the Soviet Union but of the current Russian state. "When I started working there," Radzinsky said, "I realized that it is impossible for them, at this stage, to separate historical documents from active state secrets. They said to me, 'We will show you the papers from this period to this period. We can't let you just go in and rummage around.' Also, everything is mixed up. They have only just begun to sort and classify documents. Files are mislabeled or unlabeled. In my book, I printed material from the archives which they didn't know they had. When they read it in my book, they asked me, 'Where in our archive did you find this?' "

Radzinsky did find one document that offered additional proof of Lenin's cynical mendacity in regard to the survival of the empress and her daughters. It was the memoirs of Adolf Ioffe, a Soviet diplomat serving in Berlin at the time of the murders. Curious about the official story that only Nicholas had been killed, Ioffe later asked Felix Dzerzhinsky, head of the Cheka. Dzerzhinsky admitted that the entire family was dead, adding that Lenin had categorically forbidden that Ioffe be told. "Better if Ioffe knows nothing," Lenin had said. "It will be easier for him to lie."

This document did not surprise Soloviev. "Let me give you another example of Lenin's thinking," he said. "In 1912 or 1913, there was a terrorist attack on a minor member of the Spanish royal family. Lenin was contemptuous. 'We must not be concerned with individual terror,' he said. 'If one must eliminate, one must eliminate the whole dynasty, not hunt down one person.' Again, in 1918, the fact that they did not immediately announce that they had killed everyone was not connected to any moral criteria. Officially, they said that they had executed only Nicholas for a good reason. Let us imagine that they had announced that they had eliminated everyone. In monarchist circles there immediately would have arisen the question of a new tsar. Lenin did not want opposition to crystallize around a single successor to Nicholas. So he allowed everyone to wonder who was alive and who was dead. And where those still living might be. During the Civil War, the White Army leaders of monarchist persuasion did not know on whom they should focus. So Lenin operated on two fronts: he killed all the members of the Imperial family and many other Romanovs, but he also dangled the idea that some of the immediate family remained alive. Later, when Soviet power had gained strength, when the possibility of a monarchist or any other kind of counter-revolution had disappeared, the Communists felt free to announce what they actually had done. Not only announce, but boast about the fact that they had killed children."

These matters were beyond the charge of the government commission on validation and burial of the Romanov remains. But they are to remain under investigation by the Office of the Russian Public Prosecutor. "When I have finished my investigation," promised Vladimir Soloviev, "I will present my findings."

CHAPTER 12

BURYING
THE TSAR

The last ceremonial burial of a Russian tsar took place in 1894, when Tsar Alexander III, father of Nicholas II, was interred in the Cathedral of St. Peter and St. Paul in St. Petersburg. A century later, the Russian government commission was completing its findings and recommendations regarding the burial of Nicholas II. Thereafter, the patriarch of the Russian Orthodox Church and the Council of Ministers and president of the Russian Federation were to make their decisions: the church would decide how, and the government where and when, the last Russian tsar and his family were to be buried.

"We are waiting for the scientists to finish their work," said Edvard Radzinsky. "Once the scientists have assured the commission absolutely that these bones are valid, the Patriarchal Orthodox Church must determine what ritual will be used in the burial service. There is one ritual if Nicholas is to become a saint, another if he is not to become a saint. The Church Abroad already has made Nicholas a saint. So our church has a big problem."

Alexander Avdonin, whose small working space is filled with pictures of Nicholas II, attempted to explain the dilemma confronting the Patriarchal Church: "Remember that—unlike the Church Abroad—our church is located in the country where these events took place," he said. "Here, many people consider that Nicholas II himself was guilty of permitting the revolution and therefore was at least partly responsible for his own death. If this is true, should he be canonized? How will our people react to this? After all, one must not forget that our people are not thrilled with Nicholas II. Over seventy years, respect for him has been destroyed. The truth is that he was a weak emperor. The fact that he was a good person, a kind man, who treated his family well, this cannot take away his guilt for his poor governing of our country. It is a different matter for the others who died with him. They, emphatically, are not guilty. They, indeed, are martyrs."

Metropolitan Euvenaly, the church's representative on the government commission, was the official primarily charged with the question of canonization. Euvenaly, according to Avdonin, "personally examines everything that has to do with the remains. However"—Avdonin's expression changed—"the church has known about the remains for four years. During this time not once did anyone from the Moscow patriarchate come even to look at the remains. Not one priest! Not even a deacon!"

Avdonin was correct that mixed feelings exist about Nicholas II in contemporary, post-Communist Russia, but he was mistaken when he said that, according to Orthodox doctrine, Nicholas's performance as a ruler affected the question of his martyrdom. "Martyrdom has nothing to do with the personal actions of a person," explained Father Vladimir Shishkoff, a priest of the Orthodox Church Abroad. "It only has to do with why and how that person died. In the case of Nicholas II, it is irrelevant what kind of a ruler he was, what he did or did not achieve as tsar. Nicholas became a martyr because he was brutally killed for no other reason than that he was ruler of the country." Father Shishkoff did not condemn the Moscow Patriarchal Church for taking its time in coming to its decision. "The truth," he admitted, "is that before our Church Abroad made Nicholas II a saint in 1981, we had a lot of resistance from people here, including priests. They used exactly the same arguments against the canonization of Tsar Nicholas."

❖

The Russian government's decision, once the bones have been scientifically verified, will be where to bury them. Officially, the decision is between two cities: Ekaterinburg, where the family was murdered and the bones were found, and St. Petersburg, where for three hundred years Romanov tsars and empresses have been buried. Many factors have been considered, including questions of religion and historical tradition, but essentially the decision will rest on sheer political power. Here, St. Petersburg, whose mayor, Anatoly Sobchak, was vice chairman of the commission and a powerful political ally of Boris Yeltsin, has an overwhelming advantage. But Ekaterinburg, although talk of tourist hotels and restaurant complexes has faded, still continues to hope.

Bishop Basil Rodzianko of Washington, D.C., who had been to Ekaterinburg and seen the remains, insisted that the Romanovs should be buried in that city, where they lay in a grave for seventy-three years. The decision, he said, already has been made by God: "The bones should not be separated from the bodies. The bodies are there in different form, but they are there in the soil. Therefore, to take the bones away and place them in St. Petersburg means a dismembering of the bodies. To me, this is sacrilege." Bishop Basil condemned the plan to inter the Romanovs in the Cathedral of St. Peter and St. Paul, which, he said, is a "purely earthly, purely secular place; it has nothing to do with the church or religion. Burying them there would be only a political rehabilitation. 'We killed them,' the state says. 'Now we rehabilitate them and accuse Lenin and others of this crime.' "

If the family is canonized, Bishop Basil went on to explain, there would be not a burial service but an Orthodox service of glorification. The bones, instead of being placed in coffins or vaults, would become relics, and fragments of these relics would be distributed and placed in the altars of Orthodox churches. Every Orthodox church has a piece of a relic in the altar; without this a service cannot be celebrated. But if there is not a canonization, he says, "they should be buried in Ekaterinburg. And they should all be buried together."

❖

None of the surviving Romanovs was asked to sit on the commission discussing the burial of their relatives. The Romanovs communicated their views to President Yeltsin, to commission chairman Yarov, to the patriarch, and to Investigator Soloviev, but the family's voice was weakened by the fact that it was split; the two branches dislike each other intensely, and each vehemently objected to claims of primacy by the other. The Grand Duchess Maria Vladimirovna, who lives in Madrid and sees herself as the pretender to the throne—on behalf of either herself or her fourteen-year-old son, George—proposed that the remains be divided into three groups: Tsar Nicholas and Empress Alexandra to be buried with earlier tsars in the Cathedral of St. Peter and St. Paul in St. Petersburg; the three daughters to be interred among the grand dukes now buried in a vault next to the cathedral; the doctor and the three servants to be buried in Ekaterinburg.

This proposal shocked Maria's cousins, the numerous Romanov princes and princesses led by Prince Nicholas Romanov, head of the Romanov Family Association, who lives in Switzerland. Their view was that all of the remains should be left in Ekaterinburg and buried together. "It would be a crime to split them up," said Prince Rostislav Romanov, a London investment banker who is a grandnephew of Nicholas II. "They died together and they should be buried together. It would be intolerable for the commission and the government to start rejecting these people as unimportant. Further, it makes sense to leave them in Ekaterinburg. If you're going to canonize them in martyrdom, why not bury them where they were martyred? If you bury them in St. Petersburg with the other tsars, you're pretending that nothing ever happened. Besides, you could make an awfully good argument that the future of Russia lies in the east, so it would be symbolic."

Prince Nicholas Romanov, the head of the family, passionately insisted that the remains not be divided. "I have written twice to the patriarch," he said. "I have spoken to government ministers, and I've said it in public on Russian television: we Romanovs want everybody, every victim of that massacre, to be buried together, in the same place, in the same cathedral, and, I'd say, in the same tomb. You want to bury the tsar in the Peter and Paul Fortress cathedral? Good! Then bury the doctor, the maid, and the cook with them, in the tsar's mausoleum. They have been lying together for seventy-three years. They are the only ones who never betrayed the family. They deserve to be honored at the same time, in the same place. If present-day Russians don't understand this, then, even if some Romanovs go to this funeral, I will not."

Nikolai Nevolin, the forensic specialist who for almost four years kept watch over the remains in the Ekaterinburg morgue, still hoped that they would be buried in his city. "The Romanovs were executed here and our city would like to have some sort of memorial. But there are two other cities in our country, Moscow and St. Petersburg, who during the seventy-four years of the Soviet regime have always pulled all the blankets on top of themselves. Now, they are trying to take everything again." When Nevolin was told that most of the surviving members of the Romanov family believed the remains should be buried in Ekaterinburg, he was astonished. "I didn't know this," he said. "If this were to happen here, I would be so beholden I cannot even begin to express it. You know, I was born here in the Urals. I am a patriot of my region."

Boris Yeltsin also was born in the Urals, but he has moved onto a wider stage, where his fragile presidency needs all the buttressing it can get. Politically, the support of Anatoly Sobchak is essential to Yeltsin, and Sobchak has set his heart on burying the remains in St. Petersburg. The likeliest possibility, therefore, is that Yeltsin will remain in the background until the commission makes its recommendations and then will ratify whatever site the commission recommends. Once this is done, however, Yeltsin will place himself at the center of the Russian politicians and church officials, and the visiting royal and other persons attending the burial.

Three dates for the burial were chosen and then discarded. Originally, the ceremony was scheduled for May 18, 1994, Nicholas's birthday, which, coming ten months after Doctors Gill and Ivanov had verified the bones at Aldermaston, seemed sufficient time to make arrangements. Then, in April 1994, the Moscow Patriarchal Church demanded additional research, including the exhumation of Grand Duke George. The date slid back to July 3, 1994. When that day arrived with George still unmolested in his tomb, the burial was rescheduled again, this time for March 5, 1995. This new date was religiously appropriate: in the Russian Orthodox calendar it was the pre-Lenten Day of Repentance; by burying the tsar and his family on that day, the Russian government, the church, and the people could ask forgiveness, not only for the killing of the Imperial family but for the murder of millions of others since 1918. This kind of public repentance, a nationwide exorcism of historical guilt, was the kind of ceremony over which President Yeltsin might wish to preside. In November 1994, that date was canceled. No new date has been set.

The years went by, and Alexander Avdonin waited. While the scientists argued, the commission pondered, the church leaders demanded additional proof, and the emigres hurled accusations, the earthly remains of the last Russian emperor, his wife, three of his daughters, and four faithful Russian followers continued to lie on metal tables in a little room on the second floor of a morgue in Ekaterinburg. Avdonin cannot understand why this is permitted. "This family was slandered while they lived, then horribly murdered," he said. "For many years they lay in a pit where cars drove over them. Now they have been brought out. The discovery has tremendous historical meaning. These remains should be the source of unification of our people, who were split by the revolution. But they still cause division. These remains could unite the churches—our church and the church abroad—but they do not. They could unite the scientists, but, again, nothing is working out. People abroad do not believe—Koltypin, and Scherbatow and Magerovsky—they foment various kinds of disinformation and distortion. This is not the way it should be."

Since the exhumation, Avdonin has tried to set aside as a memorial site the place where the bones were discovered. His small foundation, Obretenye, is dedicated to acquiring the land from the local authorities and then creating a park and a monument. He wants to erect a stone cross, a memorial plaque, and, eventually, when there is money, a chapel. "You understand, their blood and bodies are still right here, part of the soil," he said. He turned and pointed to a place of tossed garbage, churned mud, and pools of dark water.

Tsar Alexander III died of nephritis in November 1894 in the Crimea at the age of forty-nine. As his funeral train rolled north across the Ukraine and Russia, peasants gathered and removed their hats along the track. In the cities of Kharkov, Kursk, Orel, and Tula, the train halted for religious services. In Moscow, the coffin was transferred to a hearse to be carried to the Kremlin. Low clouds whipped across a gray November sky, and splinters of sleet bit into the faces of Muscovites who lined the streets to watch the cortege. Ten times before reaching the Kremlin, the procession stopped and litanies were sung from the steps of ten churches. In St. Petersburg, red-and-gold court carriages draped in black waited at the station for the body and the family. For four hours, the cortege advanced slowly across the city to the Cathedral of St. Peter and St. Paul, where the Romanov tsars and empresses were buried. Throughout the city, the only sounds were the beat of muffled drums, the clatter of hooves, the rumble of iron carriage wheels, and the tolling of bells. Sixty-one royal personages, including three kings, arrived to join the family mourners. The ministers of the Imperial government, the commanders of the Russian army and navy, the provincial governors, and 460 delegates from cities and towns across Russia came to pay their respects. For seventeen days, the body of the emperor lay exposed in its coffin while tens of thousands of people shuffled past. On November 19, 1894, the tsar was interred.

One week later, briefly setting aside the atmosphere of mourning and without a reception or a honeymoon, the new, twenty-six-year-old Tsar Nicholas II married his twenty-two-year-old German fiancée, Alexandra Feodorovna.

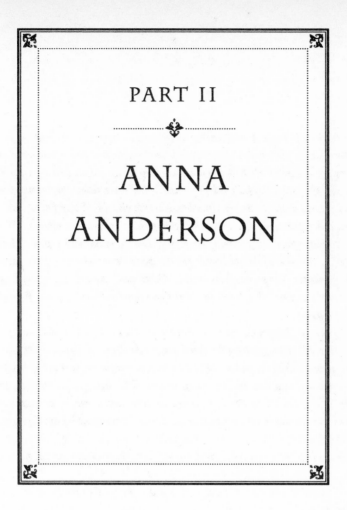

PART II

ANNA ANDERSON

Here comes a couple of men tearing up the path as tight as they could foot it.... One of these fellows was about seventy or upwards and had a bald head and very grey whiskers. He had an old battered-up slouch hat on, and a greasy blue woolen shirt, and ragged old blue jeans.... The other fellow was about thirty, and dressed about as ornery. After breakfast we all laid off and talked, and the first thing that comes out is that these chaps didn't know one another....

Nobody never said anything for awhile; then the young man hove a sigh and says,... "Ah, you would not believe me; the world never believes—let it pass— 'tis no matter. The secret of my birth ... Gentlemen," says the young man, very solemn, "I will reveal it to you, for I feel I may have confidence in you. By rights I am a duke!"

Jim's eyes bugged out when he heard that; and I reckon mine did, too.

"Yes, my great-grandfather, eldest son of the Duke of Bridgewater, fled to this country about the end of the last century, to breathe the pure air of freedom; married here and died, leaving a son, his own father dying about the same time. The second son of the late duke seized the titles and estates—the infant real duke was ignored. I am the lineal descendant of that infant—I am the rightful Duke of Bridgewater; and here I am, forlorn, torn from my high estate, hunted of men, despised by the cold world, ragged, worn, heartbroken, and degraded to the companionship of felons on a raft."

Jim pitied him ever so much and so did I. We tried to comfort him.... He said we ought to bow when we spoke to him, and say "Your Grace," or "My Lord," or "Your Lordship...." Well, that was easy so we done it.... But the old man got pretty silent by and by.... So, along in the afternoon, he says, "Looky here, Bilgewater.... I'm sorry for you, but you ain't the only person that's had troubles like that."

"No?"

"No, you ain't the only person that's had a secret of his birth.... Bilgewater, kin I trust you?... Bilgewater, I am the late Dauphin.... Yes, my friend, it is too true—your eyes is lookin' at this very moment on the poor disappeared

Dauphin, Looy the Seventeen, son of Looy the Sixteen and Marry Antonette....
Yes, gentlemen, you see before you, in blue jeans and misery, the wanderin', ex-
iled, trampled-on, and sufferin' rightful King of France."
   ... He said it often made him feel easier and better for awhile if people ... got
down on one knee to speak to him, and always called him "Your Majesty" and
waited on him first at meals, and didn't sit down in his presence till he asked
them.... So Jim and me set to majestying him.... This done him heaps of good,
and so he got cheerful and comfortable. But the duke kind of soured on him....

Mark Twain, THE ADVENTURES OF HUCKLEBERRY FINN

CHAPTER 13

THE
IMPOSTORS

The mysterious disappearance of the Russian Imperial family in July 1918 created fertile soil for the sprouting of delusion, fabrication, sham, romance, burlesque, travesty, and humbug. Since then, a long, occasionally colorful, frequently pathetic line of claimants and impostors has glided and stumbled across the century. Their stories have a common beginning: among the executioners in Ekaterinburg there allegedly existed a man, or men, of compassion—even Yurovsky was assigned this role—who secretly helped one Romanov, or two, or perhaps the entire family to escape. A recurring motive in many of these impostures was the belief that Tsar Nicholas II left a fortune behind in a foreign bank. As for delusion, who would not choose being a grand duke to real life as a gulag prisoner, a horse trainer, or even a famous spy? And being treated as a grand duchess must be preferable to being a factory worker or a milliner. Public support, naturally, is essential to these masquerades. For many years, a charming fellow adorned the society of Scottsdale, Arizona, wearing the name of Alexis Nicholaevich Romanov. When a Phoenix newspaperman was asked whether people in Scottsdale really believed that the man sitting next to them at dinner was the tsarevich, the newspaperman replied, "They wanted to. They *wanted* to."

These legends originated in and were nourished by the "disinformation" spoken, published, and broadcast by Lenin's government: Nicholas had been killed, but his wife and children were safe; Alexis had been executed along with his father; the Kremlin did not know where the women were—they were missing in the chaos of the civil war; the Soviet foreign minister supposed that the daughters were in America. This stream of disinformation continued until, as Investigator Soloviev noted, the regime felt itself secure enough to boast that everyone, children included, had been simultaneously murdered. Given the constant alterations and amendments to its tales, few outside the Soviet Union believed anything the Soviet government said.

Sokolov's investigation, not finding the bodies, further opened the door to doubt. Some accepted without question his belief that eleven people had been killed and their bodies totally destroyed. Others accepted his findings but had reservations. Still others rejected Sokolov absolutely. White Russian emigres and Western newspapers passed back and forth rumors that the murders had been a hoax. In 1920, the tsar was said to have been seen in the streets of London, his hair snow white. Another story placed him in Rome, hidden in the Vatican by the pope. The entire Imperial family was said to be aboard a ship cruising eternally through the waters of the White Sea, never touching land.

The confusion over the death of the Imperial family, and the multitude of contradictory stories in the Soviet Union and the West, made almost inevitable what happened next. Over the years, dozens of claimants stepped forward, presenting themselves as this or that member of the Imperial family. Nicholas and Alexandra did not reappear (although in one version, they were reported to have escaped to Poland), but all of the five children appeared in different times and places. The Soviet Union (now Russia and other countries of the Commonwealth of Independent States) produced the largest assemblage:

- A young woman claiming to be Anastasia, whose documents named her as Nadezhda Ivanova Vasilyeva, appeared in Siberia in

1920, trying to make her way to China. She was arrested and shuttled between prisons in Nizhny Novgorod, Moscow, Leningrad, and, finally, an island gulag in the White Sea. In 1934, she was dispatched to a prison hospital in Kazan, from where she wrote letters in French and German to King George V ("Uncle George") pleading for help. For a brief period in the hospital, she changed her story and said that she was the daughter of a Riga merchant. She died in an asylum in 1971, but, according to the head of the Kazan hospital, "except for her claim that she was Anastasia, she was completely sane."

· Not long ago, Edvard Radzinsky traveled "one day by train, one day by bus, one day by horse" to a remote village in the Urals which believed that it had given refuge in 1919 to the tsar's two youngest daughters, Marie and Anastasia. The grand duchesses, Radzinsky was told, had lived together as nuns "in terrible poverty, afraid every day," sheltered by the local priest, until they died, both in 1964. The villagers showed Radzinsky the tombstones inscribed "Marie Nicholaevna" and "Anastasia Nicholaevna."

· Radzinsky himself gave some credence to a story he was told about a former gulag prisoner named Filipp Grigorievich Semyonov, who claimed to have been the Tsarevich Alexis. Described as "a rather tall man, somewhat stout, sloping shoulders, slightly round-shouldered ... a long, pale face, blue or grey slightly bulging eyes, a high forehead," Semyonov had served in the Red Army as a cavalryman, studied economics in Baku, and worked as an economist in Central Asia. In 1949, he turned up in a psychiatric hospital where he was classified as an "acute psychotic." Questioned by Soviet doctors, the patient knew more about the names and titles of the Imperial family, the Imperial palaces, and court protocol and ceremonies than his interrogators. He also had a cryptorchidism (one undescended testicle), which the examining physician said he had been told was the case with the tsarevich. His hemophilia, apparently untroublesome during his years in the Red cavalry, "returned," Radzinsky said, "two months before his death."

The Semyonov story attracted the attention of Vladimir Soloviev and the Office of the Public Prosecutor. "Semyonov was a puzzling, very doubtful person," Soloviev said. "He was arrested during the war. Men leaving for the front were given money, and he stole that money, one hundred thousand rubles. He was sentenced to death, and then he remembered that he was the tsarevich. They sent him to a mental hospital, and that is how he avoided the death penalty. He wound up as a worker in the morgue, the lowest position, carrying corpses." Radzinsky possessed a photograph of Semyonov, which, in the playwright's view, bore a similarity to the thirteen-year-old tsarevich. In the opinion of others, there was no resemblance.

· Alexander Avdonin had several large files filled with letters and photographs sent by the "children" and then the "grandchildren" of Nicholas II. Turning through them, he said, "Here is Alexis and here is his daughter.... This is Marie Nicholaevna.... Here is the daughter of Olga Nicholaevna; she is one of two daughters of Olga.... There is Anastasia...there is the daughter of Anastasia...and there is the grandson of Anastasia.... Here is another Anastasia." Avdonin did not mock these people; because they wrote to him mostly pitiable letters, he was sympathetic. "I wish that we could afford to do blood testing or DNA testing on all of them," he said. "So that they would know who they are. And who they are not."

In Europe, other claimants appeared. A woman named Marga Boodts, living in a villa on Lake Como in Italy, declared that she was the tsar's oldest daughter, Grand Duchess Olga; the money supporting her was said to come from the pope and the former kaiser.

Another daughter, Grand Duchess Tatiana, was reported to have been rescued from Siberia by British agents in an airplane and flown to Vladivostok, then carried across the Pacific to Canada in a Japanese battleship, then escorted across Canada and across the Atlantic to England, arriving one month after the executions in Ekaterinburg. A different story depicts Tatiana as a belly dancer and prostitute in Constantinople, from which plight she was rescued by a British officer who married her. This woman, Larissa Feodorovna Tudor, died in 1927 and is buried in a graveyard in Kent.

The tsar's third daughter, Marie, is said to have escaped to Rumania, where she married and bore a child named Olga-Beata. Olga-Beata, in turn, had a son, who lived in Madrid as Prince Alexis d'Anjou de Bourbon-Condé Romanov-Dolgoruky. In 1994, the prince proclaimed himself "His Imperial and Royal Highness, Hereditary Grand Duke and Tsarevich of Russia, King of Ukraine, and Grand Duke of Kiev." In 1971, the Dolgoruky family and the Association of Descendants of the Russian Nobility of Belgium brought an action in a Belgian court against "Prince Alexis," charging that he was in fact a Belgian citizen named Alex Brimeyer. The court sentenced Brimeyer-Dolgoruky-Romanov to eighteen months in jail. In 1995, he died in Spain.

After the Second World War, a Tsarevich Alexis appeared in Ulm, Germany. This claimant had served as a major in the Red Air Force, biding his time, he said, to escape from the Soviet Union. Once in Ulm, he worked for many years as a plant technician, not revealing his true identity until his final years.

Other tsareviches sprang up in North America. Mrs. Sandra Romanov of Vancouver, British Columbia, believes that her husband, Alexei Tammet-Romanov, who died of leukemia in 1977, was the son of the tsar. She is willing to have his body exhumed so that a DNA test can be performed.

There was the robust Prince Alexis Romanov, who lived his last thirty years in Scottsdale, Arizona, and died in 1986. This entrepreneurial tsarevich operated a perfume and jewelry store and marketed a brand of vodka called Alexis. According to the label, it was "a special distillation to the specification of Prince Alexis Romanov, who is a direct descendant of Tsar Nicholas Romanov, Tsar of All the Russias." Prince Alexis lived colorfully, dating movie stars, marrying five times, and earning a reputation as a polo player. Polo is a violent sport; he admitted that, over forty years, he had suffered eleven broken bones. His fifth and final wife fell in love with him when she first saw him on horseback. "He was the most elegant rider I have ever seen," she said. "He looked like part of the horse. When he rode in the lot next to the Hilton, traffic would be tied up from people stopping to watch."

Recently, a son of another Tsarevich Alexis, who says that his father was assassinated in Chicago by the KGB, appeared in Washington, D.C. He says that he had secret meetings with Vice President Dan Quayle and Secretary of State James A. Baker III and that they told him, "We know who you are. Hold yourself in readiness."

In the early 1960s, two claimants appeared in the United States who managed to attract the attention of national newspapers and publishing houses. Ultimately, they met. One was an Alexis, the other an Anastasia.

On April 1, 1958, the American ambassador in Bern, Switzerland, received an anonymous letter written in German, postmarked in Zurich. The author, describing himself as a senior official in a Soviet Bloc national intelligence service, offered his services to the U.S. government and asked that his letter be forwarded to FBI director J. Edgar Hoover. For twenty-four months, this agent, using the code name Heckenschuetze (German for sharpshooter or sniper), passed more than two thousand microfilm documents to the Central Intelligence Agency. Unwilling to reveal his name or country of origin, this spy exposed a number of KGB moles planted inside Western governments and intelligence agencies; these agents included Stig Wennerström, George Blake, Gordon Lonsdale, Israel Beer, Heinz Felfe, and John Vassal.

The mystery as to the agent's identity seemed to have ended in December 1960, when a man speaking English telephoned the U.S. Consulate in West Berlin and announced that he was Heckenschuetze. Saying that his life was threatened, he declared that he was coming over. On Christmas Day, Heckenschuetze crossed into West Berlin. He turned out to be a husky, dark-haired man with blue eyes, a protruding lower lip, and a flourishing guardsman's mustache. The defector presented his name and identity papers. He was, apparently, Lt. Col. Michael Goleniewski, a senior officer of Polish Army Military Intelligence. Later, Goleniewski elaborated: "From 1957 to 1960, I was the head of the Technical and Scientific Department of the Polish Secret Service. This function led me to foreign travel, which was very important for my clandestine activities. I had close ties with influential people in the KGB without ever having belonged to it." An American intelligence official explained, "Goleniewski was in Polish Military Intelligence. But at the same time he was employed by the Russians to keep tabs on all Polish intelligence services and personalities in Poland and in the West."

Colonel Goleniewski was shocked and displeased by the reception party which greeted him. He had expected to be met by agents of the FBI. Through all his months of service, he had believed that he was dealing directly with FBI director J. Edgar Hoover. Although he knew that by law the CIA is responsible for espionage conducted by the United States outside American territory, Goleniewski had deliberately intended to bypass it in the belief that it had been infiltrated by Soviet agents. His mistake about the identity of his American handlers had been accepted and encouraged: all messages sent back to him had been signed "Hoover." Nevertheless, the men waiting in Berlin to receive him were agents of the CIA. Colonel Goleniewski never met Hoover; the nearest he got was a tour of the FBI building in Washington, in which he was shown the Dillinger and Bonnie and Clyde exhibits, a display on the crime laboratory and fingerprints, and a number of portraits and photographs of J. Edgar Hoover.

On January 12, 1961, Goleniewski arrived in the United States from Germany on a U.S. military plane. Given an employment contract and a stipend from the U.S. government, he worked for almost three years with CIA debriefing officers, describing Soviet intelligence techniques and operations and pinpointing the names of Communist agents in various Western countries. On September 30, 1961, he had a one-hour meeting with CIA director Allen Dulles. The agency had not yet moved into its quarters in Langley, Virginia, and the only detail the visitor remembered was Dulles's concern that his new office would lack sufficient wall space to mount his extensive collection of pipes. The conversation, according to Goleniewski, was vague and noncommittal.

Because the Polish government, on learning of his defection, had sentenced him to death in absentia, the CIA placed him in a well-secured apartment in Kew Gardens, Queens. In order to give Goleniewski the protection of U.S. citizenship, the agency negotiated with the House and Senate committees on immigration and nationality. "The beneficiary, Michael Goleniewski, a native and citizen of Poland, was born August 16, 1922, in Nieswiez," the CIA told the House Immigration Subcommittee. "He completed three years of law at the University of Poznan and, in 1956, received a master's degree in political science from the University of Warsaw. He enlisted in the Polish Army in 1945 and was commissioned a lieutenant colonel in 1955." On July 10, 1963, a private bill, H.R. 5507, was introduced. The bill declared, "The beneficiary is a 40-year-old native and citizen of Poland who has been admitted to the United States for permanent residence and is employed by the U.S. Government.... His services to the United States are rated as truly significant." The bill passed both houses of Congress, and Michael Goleniewski became a citizen of the United States.

This, however, was not the conclusion to the case. At some point during his months with the CIA, Goleniewski told his debriefing officers another tale. Goleniewski, the defector informed them, was a cover name he had used while living in Poland and working in Polish intelligence. His true identity, he said, was Grand Duke Alexei Nicholaevich Romanov; he was, he announced, the Russian tsarevich presumed to have been killed in Ekaterinburg.

Instead of shooting the family in the cellar, according to Goleniewski, Yurovsky had helped them to escape. He shepherded them, disguised as poor refugees, out of Russia. After months of travel through Turkey, Greece, and Austria, they found their way to Warsaw. Why Warsaw? "My father thought it over very carefully," Goleniewski said. "He chose Poland because there were a large number of Russians in the cities and on the farms. He thought we could blend into the background without attracting attention. He shaved off his beard and mustache, and nobody recognized him. In 1924, we moved from Warsaw to a country village near Poznan, close to the German border."

That same year, he said, his mother, Empress Alexandra, died, and the tsar sent Anastasia to America to withdraw funds from a bank in Detroit. She never returned to Poland. Subsequently, Olga and Tatiana moved to Germany. Nicholas, Alexis, and his sister Marie remained near Poznan through the Second World War, and for a time the tsar served in the Polish Underground. Goleniewski grew up in Poznan. In 1945, after the war, friends arranged his admission into the Polish Army, and he began his career in intelligence. In 1952, at the age of eighty-four, Nicholas II died. At the time of his own defection, Goleniewski said, all four of his sisters were alive, and he was in contact with them.

Two questions arose: What was Goleniewski's age? And what was the condition of his hemophilia? Goleniewski had told the CIA and the U.S. Congress that he was born in 1922, whereas the Tsarevich Alexis was born in 1904. A difference of eighteen years is difficult to hide, and Colonel Goleniewski's age in 1961 appeared much closer to thirty-nine than to fifty-seven. Goleniewski explained. His hemophilia had been confirmed, he said, by Dr. Alexander S. Wiener of Brooklyn, a codiscoverer of the Rh factor in blood.* His youthful appearance he ascribed to a rare suspension of growth in childhood caused by his illness; hemophilia, he said, had meant that he was a child "twice over."

Having revealed his Imperial identity, Colonel Goleniewski was ready to collect his inheritance. "After the 1905 war with Japan," he said, "my father started depositing money in Western countries." In New York, he named the Chase Bank, Morgan Guaranty, J. P. Morgan & Co., Hanover, and Manufacturer's Trust; in London, the Bank of England, Baring Brothers, Barclays Bank, and Lloyds Bank; in Paris, the Bank of France and Rothschild Bank; in Berlin, the Mendelssohn Bank. "The sum amounts to $400 million in the United States alone," Goleniewski declared. "Up to twice that amount is deposited in other countries. I won't demand every nickel, but I want a

---

*Dr. Wiener died many years ago, and his files have vanished. One of his colleagues, Dr. Richard Rosenfield, said, "I'm not at all sure that Al Wiener was competent to make such a diagnosis. It was not his area of expertise at all. He tried to get by with everything in clinical medicine, but he was more or less incompetent except in the field of blood typing, and there, of course, he was exceptionally good."

fair amount. If I can't get it, I will go to court and a lot of important names will come out."

Goleniewski's claim that he was the tsarevich embarrassed the CIA. He insisted on being addressed as a grand duke. He had a violent temper. Director Dulles quickly washed his hands of the former agent. Asked by a reporter about Goleniewski's claim, Dulles replied, "The story may all be true or it may not be. I do not care to discuss the subject further." Eventually, a decision was made: whatever the value of Goleniewski's services to the agency, the CIA could not be put in the position of supporting his claim to the tsar's fortune. Late in 1964, the agency put Goleniewski on a pension and severed all connections with its former spy.

Looking back on the CIA's relationship with Goleniewski, a former senior officer of the agency, now retired, remembered meeting the Polish agent twice. "I went up to see if I could pour oil on troubled waters. It was no use; he was around the bend. But I will say this: the material he provided us was very good indeed. There was no nonsense. It was not the product of a fevered imagination. It was the real stuff." Was Goleniewski, as *The New York Times* had once described him, the most productive agent in the history of the CIA? "No, that's terribly exaggerated. But he provided very clear, precise identification. It led to some serious arrests."

During Goleniewski's final year at the CIA, the press became involved. For three years, his story had been kept out of the newspapers, but when his private citizenship bill went up to Capitol Hill, the responsible congressional subcommittee wanted the CIA to produce the defector for interrogation. "I want to see a live body," said the subcommittee chairman. The agency refused to allow Goleniewski to appear before the committee. The former spy became enraged and went to the press. He gained a willing ear in *New York Journal-American* reporter Guy Richards. Richards found Goleniewski "striding energetically back and forth in his apartment" and described him as "41, a husky, handsome, Polish-born agent, who resembles the Hollywood prototype of the suave spy."

Meanwhile, Goleniewski was twice subpoenaed to appear before secret sessions of the Senate Internal Security Subcommittee. The appearances never took place. After several postponements, the sub-committee decided not to put Goleniewski in the witness chair. Instead, Jay Sourwine, the committee counsel, questioned witnesses from the State Department who testified to the invariable accuracy and importance of the intelligence information Goleniewski had supplied. Sourwine said that the reason Goleniewski had not been questioned directly was that he insisted on testifying first about his Romanov identity. The senators, he said, had decided that this would "not be appropriate."

Depressed by the Senate's refusal to hear his testimony, Goleniewski quickly became the center of another storm. On September 30, 1964, a few hours before the birth of their daughter, Tatiana, he married thirty-five-year-old Irmgard Kampf, a German Protestant with whom he had been living. On his wedding license and in the church marriage register, Goleniewski signed his name as Alexis Nicholaevich Romanov, son of Nicholas Alexandrovich Romanov and Alexandra Feodorovna Romanov, née von Hesse. He listed his birthday as August 12, 1904, and his birthplace as Peterhof, Russia. Two middle-aged women, whom he described as his "sisters, Olga and Tatiana," came from Germany for the wedding. The ceremony was performed in his apartment by the very reverend archpriest and protopresbyter of the Synod of Bishops of the Russian Orthodox Church Abroad, Count George P. Grabbe, better known as Father George. (Father George was a nephew of Maj. Gen. Count Alexander Grabbe, commander of Tsar Nicholas II's Cossack horse guards.) A photograph taken that day shows a bearded Grabbe seated next to the pregnant bride, the groom, and the two "sisters," whose resemblance to the grand duchesses—even given the passage of many decades—is nonexistent.

The storm raged not so much around Goleniewski—whose claim to be the tsarevich had long since been dismissed as "absurd," "outrageous," and "a stupid Soviet fabrication" by the Russian emigre community in America—as around Father George. The priest was ferociously attacked in the Russian-American press. Grabbe's ecclesiastical superiors forbade him to baptize little Tatiana. He was obliged to repeat over and over that the name Romanov was as common in

Russia as Smith in America, that as a priest he could not refuse to marry a couple who were otherwise qualified, that Goleniewski could not possibly be *that* Alexis Nicholaevich Romanov, and that his performance of the wedding in no way signified church recognition of the groom's claim to identity.

At the time, Father George's explanations failed to convince his accusers, especially when it became known—by way of a three-column ad in the *Journal-American,* supposedly paid for by Colonel Goleniewski—that, before he agreed to perform the ceremony, he had visited Goleniewski five times in his Queens apartment. As a result of his action, Grabbe was asked to resign from all Russian emigre organizations; for a while, no one would speak to him.

Thirty years later, Father George, now called Bishop Gregory and retired, explained why he had done what he did. On September 30, 1964, he received a call from Goleniewski at five o'clock in the morning, saying that his wife was about to give birth and that he possessed a marriage license. Father George went to Goleniewski's apartment, where he found the expectant couple and a publisher named Robert Speller waiting. Goleniewski handed the priest a marriage license made out in the name of Alexis Nicholaevich Romanov and a court decree showing that he had changed his name from Michael Goleniewski to Alexis Romanov. "I could have walked out," admitted Bishop Gregory. "Perhaps I should have. But, given the circumstances, I felt I had no choice. When a child is about to be born out of wedlock, a priest has a responsibility. The wife went directly to Manhasset Hospital and gave birth." Many years later, the child born that day wrote to Bishop Gregory, asking the bishop to help her find her father. "I didn't answer," said Bishop Gregory. "I didn't want to be mixed up with him anymore."

Goleniewski's temper and mental stability worsened. He severed his relationships with every American he had known, declaring, "You are dismissed!" He accused Guy Richards of "criminal libel." He continued to live in Queens on a U.S. government pension, which he complained was only five hundred dollars a month, the equivalent of a Polish colonel's pension. In 1966, he began writing open letters to the director of the CIA, to Attorney General Ramsey Clark, to the U.S. Civil Liberties Union, and to the International Red Cross. "I am no longer able to pay the monthly rent for my apartment arranged by the CIA," he complained. "I have been deprived of necessary and expensive medical help. I have been deprived of any possibilities to express my opinions through the free press." He demanded fifty thousand dollars in arrears salary payment and one hundred thousand dollars in reimbursement for loss of property in Poland.

During the 1970s, Colonel Goleniewski published from his home a monthly bulletin titled *Double Eagle,* "dedicated to the national independence and security of the United States and the survival of Christian Civilization." In it, he titled himself "His Imperial Highness, the Heir to the All-Russian Imperial Throne, Tsarevich and Grand Duke Alexis Nicholaevich Romanoff of Russia, the August Ataman and Head of the Russian Imperial House of Romanoff, etc., Knight of the OSA, OSG, OSJ, etc. and of SOS, FLH, etc." The bulletin was a twenty-page, densely typed, unparagraphed cataract of abuse against "Jewish bankers from London," "aristocratic thieves," "embezzlers," "ganglords and transcontinental racketeers," and "cannibalistic usurers." Colonel Goleniewski declared that the Rockefellers were the "biggest crooks who ever existed" and that on his list of Soviet agents passed to the CIA in 1961 had been a university professor named Henry Kissinger.

In 1981, the Russian Orthodox Church Abroad canonized all the immediate members of the last Russian Imperial family, including the Tsarevich Alexis. This ceremony, possible only because the church considered all of the family to have been martyred in death, provoked an outburst from Colonel Goleniewski. He declared the Church Abroad—a fiercely anti-Communist institution—to have been "thoroughly penetrated by the KGB" in order to carry out this plot against his rightful inheritance. Thereafter, Goleniewski became less visible. In August 1993, a former Polish intelligence officer wrote in a Polish newspaper that his onetime colleague Michael Goleniewski had died in New York on July 12, 1993. The U.S. Central Intelligence Agency does not know what became of its former agent Heckenschuetze.

❧

On October 18, 1963, the cover of *Life*, the nation's most prominent and widely read weekly magazine, displayed a picture of Nicholas II's five children. The headline was "THE CASE OF A NEW ANASTASIA: IS A LADY FROM CHICAGO THE TSAR'S DAUGHTER?" Inside, across ten pages, *Life* excerpted a new book, *Anastasia, the Autobiography of the Grand Duchess of Russia*, and summarized the life of its author, a woman who called herself Eugenia Smith. For forty years this woman had lived in Illinois, the final seventeen as the permanent guest of a wealthy woman, Mrs. William Emery, whose family owned the Chicago Rawhide Company. Mrs. Emery believed that her house-guest was Grand Duchess Anastasia. She took Mrs. Smith on trips to Europe and always solemnly celebrated her birthday on June 18, Anastasia's birthday. Mrs. Smith lived with Mrs. Emery from 1945 until June 1963, when, having inherited money from her benefactress, she moved to New York City to help with the publication of her book.

During her years in Illinois, Mrs. Smith received only slight attention from the press and public. She had no support from a local Romanov, but here the fault was her own. When stories appeared, announcing that Grand Duchess Anastasia was living in Elmhurst, Prince Rostislav of Russia, Nicholas II's nephew, also happened to be living in Chicago. His first wife, Alexandra, had divorced him and married Lawrence Armour, a banker. Mrs. Armour heard that one of her former husband's relatives was living nearby in Elmhurst, so she phoned and invited Mrs. Smith to lunch. The party, she said, would also include her ex-husband, because Prince Rostislav was eager to see his cousin Anastasia, who had been a childhood playmate. Three times Mrs. Armour issued this invitation; each time Mrs. Smith developed a headache and declined to go, explaining that she was too nervous to see her cousin.

When Eugenia Smith first brought her manuscript to her publisher, Robert Speller & Sons in New York, she did not claim to be Grand Duchess Anastasia. Instead, she said that she had been a friend of the grand duchess, who, before she died in 1920, had entrusted her with personal notes. Soon afterward, Mrs. Smith amended her tale:

now she became the grand duchess. She said that she had escaped from Ekaterinburg and Russia to Rumania. In October 1918—three months after the Ekaterinburg massacre—she married a Croatian Catholic, Marijan Smetisko. One child, a daughter, had died in infancy. In 1922, she received her husband's permission to come to America; her immigration papers that year listed her as Eugenia Smetisko. She landed in New York, stopped briefly in Detroit, and then went to Chicago. Her marriage dissolved a few years later, and she became a salesgirl, a model, a milliner, a lecturer, and a seller of perfume. During World War II, she became a U.S. citizen and worked in a defense plant. After the war, she moved in with Mrs. Emery.

Life presented the story as a mystery, still unsolved, and offered evidence for and against its subject. A polygraph expert, hired by the magazine, questioned Mrs. Smith for thirty hours and then declared that he was virtually positive his subject was Anastasia. Two anthropologists, comparing photographs of Anastasia and Mrs. Smith, declared that they could not possibly be pictures of the same woman. A graphologist, studying handwriting samples, agreed with the anthropologists. Princess Nina Chavchavzdze, a cousin who had played with Anastasia in Russia until both were thirteen, met Mrs. Smith and also concluded that she was bogus. Tatiana Botkin, daughter of the tsar's doctor, killed with the family, read Mrs. Smith's book and compiled a twenty-page list of specific errors; she also pointed out a number of remarkable similarities between passages in her own book about the Imperial family and passages in Mrs. Smith's book. *Life* located a Croatian named Marijan Smetisko through the address listed in Mrs. Smith's immigration papers; he said that he had never known any woman named Eugenia and had never been married to anyone other than his current wife.

Two months after the *Life* article was published, Colonel Goleniewski appeared on Eugenia Smith's doorstep. At that time, Goleniewski was still under wraps at the CIA, and no one in America outside the intelligence agency and the FBI had heard of him. On December 28, 1963, he phoned Mrs. Smith's publisher and asked for an appointment to see her. He did not use the name Goleniewski; instead, he called himself Mr. Borg. Mrs. Smith agreed, and a meeting between the two pretenders, supposedly brother and sister, took place on December 31. Goleniewski said that he had been trying for two years to get the CIA to help him find his sister in America. He told her briefly about his life and brought her up to date on their family: "Your sister Marie is in Warsaw.... Mother died in Warsaw.... In 1952, I buried our father with my own hands. He was a very good Russian man.... I was two times a child because of my sickness."

Mrs. Smith listened for a while and then burst out passionately, "He knows. He knows. He is my brother Alexis. My darling. My darling."

This emotional meeting was followed by three more during the next several weeks, during which time Mrs. Smith called Goleniewski "my brother, Alexis." But an awkward fact intruded on their relationship: in her book, Mrs. Smith had said that she was the only Romanov to survive Ekaterinburg. Her publisher pointed out that public recognition of the man as her brother would require Mrs. Smith to admit that she had not told the truth. Mrs. Smith refused to change her story, and, inevitably, the relationship between the "siblings" began to deteriorate.

Michael Goleniewski and Eugenia Smith did not see each other again, but he continued to assert that she was his sister Anastasia. Later, he reported that she had died in New York City in 1968. She was murdered, he said, after a visit by "very powerful men...two of them were Rockefellers."*

The women who claimed to be Grand Duchess Anastasia were challenged by relatives who tested their memories, anthropologists who measured their faces, and graphologists who studied their handwriting. The men aspiring to be accepted as the Tsarevich Alexis faced a more difficult test. Nicholas II's only son suffered from hemophilia. This is a hereditary, noncurable disease, transmitted by mothers to

*In fact, in 1995, Eugenia Smith was still alive, living in Newport, R.I. Asked whether she wished to give blood so that her DNA profile could be compared to that of Empress Alexandra and the three Imperial daughters, she declined.

their sons. It meant that the tsarevich's blood did not clot as does most people's. A bump or bruise rupturing a tiny vessel beneath the skin could begin a slow seepage of blood into surrounding muscle and tissue. Instead of clotting quickly, the blood would have continued to flow, creating a swelling or hematoma, sometimes as big as an orange or a grapefruit. There were no transfusions of blood or blood fraction—as there are today—which could halt the bleeding. Eventually, when the skin was filled with blood, pressure on the torn vessel would slow the hemorrhage and allow a clot to form. Then, over weeks, the process of reabsorption would take place, turning the skin from a shiny purple to a mottled yellow-green. A simple scratch on a finger was not dangerous. Minor cuts and scratches anywhere on the surface of the body were treated with pressure and tight bandaging, which pinched off the blood and permitted the flesh to heal over. Exceptions were hemorrhages inside the mouth or nose, areas which could not be bandaged.

The permanent crippling effect of Alexis's hemophilia came from bleeding into the joints. Blood entering the confined space of an elbow, a knee, or an ankle caused pressure on the nerves, which inflicted intense pain. Sometimes the cause of the injury was apparent, sometimes not. In either case, Alexis awakened in the morning and called out, "Mama, I cannot walk today" or "Mama, I cannot bend my elbow." At first, as the limb flexed, leaving the largest possible area in the joint socket for the inflowing fluids, the pain was small. Then, as the space filled, it began to hurt. When the pain obliterated everything else from his consciousness, Alexis still was able to cry, "Mama, help me, help me!" Doctors were summoned, ice packs applied, prayers offered. Nothing helped. Then Gregory Rasputin, the Siberian peasant reported to have miraculous powers of faith healing, was brought to Alexandra.

Each bleeding episode added to the damage. Once inside a joint, blood had a corrosive effect, destroying bone, cartilage, and tissue. As bone formation changed, limbs locked in bent positions. There was no rehabilitation other than rest and waiting for the hematoma to be reabsorbed. The best therapy was constant exercise and massage, but this risked recommencing the hemorrhage. When Alexis reached age five, two sailors from the Imperial navy were assigned to protect him every minute. When he was sick, they carried him; many photographs and movies of Imperial ceremonies under Nicholas II depict the tsar and the empress walking along, nodding and bowing, followed by a large sailor carrying a handsome six-, eight-, or ten-year-old boy.

When the revolution came, this protection and care were stripped away. One of the two sailor-attendants deserted; the other eventually was taken and shot. Alexis was well during the first seven months of the family's imprisonment in Tobolsk. Then, in April, seeking an outlet for his energy, he carried a sled to the top of an indoor staircase and rode it down. He fell and began to bleed into the groin. During the remaining four months of his life, he could not walk. When a troop of cavalry arrived in Tobolsk, sent by Moscow to bring the Imperial family to the capital, Alexis was too ill to travel and was left behind. Three weeks later, he joined his parents in Ekaterinburg. During the family's final imprisonment in the Ipatiev House, Alexis remained most of the day in bed in his parents' room. On the night of July 16, 1918, when Yurovsky came for the family, Nicholas carried his son down the stairs into the cellar.

It is inconceivable that a hemophiliac could survive the carnage in Ipatiev's cellar. Nevertheless, if—somehow—Alexis had been saved and had been carried thousands of miles to political safety, his medical prospects still would have been dismal. Hemophiliacs born at the beginning of this century spent much of their lives in beds and wheelchairs, their limbs contorted by permanent joint damage. Many perished by the time they were twenty; most others were dead before thirty. Today, hemophilia can be treated, but it cannot be cured.

CHAPTER 14

❖

THE
CLAIMANT

Mrs. Tchaikovsky is either Grand Duchess Anastasia or a miracle.

—Ambassador Sergei Botkin, president of the
Russian Refugee Office in Berlin, 1926

One Romanov claim stood apart from the others. From her appearance in 1920 to her death in 1984, the identity of the woman known variously as Fräulein Unbekannt (Miss Unknown), Mrs. Alexander Tschaikovsky, Anna Anderson, Anastasia Manahan, and Franziska Schanzkowska was one of the celebrated mysteries of the twentieth century. She insisted that she was Grand Duchess Anastasia, Nicholas II's youngest daughter. The survivors of the revolution, some of whom had known Anastasia well, disagreed passionately among themselves about the legitimacy of this claim. Aunts, uncles, cousins, grand dukes, grand duchesses, former ladies-in-waiting, former nursemaids, tutors, army officers, officers of the Imperial yacht, even Nicholas II's former mistress, were called upon or presented themselves to give opinions. They made declarations, signed affidavits, gave interviews, and wrote books. Her cause called up devotion and personal sacrifice from an international legion of supporters. At the same time, it brought down, upon her, her supporters, and her opponents, denunciation, lawsuits, and, in some cases, financial ruin. When she died, the solution appeared no closer than it had been sixty-four years earlier, when she first appeared.

At nine o'clock on the night of February 17, 1920—nineteen months after the murders in Ekaterinburg—a young woman jumped twenty feet from a bridge into the Landwehr Canal in Berlin. A policeman saw her, rescued her, and took her to a hospital. She had no purse, no papers, no identification of any kind. Questioned when she recovered, she refused to say who she was, where she lived, or how she supported herself. When the police persisted, she pulled a blanket over her face and turned to the wall. After six weeks, she was sent to Dalldorf Mental Asylum as Fräulein Unbekannt and placed in a ward with fourteen other women. On arrival, her height was five feet, two inches, her weight, 110 pounds. Medical examination showed that her body was covered with scars and, so the doctors believed, that she was not a virgin. Her teeth were in poor condition, and seven or eight were extracted by asylum dentists.

She remained in Dalldorf for over two years. After months of silence, she began to talk to some of the nurses. Later, one—a Russian-speaking German—said that she spoke Russian "like a native." In the autumn of 1921, turning through an illustrated magazine containing pictures of the Russian Imperial family, the patient asked another nurse whether she noticed any resemblance between herself and the tsar's youngest daughter. When the nurse agreed that there was a resemblance, the patient declared that she was Grand Duchess Anastasia. Word filtered out of the hospital that Grand Duchess *Tatiana* was present, and Baroness Buxhoevden, a former lady-in-waiting to Empress Alexandra, came to see her. When the patient refused to speak and hid beneath her blanket, the baroness roughly pulled back the cover and then stormed away, declaring, "She's too short to be Tatiana." Subsequently, the patient told her nurses again that she was

Anastasia. At the end of May 1922, Fräulein Unbekannt left Dalldorf and went to live in a small Berlin apartment with a Russian Baltic baron and his wife. Soon the baron's parlor was filled with other Russian emigres eager to see her for themselves and listen to her story.

According to her, when the bodies of her family were being carried from the cellar, one of the soldiers noticed that, although unconscious, she was still alive. This man, a Pole who assumed the name of Alexander Tschaikovsky, carried her, assisted by his brother Sergei, to his house in Ekaterinburg. Soon after, Alexander, Sergei, their mother, sister, and the semiconscious young woman fled Ekaterinburg in a peasant cart. Four and a half months and two thousand miles later, they crossed the border into Rumania and settled in Bucharest. There, to her distress, the young woman discovered that she was pregnant. Tschaikovsky confessed to rape. When the child, a son, was born out of wedlock, the mother wanted only to be rid of it. At the age of three months, the baby was handed over to Tschaikovsky's mother and sister. "My only desire was that it would be taken away," the baby's mother said. The infant was placed in an orphanage and, thereafter, vanished from history and legend. At some point, according to one version of this tale, the mother and Alexander Tschaikovsky were married in a ceremony supposedly performed in a Roman Catholic church. Not long after, she said, Tschaikovsky was killed in a street fight in Bucharest.

The young woman said that she decided to go to Berlin to ask for help from Empress Alexandra's sister Princess Irene of Prussia, who was Grand Duchess Anastasia's godmother as well as her aunt. Because she had no passport and no money, a male companion, possibly Sergei Tschaikovsky, helped her to walk across Europe, crossing borders at night to avoid detection. Reaching Berlin, she went to Princess Irene's Netherlands Palace. Standing alone before the gates, she decided that her aunt probably was not at home and that no one inside would recognize her. In a moment of despair, she threw herself into the canal.

That was her story of her escape. A subsequent check of the names of the guards at the Ipatiev House revealed no Alexander Tschaikovsky, nor, indeed, was there a family named Tschaikovsky living in or near Ekaterinburg in 1918. During the 1920s, researchers in Bucharest discovered no trace of any Tschaikovsky living in that city, nor any record of a marriage and birth recorded under that name, nor any record of a murder or death in the streets or anywhere else of a man by the name. For Grand Duchess Anastasia to have spent months in Bucharest and not have appealed to Queen Marie of Rumania, who was a first cousin of both her father and her mother, whom she had seen in June 1914, when there was talk of a marriage between the Russian and Rumanian families, was, according to Marie's daughter, "unexplainable."

The claimant later said that she did not go to the queen in Bucharest because she was pregnant and ashamed. Anastasia's aunt Grand Duchess Olga rejected that excuse, saying, "In 1918 or 1919, Queen Marie would have recognized Anastasia on the spot.... Marie would never have been shocked at anything, and a niece of mine would have known it.... *My* niece would have known that her condition would indeed have shocked [Princess] Irene." Thus, Olga found it unthinkable that a daughter of the tsar would turn her back on Queen Marie and walk across Europe to seek out Princess Irene.

All in all, "the escape" was perhaps the least verifiable of the chapters of the Anastasia legend; it had to be accepted on faith—as it was by her supporters—or rejected as wildly improbable—as it was by her opponents. In the end, it was no longer an issue. Those on either side of the argument were not interested in how she got away from the cellar. They wanted to know who she was.

Anastasia Nicholaevna, the fourth and youngest daughter of Tsar Nicholas II and Empress Alexandra, was born on June 18, 1901. Her older sisters Olga and Tatiana occupied the positions of authority among the Imperial children; her third sister, Marie, was gentle, merry, and flirtatious; this left Anastasia, a short, dumpy, blue-eyed child, to make her family reputation as a rebel and a wag. When the saluting cannon on the Imperial yacht fired at sunset, Anastasia retreated into a corner, stuck her fingers in her ears, widened her eyes, and lolled her tongue in mock terror. Quick-witted and comical, she was also stubborn, mischievous, and impertinent. The same gift of ear and tongue that made her quickest among her sisters to pick up good pronunciation in foreign languages equipped her admirably as a mimic. She aped, sometimes cruelly, the speech and mannerisms of those about her. She climbed trees, refusing to come down until specifically commanded to do so by her father. She rarely cried. Her aunt Grand Duchess Olga remembered a time when Anastasia was teasing so ruthlessly that she slapped the child. The little girl's face went crimson, but instead of crying she ran soundlessly out of the room. Sometimes, Anastasia's practical jokes went too far. Once she rolled a rock into a snowball and threw it at Tatiana. The missile hit her sister in the face and knocked her, stunned, to the ground. Frightened, at last Anastasia cried.

As daughters of a Russian tsar, without a range of friends, the four grand duchesses were closer than most sisters. Olga, the eldest, was only six years older than Anastasia, the youngest. In adolescence, the four proclaimed their unity by choosing for themselves a single autograph, OTMA, derived from the first letter of each of their names. As OTMA, they jointly signed letters and gave gifts. They were brought up simply. They slept in hard camp beds without pillows and began each day with a cold bath. They worked alongside maids making their beds. They made requests rather than gave commands: "If it isn't too difficult for you, my mother asks you to come." Within the household, they were addressed not as Your Imperial Highness but in simple Russian fashion as Olga Nicholaevna or Anastasia Nicholaevna. Among themselves, to their father, and to the servants, they spoke Russian. To their mother, who was brought up in England by her grandmother Queen Victoria, they spoke English.

To those who knew them, the appearance and characteristics of the four grand duchesses were clearly distinct. Baroness Buxhoevden remembered Anastasia's "fair hair, fine eyes, and dark eyebrows that nearly met.... She was rather short even at seventeen and ... decidedly fat.... the originator of all mischief." Tatiana Botkin, the daughter of the family doctor killed in the cellar, recalled Anastasia's "luminous blue eyes" and that she was "lively, rough, mischievous.... When Anastasia Nicholaevna laughed, she would never turn her head to look at you. She would glance at you from the corner of her eye with a roguish look." Gleb Botkin, Tatiana's younger brother, remembered Anastasia's hair, "blond with a slightly reddish luster, long, wavy, and soft. Her features were irregular. Her nose was rather long and her mouth quite wide. She had a small, straight chin." He also remembered her as autocratic and not in the least interested in what others thought of her. Anastasia's cousin Princess Xenia, two years younger, recollected the youngest grand duchess as a playmate who was "frightfully temperamental, wild and rough," who "cheated at games, kicked, scratched, and pulled hair."

For eight years after being plucked from the canal, the claimant lived mostly in Germany. Beginning in 1922, members of the former German Imperial family, the Hohenzollerns, came to discover whether this was, in fact, their Russian relative. The first was Anastasia's aunt Princess Irene of Prussia, married to the brother of the former kaiser. Aunt Irene had not seen her niece since 1913, before the outbreak of war between Germany and Russia, when Anastasia was twelve. Nine years had passed, enough to create difficulties in any remembrance, particularly of a sick person who had been through physical and emotional trauma. But Mrs. Tschaikovsky, as she now called herself, did not give her purported aunt a fair chance. Introduced under a false name, the princess stared hard across a table at the patient. Frightened, Mrs. Tschaikovsky jumped up and ran from the room. Princess Irene followed, but the patient turned away, put her face in her hands, and refused to speak. "She did not even answer when I asked her to say a word or give me a sign that she recognized me," Princess Irene said. Offended by this behavior, the princess departed.

"I saw immediately that she could not be one of my nieces," Irene wrote. "Even though I had not seen them for nine years, the fundamental facial characteristics could not have altered to that degree, in particular the position of the eyes, the ears, and so forth." Later Princess Irene appeared less certain. "I could not have made a mistake," she insisted when challenged by a nephew who believed in the claimant. "She *is* similar. She *is* similar. But what does that mean if it is not she?" Confused and distraught, the princess wept. But she never returned to visit Mrs. Tschaikovsky.

Gradually, other members of the former German Imperial family followed. In 1925, Crown Princess Cecilie, the former kaiser's daughter-in-law, called on the claimant. Cecilie was "struck at first by the young person's resemblance to the tsar's mother and to the tsar himself, but I could see nothing of the tsarina in her." Again, Mrs. Tschaikovsky provided no help. "It was virtually impossible to communicate with the young person," Cecilie observed. "She remained completely silent, either from obstinacy or because she was totally bewildered." Subsequently, Crown Princess Cecilie's opinion wavered, as had Princess Irene's. "I almost believe it must be she," Cecilie declared. But, as Anastasia's Aunt Irene and her Uncle Ernest of Hesse opposed the claim, Cecilie decided that "it was not my business to follow up the question of her identity." By 1952, after three subsequent visits to the claimant, the crown princess had changed her mind. "Today, I am convinced she is the tsar's youngest daughter," she said. "I detect her mother's features in her." Responding to a birthday gift, Cecilie wrote to the claimant, "God bless you with a tender kiss from your loving Aunt Cecilie." Princess Cecilie told her daughter-in-law, Princess Kyra of Russia, married to her son Prince Louis Ferdinand, by then the Hohenzollern pretender, "This [the claimant] is your cousin." Louis Ferdinand and Kyra did not agree. Across the bottom of Cecilie's affidavit testifying to the claimant's legitimacy, Louis Ferdinand scrawled in large pen strokes: "Kyra and I find no resemblance."

Meanwhile, another Hohenzollern, Princess Irene's son Prince Sigismund of Prussia, dispatched from his home in Costa Rica a list of eighteen questions for the claimant to answer. They were secret things from their childhood, he said, which only his first cousin Anastasia could know. The claimant answered sufficiently well for Sigismund, sight unseen, to announce, "This has convinced me. She is undoubtedly Anastasia of Russia."* Even the old ex-Kaiser Wilhelm II, living in exile in Holland, sent his second wife, Empress Hermine, to visit the

---

*The few people who subsequently saw the questions and answers always refused to describe them.

claimant in a German sanatorium. No statement was issued, but from this august quarter, silence was assumed to mean assent.

The character of the young woman her purported relatives saw during these years was often unappealing. If she could be moody and rudely uncommunicative to a visiting Russian baroness or to German princesses, her behavior was far worse toward people who took her in and tried to help. In their presence, she was irritable, demanding, and despotic. Her temper was ferocious. "She gets so angry sometimes that she becomes simply frightening," said one of her hostesses. "Her eyes acquire a fierce expression and she just trembles." At such moments, she would threaten to "pave the streets with the skulls of her enemies" and to "hang all her relatives from lampposts for their treason." She had no home or money, but usually it was she who would terminate a visit, storming out the door, hurling imprecations. Always, there was somewhere else to go. She moved endlessly from family to family, house to house, and, eventually, castle to castle. During the sixty-four years the claimant lived after being pulled from the canal, she was always dependent on benevolence and charity.

Poor health provided a partial excuse for her behavior. Particularly in the early years, she was always ill, shuttling in and out of hospitals, asylums, and sanatoria. In 1925, suffering from tuberculosis of the bone, she nearly died. Her mental health, also, was unstable. Her nerves were shattered and her memory impaired; this was the reason, her supporters said, that she had forgotten both Russian and English and spoke exclusively in German. Tatiana Botkin gave this explanation: "Her attitude is childlike, and altogether she cannot be reckoned with as an adult, responsible person, but must be led and directed as a child. She has not only forgotten languages, but she has in general lost the power of accurate narration, although not of thought. Even the simplest stories... she tells incoherently and incorrectly; they are really only words strung together in impossibly ungrammatical German.... Her defect is obviously in the region of the memory and in eye trouble. She says that, after her illness, she forgot how to tell time and had laboriously to learn it again."

The claimant's inability—or refusal—to speak Russian constituted a major stumbling block in her effort to be recognized as Anastasia. There were those, like the nurse at Dalldorf, who said that they had heard her speak "Russian like a native...she used whole, complete, connected sentences without any impediments." A doctor's report during the same period declared: "In her sleep, she speaks Russian with good pronunciation; mostly unessential things." More often, she gave the impression that she understood Russian, although she did not speak it. The Russian surgeon who operated on her tubercular arm in 1925 said, "Before the operation, I spoke Russian with her, and she answered all my questions, although in German."

Her supporters were divided: some, like Tatiana Botkin, blamed her *inability* to speak Russian on damage to her brain and consequent memory loss; others said that her *refusal* to speak her native language was the result of psychological inhibition caused by the trauma of imprisonment and the night in the cellar. The claimant herself explained that in Ekaterinburg the family was compelled to speak Russian so that the omnipresent guards could listen to their conversation; the language of the guards was rough, vile, and frequently obscene; the last words she heard in the cellar were Russian. Russian, to her, was the language of humiliation, terror, and death. Among her opponents, naturally, it was said that she did not speak Russian because she could not. The issue was never resolved. In 1965, a frustrated German judge tried singing Russian songs to her to determine whether she understood. She listened to him, impervious.

The most important potential witnesses were, of course, the principal members of the family she claimed to be her own, the Romanovs. Anastasia's grandmother the Dowager Empress Marie had survived the revolution and returned to live in her native Denmark. The old woman, the senior surviving member of the dynasty, having refused to listen to reports of the death of her son and his family, had no interest in stories that one of her granddaughters, having borne a child out of wedlock, had appeared in Berlin. Empress Marie's older daughter, Grand Duchess Xenia, living in London as a permanent guest of King George V, was not interested either. But the younger of Marie's two daughters, Grand Duchess Olga, refused to turn her back, unseeing, on a young woman who might be her cherished Malenkaya (Little One).

In their youthful Aunt Olga Alexandrovna, the four young grand duchesses had had a special friend and benefactress. Every Saturday, she came from St. Petersburg to spend the day with her nieces at Tsarskoe Selo. Convinced that the young women needed to get away from the palace, she persuaded Empress Alexandra to let her take them to the city. Accordingly, every Sunday morning, the aunt and her four excited nieces boarded a train for the capital. The first stop was a formal luncheon with their grandmother the dowager empress. From there, they went on to tea, games, and dancing with other young people at Olga Alexandrovna's house. "The girls enjoyed every minute of it," the grand duchess wrote over fifty years later. "Especially my dear goddaughter [Anastasia]. I can still hear her laughter rippling all over the room. Dancing, music, games—she threw herself wholeheartedly into them all."

Olga Alexandrovna herself had not had a happy early life. Wed at nineteen to Prince Peter of Oldenburg, a man not interested in women, she obtained, after fifteen years of unconsummated marriage, her brother's permission for annulment. In 1916, she married the man she loved, a commoner, Colonel Nicholas Kulikovsky. After the revolution, Olga, her husband, and their two sons, Tikhon and Guri, settled in Denmark with her mother, the dowager empress. When news came of the claimant's appearance, Grand Duchess Olga wrote to Pierre Gilliard, the former tutor of French to the Imperial children: "Please go at once to Berlin to see the poor lady. Suppose she really were the little one.... It would be such a disgrace if she were living all alone in her misery.... If it really is she, please send me a wire and I will come to Berlin to meet you."

Gilliard was superbly qualified to carry out this mission. He knew the children of the Russian Imperial family better than any of those who had yet seen the claimant. For thirteen years, he had lived in the inner circle of the Imperial household, tutoring the young grand duchesses and the tsarevich several times a week. Gilliard's dedication to the family was absolute. He followed them to Siberia and spent the winter with them in Tobolsk, continuing to give lessons, arranging French plays for his pupils to act in, and sawing wood in the courtyard with Nicholas and the tsarevich. He traveled with the family to Ekaterinburg, where only forcible separation by the Ural Soviet prevented him from joining them in the Ipatiev House. After the carnage in the cellar and the fall of the town to the Whites, Gilliard assisted Nicholas Sokolov in his investigation. Sifting through the grim remnants of the Four Brothers mine shaft, he cried out, "But the children? The children?" Gilliard left Russia in the company of the young grand duchesses' maid, Alexandra Tegleva, called Shura. Returning to his native Switzerland in 1919, he married Shura and took up a professorship at the University of Lausanne.

When Pierre Gilliard received Grand Duchess Olga's letter, he and his wife departed immediately for Berlin. The person they found in St. Mary's Hospital was feverish, delirious, and hallucinating. A tubercular infection in her left arm, aggravated by a staphylococcus infection, had created an excruciating open wound. The arm itself had swollen "to a shapeless mass," while the patient had shrunk to skeletal thinness. While the Gilliards sat by the bed, Shura asked to look at the patient's feet. Grand Duchess Anastasia had suffered from a condition known as hallux valgus, a malformation of the joints at the root of both big toes which gave the impression that the enlarged knuckle was bent to one side. "The feet look like the Grand Duchess's," said Shura, when the blanket was removed. "With her [Anastasia] it was the same as here; the right foot was worse than the left." Because the claimant was so ill, Gilliard insisted that she be moved to a better hospital. "The most important thing at the moment," he said, "is to keep her alive. We will both come back as soon as her condition improves." In a private clinic, a Russian surgeon removed the muscles and part of the bone of the left elbow, inserting a silver joint, which left bone permanently exposed. For weeks, the patient battled pain with repeated injections of morphine. Her weight dropped to under seventy-five pounds.

Three months later, Gilliard and his wife returned. First, Gilliard alone sat by the patient's bed and said, "Please chat with me a little.

Tell me everything you know about your past." The claimant was shocked and angry. "I do not know how to chat," she retorted. "Do you think that if someone had tried to kill you, as they did me, you would know much from before?" Gilliard left. That afternoon, a woman in a violet cloak entered the room, came up to the bed, smiled, and offered her hand. It was Grand Duchess Olga. She came again the next morning, and the two continued to talk, Olga in Russian, the patient in German. In the afternoon, Shura appeared. When the patient covered her hand with eau de cologne, Shura remembered that Grand Duchess Anastasia, "who was mad about perfume," often had done the same thing. Standing on the balcony watching this scene, Olga said to one of the claimant's friends, "Our Little One and Shura seem very happy to have found one another again. I am so happy that I came, and I did it even though Mamma did not want me to. She was so angry with me.... And then my sister [Grand Duchess Xenia] wired me from England saying that under no circumstances should I come to see the Little One." When Gilliard returned, he too seemed swept along by the belief that a family had been reunited. "I want to do everything I can to help the grand duchess," he said. Turning to the surgeon who had operated on her, he asked, "What is Her Imperial Highness's condition?" The doctor replied that her life was still in danger.

The next day, the third of this visit, Gilliard attempted again to question the patient about the past, especially Siberia. He had little success, and the visitors decided to leave. As Grand Duchess Olga departed, the patient burst into tears. Olga kissed her on both cheeks, saying, "Don't cry. I will write. You must get well. That is the main thing." As she left, the grand duchess told the Danish ambassador, who had escorted her, "My reason cannot grasp it, but my heart tells me that the Little One is Anastasia." Shura departed weeping. "I loved her so much!" she sobbed. "I loved her so much! Why do I love this patient just as much? Can you tell me that?" Gilliard kept his feelings and opinions under tighter control, declaring as he left, "We are going away without being able to say that she is *not* Grand Duchess Anastasia Nicholaevna."

The affection displayed during the visit continued to cheer the patient for several months. From Copenhagen, Grand Duchess Olga wrote five notes filled with endearments and concern. The first set the tone: "I am sending you all my love, am thinking of you all the time. It is so sad to go away, knowing that you are ill and suffering and lonely. Don't be afraid. You are not alone now and we shall not abandon you.... Eat a lot and drink cream." Olga's third note was accompanied by a gift: "I am sending to my little patient my own silk shawl, which is very warm. I hope that you will wrap this shawl around your shoulders and arms and that it will keep you warm during the cold of winter. I bought this shawl in Yalta before the war." The shawl was pure silk, rose colored, six feet long and four feet wide. But after the fifth letter, no more ever came.

The truth was that Olga, kindhearted, generous, and subject to powerful influence, was not sure. The night she returned to Copenhagen, even as she was writing the first of her notes to the patient in Berlin, Olga also wrote to Mrs. Tschaikovsky's supporter, Ambassador Zahle: "I have had very long conversations with my mother and Uncle Waldemar all about our poor little friend. I can't tell you how fond I got of her—whoever she is. My feeling is that she is not the one she believes—but one can't say she is not as a fact—as there are many strange and inexplicable facts not cleared up."

Thirty years later, looking back, Grand Duchess Olga was more decisively negative: "My beloved Anastasia was fifteen when I saw her for the last time in 1916. She would have been twenty-four in 1925. I thought Mrs. Anderson looked much older than that. Of course, one had to make allowances for a very long illness.... All the same, my niece's features could not possibly have altered out of all recognition. The nose, the mouth, the eyes were all different." Long before Grand Duchess Olga made this statement, however, the claimant had spoken the last word on their relationship. "It is now I who will not receive her," said Mrs. Tschaikovsky.

Rejection, even tentative, by Grand Duchess Olga, the Romanov survivor who had known Anastasia best and the only one until then who had troubled to come to see her, was a blow to the claimant's cause. The aunt's opinion was taken as decisively negative by most of the family and by virtually all Russian emigres. Pierre Gilliard added ammunition to the opposition cause. He gave lectures and wrote articles and eventually a book, *The False Anastasia*. He declared that he had known at first glance that the claimant was not his former pupil: "The patient had a long nose, strongly turned up at the end, a very large mouth, thick and fleshy lips; the grand duchess, on the other hand, had a short, sharp nose, a much smaller mouth and fine lips.... Apart from the color of the eyes, we could find nothing to make us believe that this was the grand duchess." Everything the claimant knew about the intimate life of the Imperial family, Gilliard said, she had read in published memoirs or seen in photographs. He denounced Mrs. Tschaikovsky as "a vulgar adventuress" and "a first rate actress."

In the years following Grand Duchess Olga's rejection, only two Romanovs declared in the claimant's favor. One was Grand Duke Andrew, Nicholas II's first cousin, who had seen the young Anastasia occasionally at family lunches. Troubled by Mrs. Tschaikovsky's claim, he received Empress Marie's permission to take charge of the investigation. In January 1928, he spent two days with the claimant. After the first meeting, he cried happily, "I have seen Nicky's daughter! I have seen Nicky's daughter!" Later, he wrote to Grand Duchess Olga, "I have observed her carefully at close quarters, and to the best of my conscience I must acknowledge that Anastasia Tschaikovsky is none other than my niece the Grand Duchess Anastasia Nicholaevna. I recognized her at once, and further observation only confirmed my first impression. For me there is definitely no doubt: it is Anastasia." On this same occasion, Grand Duke Andrew's wife, the former prima ballerina Mathilde Kschessinska, also met the claimant. In 1967, after Andrew's death, his ninety-five-year-old widow, who three quarters of a century before had been the youthful Nicholas II's mistress, was asked about the claimant. "I am still certain it was she," Madame Kschessinska replied. "When she looked at me, you understand, with those eyes, that was it. It was the emperor... it was the emperor's look. Anyone who saw the emperor's eyes will never forget them."

The other Romanov who endorsed the claimant was Anastasia's cousin Princess Xenia of Russia, who at eighteen had married an American tin mining heir, William B. Leeds, and moved to his Long

Island estate in Oyster Bay. Xenia was two years younger than Anastasia and had last seen her in the Crimea in 1913, when she was ten and Anastasia twelve. Fourteen years had passed, but Xenia, having invited Mrs. Tschaikovsky to stay with her and having closely observed the claimant over a period of six months, declared, "I am firmly convinced." Princess Xenia's older sister, Princess Nina, also met the claimant and was more cautious. "Whoever she is," said Princess Nina, "she is a lady of good society."

The ultimate arbiter in the Romanov family was the Dowager Empress Marie, and, despite the old woman's oft-reiterated hostility, Mrs. Tschaikovsky continued to hope that Marie would change her mind. "My grandmamma, she will know me," the claimant believed. It fell to Tatiana Botkin to break the news that the empress would never receive her, that her grandmother wanted nothing to do with her, and that Mrs. Tschaikovsky should give up waiting for an invitation to Copenhagen. "Why do they reject me? What have I done?" the claimant cried out. She was told it was, in part, because of her illegitimate child. "I have not seen my child since he was three months old," Mrs. Tschaikovsky protested. "Do you think I would allow any little bastard to proclaim himself the grandson of the tsar and the emperor of Russia?" But the dowager did not relent, and, to the claimant's distress, Empress Marie died in October 1928, still forbidding and silent.

Worse immediately followed. Within twenty-four hours of the funeral, a document that came to be called the Romanov Declaration was published. Signed by twelve members of the Russian Imperial family, along with Empress Alexandra's brother and two of her sisters, it announced their "unanimous conviction that the woman now living in the U.S.A. [Mrs. Tschaikovsky was with Princess Xenia on Long Island] is not the daughter of the tsar." The document, which cited the opinions of Grand Duchess Olga, Pierre Gilliard, and Baroness Buxhoevden, largely convinced the public that the entire family had considered the evidence and rejected the claimant. But this was not what had happened. Of forty-four living Romanovs, only twelve had signed. The two Romanovs who had accepted Mrs. Tschaikovsky's claim, Grand Duke Andrew and Princess Xenia, were not invited to sign. Of the fifteen signatories (Empress Alexandra's two sisters Princess Victoria of Battenberg and Princess Irene of Prussia and her brother, Grand Duke Ernest Louis of Hesse, had also signed the document), only two, Grand Duchess Olga and Princess Irene, had ever seen the claimant.

The Romanov Declaration was first published not in Copenhagen, where the dowager empress had died, but in Hesse-Darmstadt, the home of Grand Duke Ernest Louis of Hesse. Of all the claimant's purported relatives, Ernest was the most implacably hostile. Her supporters believed that this hostility was founded on Ernest's determination to preserve his own reputation, a determination so strong, as they saw it, that he was willing to override and suppress the identity and appeals of his sister's only surviving child.

What happened was this: In 1925, the claimant told a friend that she hoped for a visit from her "Uncle Ernie," whom she had not seen since his trip to Russia in 1916. In fact, in 1916, war was raging between Germany and Russia, and Ernest, a German general, was commanding troops on the western front. A trip to Russia, made without the knowledge of the German government or general staff, to visit his sister and his brother-in-law, the tsar, could have been construed as treason. Although the mission supposedly had been undertaken with the kaiser's blessing to attempt to arrange a separate peace, the story was deeply embarrassing to the grand duke. Having been deposed from his small throne after the war, he still hoped to get it back, and an allegation of consorting with the enemy in wartime made that unlikely possibility still less likely.

The truth about this secret mission will never be known. History has revealed no record of it. Grand Duke Ernest's diaries for this period deal with the western front, and his letters to his wife were posted from the same area. Undeniably, there was talk during this period, in both Russia and Germany, of holding discussions to terminate the carnage. According to an adviser to Grand Duke Ernest, there was a plan to go; the grand duke submitted his plan to the kaiser and was overruled. The witness did not know whether Ernest had gone ahead on his own initiative. Another witness, the British ambassador Sir George Buchanan, wrote after the war that Grand Duke Ernest had sent an emissary in the person of a Russian woman to tell the tsar that the kaiser was prepared to grant Russia generous peace terms. Nicholas locked her up. In 1966, the kaiser's stepson testified in court under oath that while in exile the kaiser had told him that Grand Duke Ernest had indeed been in Russia in 1916 to discuss the possibility of a separate peace. Also under oath, Crown Princess Cecilie declared of the Hessian visit to Russia, "I can assert from personal knowledge—the source is my father-in-law [i.e., the kaiser]—that our circles knew about it even at the time."

The truth was unprovable, but, true or false, Mrs. Tschaikovsky's statement was provocative. Had her description of "Uncle Ernie's" trip proved accurate, her claim to be Grand Duchess Anastasia would have been powerfully reinforced: who but a daughter of the tsar could have known this secret? And even if her statement was false, one may wonder how a bedridden young woman in Berlin came up with such an intricate dynastic and diplomatic tale.

Grand Duke Ernest vehemently denied Mrs. Tschaikovsky's story, denounced its author, and set out to attack her credibility with all the considerable resources at his command. She was an "impostor," "a lunatic," "a shameless creature." Libel suits were threatened. Grand Duke Andrew was warned that continuation of his investigation into her identity could be "dangerous." Ernest made an ally of Pierre Gilliard, who soon was spending as much time in Darmstadt as he was in Lausanne. And he joined in—some said he was behind and financed—an effort to prove not only that Mrs. Tschaikovsky was *not* Grand Duchess Anastasia but that she *was* somebody else.

In March 1927, a Berlin newspaper announced that Frau Tschaikovsky, the Anastasia claimant, actually was Franziska Schanzkowska, a Polish factory worker of peasant origin. The source for this scoop was a woman named Doris Wingender, who said that Franziska had been a lodger in her mother's home until her disappearance in March 1920. Over two years later, during the summer of 1922, Doris reported, Franziska had suddenly returned and said that she had been living with a number of Russian monarchist families "who apparently mistook her for someone else." Franziska had stayed for three days, Doris continued, and while she was there, the two women had exchanged clothing: Franziska took from Doris a dark blue suit trimmed with black lace and red braid with buffalo-horn buttons and a small cornflower-blue hat sewn with six yellow flowers; she handed over a mauve dress, some monogrammed underwear, and a camel's-hair coat. Then, once again, Franziska vanished.

To verify the story, the newspaper hired a detective, Martin Knopf, who took the clothing Franziska had left behind at the Wingenders' to one of the Russian emigre households where Fräulein Unbekannt had stayed in 1922. Baron and Baroness von Kleist recognized it. "I bought the camel's hair myself," said the baron. "That's the underwear. I monogrammed it myself," cried the baroness. For the benefit of newspaper readers, "The Riddle of Anastasia" was solved. Doris Wingender helped out by supplying eyewitness descriptions of Franziska Schanzkowska: "stocky," "big-boned," "filthy and grubby," with "work-worn hands" and "black stumps" of teeth. Grand Duke Ernest of Hesse was pleased; he told the author of the newspaper series that "the outcome of this case has rolled a great stone off my heart."

But the tale was not complete. It turned out that Wingender had initiated the affair by telephoning the newspaper and asking how much her story might be worth. She was promised fifteen hundred marks for telling her tale and for confronting and making a personal identification of the claimant. The Grand Duke of Hesse's role in the episode became more visible. Information collected by Detective Knopf was making its way to Darmstadt before it reached the newspaper. "It is now known that the detective was hired by Darmstadt and not by the *Nachtausgabe*," said Grand Duke Andrew. The Duke of Leuchtenberg, where Mrs. Tschaikovsky was staying at that time, heard from the writer of the newspaper series that the Grand Duke of Hesse had paid the paper twenty-five thousand marks for its "research" into the Anastasia affair. This allegation, printed in a different Berlin paper, led to libel suits. Meanwhile, Doris Wingender's confrontation with her mother's "lodger" took place. Mrs. Tschaikovsky, faced with charges of assuming a false identity, had no choice. According to the writer for the Berlin *Nachtausgabe*, who was present with Martin Knopf, this was what happened:

The witness, Fräulein Doris Wingender, enters the room. Franziska Schanzkowska lies on the divan, her face half-covered with a blanket. The witness has barely said "Good Day" before Franziska Schanzkowska jerks up and cries in a heavily accented voice, "That [thing] must get out!" The sudden agitation, the wild rage in her voice, the horror in her eyes, leave no doubt: she has recognized the witness Wingender.

Fräulein Wingender stands as if turned to stone. She has immediately recognized the lady on the divan as Franziska Schanzkowska. That is the same face she saw day after day for years. That is the same voice, that is the same nervous trick with the handkerchief, that is the same Franziska Schanzkowska!

To add corroboration, Franziska Schanzkowska's brother Felix came a few weeks later to identify the claimant. They met in a Bavarian beer garden. As soon as he saw her, Felix declared, "That is my sister Franziska." Mrs. Tschaikovsky walked over and began to talk to him. That night, Felix was handed an affidavit identifying the claimant "beyond any doubt" as his sister. He refused to sign. "No, I won't do it," he said. "She isn't my sister." Eleven years later, in 1938, the claimant had a final confrontation with the Schanzkowski family. A decree from the Nazi regime in Berlin summoned her to a room where four Schanzkowskis, two brothers and two sisters, were waiting. She walked back and forth while the Schanzkowskis stared at her and spoke in low voices. Finally, one brother announced, "No, this lady looks too different." The meeting seemed at an end when suddenly Gertrude Schanzkowska hammered her fists on the table and shouted, "You are my sister! You are my sister! I know it! You must recognize me!" The policemen present stared at Mrs. Tschaikovsky, and, calmly, she stared back. "What am I supposed to say?" she asked. The two brothers and the other sister were embarrassed and tried to quiet Gertrude, who shouted louder, "Admit it! Admit it!" A few minutes later, everyone went home.

✣

As the 1920s came to a close, the personal confrontations were mostly over. Both sides were exhausted. Prince Waldemar of Denmark, the brother of the Dowager Empress Marie, who, despite his sister's disapproval, had been paying Mrs. Tschaikovsky's hospital and sanatorium bills, was obliged by family pressure to stop. The Danish ambassador to Germany, Herlauf Zahle, the claimant's staunchest official supporter in Berlin, was commanded by his government to terminate his activity on her behalf. "I have done my utmost so that my [Danish] royal family may be blameless in the eyes of history," Zahle said bitterly. "If the Russian Imperial family wishes one of its members to die in the gutter, there is nothing I can do."

With Zahle's support withdrawn, the claimant was offered refuge by Duke George of Leuchtenberg, a distant member of the Romanov family and the owner of Castle Seeon in Upper Bavaria. The duke adopted a middle ground: "I can't tell if she is a daughter of the tsar or not. But so long as I have the feeling that a person who belongs to my tight circle of society needs my help, I have a duty to give it." The duke's wife, Duchess Olga, had no such sentiments. For eleven months, she quarreled with their guest over the food, the servants, the linen, the tea service, and the flower arrangements. "Who does she think she is?" the duchess demanded. "I am the daughter of your emperor" came the imperious reply. The Leuchtenberg family divided: the eldest daughter, Natalie, passionately championed the claimant's authenticity; the son Dimitri and his wife, Catherine, were adamantly hostile. Floating up and down the halls, an English governess, Faith Lavington, saw "the Sick Lady" every day and admired her "purest and best English accent." Miss Lavington had an opinion: "I feel certain it is she."

When Princess Xenia offered Mrs. Tschaikovsky rest and quiet at her Long Island estate, she accepted. Six months later, this new hostess and her guest were quarreling and the pianist Sergei Rachmaninov arranged for the claimant to live in a comfortable hotel suite in Garden City, Long Island. Here, to avoid the press, she registered as Mrs. Anderson; later, she added the first name Anna, and no more was heard of Mrs. Tschaikovsky. Early in 1929, she moved in with Annie B. Jennings, a wealthy Park Avenue spinster eager to have a daughter of the tsar under her roof. For eighteen months, the onetime Fräulein Unbekannt was the toast of New York society, a fixture at dinner parties, luncheons, tea dances, and the opera. Then the pattern of destructive behavior reasserted itself. She complained about her room and the food. She developed tantrums. She attacked the servants with sticks and ran back and forth naked on the roof. She threw things out the window. She stood in the aisle of a department store and told a crowd how badly Miss Jennings was treating her. Finally, Judge Peter Schmuck of the New York Supreme Court signed an order, and two men broke down her locked door and carried her off to a mental hospital. She remained in the Four Winds Sanatorium in Katonah, New York, for over a year.

While Anna Anderson was in America, the possibility arose of a hidden tsarist fortune in the Bank of England.

The claimant's trip to America had been, primarily, the idea of Gleb Botkin, a younger son of the doctor murdered with the Imperial family. Working on Long Island as a writer and illustrator, Gleb had been asked to write articles for newspapers about the tsar's youngest daughter, whom he had known as a child. Princess Xenia read these articles and invited the woman who might be her cousin to stay with her at Oyster Bay. While the claimant was with Xenia, Gleb became her primary adviser and visited frequently. By then, Gleb and his older sister Tatiana, who had met the claimant in Europe, were convinced that she was the grand duchess. Already a skillful artist as a boy, Gleb had drawn caricatures of animals, mostly pigs, wearing elaborately detailed Russian court dress that had delighted the young grand duchesses, especially Anastasia. When he first visited the claimant at Castle Seeon, her question before receiving him was "Ask him if he has brought his funny animals." He had, and when she looked at them, apparently remembering, she laughed nostalgically. Thereafter, believing absolutely in her identity, Gleb had urged the claimant to turn her back on the hostile family in Europe and cross the Atlantic.

In America, Gleb hurled himself into her cause. When the Romanov Declaration was published, he volleyed back with a stinging letter to Grand Duchess Xenia, the older of Anastasia's two Romanov aunts:

Your Imperial Highness!
Twenty-four hours did not pass after the death of your mother... when you hastened to take another step in the conspiracy to defraud your niece....
Before the wrong which Your Imperial Highness [is] committing, even the gruesome murder of the Emperor, his family and my father by the Bolsheviks pales. It is easier to understand a crime committed by a gang of crazed and drunken savages than the calm, systematic, endless persecution of one of your own family... the Grand Duchess Anastasia Nicholaevna, whose only fault is that, being the only rightful heir to the late Emperor, she stands in the way of her greedy and unscrupulous relatives.

Gleb's letter was the final stroke in the permanent alienation of the Romanovs. Grand Duke Andrew was dismayed. "All is lost," he wrote to Gleb's sister Tatiana. "Does he realize what he has done? He has completely ruined everything." "Grand Duke Andrew also remarked that the case was beginning to take on the aspect of an intrigue for the tsar's fortune," Tatiana Botkin wrote. "This profoundly disgusted the grand duke and he did not further wish to involve his name in it."

In truth, Gleb Botkin had become concerned about money—the claimant's money, he believed—and had hired a lawyer to help her obtain it. Rumors existed of a Romanov inheritance, of millions of rubles of tsarist gold deposited in the Bank of England. In July 1928, while the claimant was a guest at Oyster Bay, Botkin asked an American lawyer, Edward Fallows, to investigate the matter. Fallows agreed, obtained the claimant's power of attorney, and commenced a search which consumed the remaining twelve years of his life. He began by having his client sign a statement declaring that, in Ekaterinburg shortly before the murders, Tsar Nicholas II had told his four daughters that before the war he had deposited 5 million rubles in the Bank of England for each of them. Next, in order to pay his own fees and provide other sums required in the case, Fallows formed a Delaware corporation under the acronym Grandanor, for "Grand Duchess Anastasia Nicholaevna of Russia." Miss Jennings's wealthy friends were invited to invest. Thus equipped, Fallows went off to London to tackle the Bank of England.*

The bank responded that it could not reveal information having to do with private deposits, including whether or not such deposits existed. First, said the bank, Mr. Fallows should go to the Court of Chancery and obtain an order that his client was indeed Grand Duchess Anastasia. Fallows went back and forth to and from Europe, spending the sums supplied by Miss Jennings and brought in by Grandanor, then working without fees, cashing in his insurance; selling his stocks, his bonds, and his house; moving his family to rented rooms. In the end, said his daughter, his efforts "killed him."

Controversy over the Romanov fortune in English banks continued after Fallows's death in 1940. In 1955, Mme. Lili Dehn, who had been one of Empress Alexandra's closest friends, declared under oath that, after the Imperial family had been arrested at Tsarskoe Selo and was expecting to be sent to England, the empress said to her, "At least we shan't have to beg, for we have a fortune in the Bank of England." This fortune has never been located. There is evidence that, during the First World War, Nicholas II brought home whatever private money he and his wife had in British banks and used it to help pay for hospitals and hospital trains. A number of aristocratic and wealthy Russian families, following the tsar's example, did the same.

After the revolution, Nicholas II's mother and two sisters lived on what they could earn from the sale of their jewelry and on the

---

*Fallows looked elsewhere in Europe for money and for evidence that the tsar's youngest daughter had escaped. On October 7, 1935, he wrote to Adolf Hitler, the German chancellor, saying that "by a miracle she escaped from Yurovsky and the other Jews who murdered her family" and that Hitler's Interior Ministry might have in its files "a confession of the Jew, Yurovsky, who was the leader of the Jewish assassins." Hitler, whom Fallows addressed as "Honored Sir" and "Esteemed Sir," never replied.

charity of their Danish and English relatives. Anna Anderson's supporters argued that the money Nicholas II set aside for his four daughters—to be used, perhaps, as dowries—would not have been brought back to Russia or distributed to aunts or a grandmother. This hope that money for the daughters still might be in safekeeping was diminished in 1960, when Sir Edward Peacock, a director of the Bank of England between 1920 and 1946, declared, "I am pretty sure there never was any money of the Imperial family of Russia in the Bank of England, nor in any other bank in England. Of course, it is difficult to say 'never,' but I am positive at least there never was any money after World War I and during my long years as director of the bank."

Even today, British bankers are accustomed to being disbelieved on this subject. John Orbell, archivist of Baring Brothers, a private London bank which held deposits of the Imperial Russian government after the revolution, is wearily polite when questioned about Romanov family money.* "People keep asking," he says. "They will not take no for an answer. It's frustrating. Listen, if there had been family money here, the fact would have come out long ago. There would have been a piece of paper, a bank statement, something. Some little clerk would have found it and stepped out and made his fortune by telling the newspapers. But nothing has ever turned up."

---

*Baring Brothers did not deny that for seventy years it held millions of pounds of Russian money. On November 7, 1917, the day the Bolsheviks seized power, the British government froze 4 million pounds deposited at Baring Brothers by the Imperial government. Over the years, interest ballooned this sum to 62 million pounds. In July 1986, in the era of *glasnost* and *perestroika*, the governments of Mikhail Gorbachev and Margaret Thatcher decided to wipe the slate clean and use this sum to pay off British holders of Russian Imperial bonds and British and Commonwealth claimants who had lost property or other assets in Russia because of the revolution. The list of claimants was very long: 37,000. The list of items of lost property was even longer: 60,000. It ran in importance from oil wells, banks, factories, insurance companies, ships, gold, and copper and coal mines to personal jewelry, furniture, automobiles, and bank balances. One claimant demanded reimbursement for five dozen pair of stockings left behind,

✤

In August 1932, Anna Anderson returned to Germany accompanied by a private nurse in a locked cabin on the liner *Deutschland*. Her Park Avenue benefactress, Annie B. Jennings, paid for this voyage, as she had paid twenty-five thousand dollars for the one-year stay at the Four Winds Sanatorium, and as she would pay for an additional six months' cure at Ilten psychiatric home near Hanover. When this cure was finished, Mrs. Anderson embarked on another seven years of wandering. She lived for several years in Hanover, spent a year in Berlin, then moved on to Bavaria, Pomerania, Westphalia, Saxony, Thuringia, even Hesse. World War II found her living in Hanover, where she endured the heavy Allied bombing. When that city was mostly destroyed, she fled to a ducal castle in the east. At the end of the war, this territory was occupied by Soviet troops, and, with the aid of a German prince and the Swedish Red Cross, she escaped to what was to become West Germany.

In 1949, from his own meager funds, Prince Frederick of Saxe-Altenburg settled her in a small former army barracks in the village of Unterlengenhardt on the edge of the Black Forest. In this modest place, surrounded by overgrown shrubbery, vines, brambles, and high weeds, guarded by four huge dogs, half St. Bernard and half

---

another for season tickets for ten performances of the opera which he was unable to attend because of the revolution. A Briton owning an orchard in Russia declared that he had awakened one morning to find his orchard filled with soldiers; his assets, the file recorded, "were consumed." Another Briton asked to be reimbursed because he had lost his parrot.

Between 1987 and 1990, these claims were investigated, values established, and exchange rates calculated. Eventually, bondholders and property owners were compensated at a rate of 54.78 percent of their original value.

The existence of this large sum of "tsarist government money" may or may not have been the source of the rumors about "Romanov family money." Even today, there are those who argue that, because the tsar was titled Autocrat of all the Russias, he personally owned Russia: land, property, bank accounts—everything. The deposits at Baring Brothers, these people say, therefore belonged to him or his heirs. Russian constitutional law does not support this opinion.

wolfhound, Anna Anderson lived for the next nineteen years. A group of educated, middle-aged German women took turns obeying her instructions and catering to her needs. She spoke to them in English, which, from that point to the end of her life, was the language she preferred to speak. Ironically, her use of English, like her nonuse of Russian, became a weapon against her. "It was not the English of someone who has spoken English since childhood—as Anastasia did," said the English writer Michael Thornton, who first went to Unterlengenhardt in 1960. "The accent was Germanic, the sentence structure German, the grammar hopeless. I knew Grand Duchess Xenia, Anastasia's aunt, who lived in London. Her English was simple, pure and refined, the English spoken by the Romanovs."

During the years at Unterlengenhardt, two final eyewitnesses stepped forward: Lili Dehn, the empress's friend; and Sidney Gibbes, the English tutor of the Imperial children. Their testimony was contradictory: "I have recognized her, physically and intuitively, through signs which do not deceive," said Madame Dehn. Gibbes disagreed. "If she is the Grand Duchess Anastasia, I am a Chinaman," he told a friend. He put his view more formally in an affidavit: "She in no way resembles the true Grand Duchess Anastasia that I had known.... I am quite satisfied that she is an impostor."[*]

During these years, the play and the film *Anastasia* appeared, bringing Anna Anderson a new, worldwide burst of publicity. When

---

[*]One witness who had known Grand Duchess Anastasia better than Lili Dehn, Baroness Buxhoevden, Pierre Gilliard, or Sidney Gibbes, and perhaps as well as Grand Duchess Olga or Shura Tegleva, was never asked to testify, by either the claimant's supporters or her opponents. This was Alexandra's closest friend, Anna Vyrubova, whose role with respect to the empress was something between that of a younger sister and an oldest child. Anna had lived in a small house across the street from the Alexander Palace in Tsarskoe Selo and spent her days with the empress and her evenings with the family. She accompanied them on vacations in the Crimea and aboard the Imperial yacht in the Baltic. She would have accompanied the family to Siberia had she not first been arrested by Alexander Kerensky and imprisoned for five months in the Peter and Paul Fortress.

Vyrubova was released, departed Russia, and lived in Finland until her death in 1964 at the age of eighty. Her testimony was never sought in the Anna

the playwrights, who had not realized that she was still alive, felt sorry for her and voluntarily paid her $30,000 of the $400,000 they were paid by Twentieth Century–Fox, she used the money to build a small, modern chalet on the site of the crumbling army barracks. Thereafter, the public, seeing pictures of Anna Anderson, complained that she did not look like Ingrid Bergman.

Her actual appearance during those years was graphically described by Mme. Dominique Auclères, a correspondent for *Le Figaro* of Paris, who first visited the claimant in Unterlengenhardt in August 1960 and subsequently became a devoted supporter:

> Suddenly, a door opened and I saw the strangest looking woman I have ever seen in my life. It was a tiny Madame Butterfly disguised as a Tyrolean. She wore a Japanese kimono; over this was an Austrian loden cloak; and over this was a black mackintosh. On top of the pointed hood of the cloak, she had perched a green felt Tyrolean hat. Her hair was light brown with streaks of grey, cut short to the level of her ears. She wore black leather gloves and had a kind of floating walk which conferred something unreal on this apparition. I noticed a slightly tipped and tilted nose (I saw her only in profile) and an eye more grey than blue. In front of her mouth, one of her black-gloved hands held a little paper fan which never moved throughout my visit.

Before she left, however, Madame Auclères caught her unawares and was able to see the mouth, "deformed by the top jaw slightly deformed to the right." The interview was in English, although, at one point when the reporter forgetfully slipped into French, her hostess responded immediately in French. Her accent, said Mme. Auclères, was "perfect."

Anderson debate because she had been a friend and disciple of Gregory Rasputin, whose behavior had scandalized Russia before the revolution. "It was our belief," said Tatiana Botkin, "that Madame Vyrubova's involvement...could only hurt Anastasia's cause in the eyes of the Russian emigration, which, for the most part, had profoundly despised Rasputin."

✤

The Anna Anderson case was the longest legal action in the German courts during the twentieth century. Beginning in 1938, when she sued to contest distribution of a small estate to Empress Alexandra's German relatives, suspended during World War II, renewed in Hamburg during the 1950s and '60s, the case finally concluded in 1970 with a rejection of her appeal by the German Supreme Court in Karlsruhe. The opposition to Anna Anderson's claim in these trials was provided by the House of Hesse, still adamant that she must be discredited. Grand Duke Ernest was dead, but his son Prince Louis took up his father's cause, along with Prince Louis's niece, Barbara Duchess of Mecklenburg. Financial backing for the Hessian case came from Lord Louis Mountbatten, the British war hero, former Viceroy of India, Chief of the Defense Staff, and uncle of the queen's husband, Prince Philip. Earl Mountbatten was Hessian; his mother, Princess Victoria of Battenberg, was Empress Alexandra's sister; the Prussian Princess Irene was his aunt; Grand Duke Ernest of Hesse was his uncle. Had Anna Anderson been legally proven to be Grand Duchess Anastasia, Mountbatten would have had to recognize her as his first cousin. He was determined not to do this and to prevent it poured thousands of pounds, inherited from his wealthy, deceased wife, into lawyers' fees.

One body of evidence, largely ignored in the early years of the Anna Anderson case, came to the fore in the German court trials of the 1950s and '60s. It was the testimony of medicine and science, and, to a surprising degree, it supported Anna Anderson's claim. In the early years after the claimant's appearance, doctors—most of them psychologists—had tended to believe her story. In 1925, Dr. Lothar Nobel, director of the Mommsen Clinic in Berlin, gave his opinion that "no mental illness of any kind exists.... It seems impossible that her knowledge of many small details is due to anything but her own personal experience. Furthermore, it is psychologically scarcely conceivable that anyone who...is playing the part of another person should behave as the patient does now."

This view that the patient was incapable of playing a role was reiterated in 1927. After the claimant had spent eight months in his sanatorium in the Bavarian Alps, the director, Dr. Saathof, declared, "It is, in my opinion, quite unthinkable that Frau Tschaikovsky is an imposter. Even at crucial moments, she has almost always behaved in the exact opposite way from what you might expect of an imposter." A similar, albeit nonprofessional, opinion was offered by Princess Xenia after observing the claimant on her Long Island estate: "One of the most convincing elements of her personality was a completely unconscious acceptance of her identity [as Grand Duchess Anastasia]. She never gave the slightest impression of acting a part."

During the Hamburg trials, the court decided to obtain physical evidence, based on science. It appointed two distinguished expert witnesses: Dr. Otto Reche, an internationally famous anthropologist and criminologist who had founded the Society of German Anthropologists, and Dr. Minna Becker, a graphologist who had assisted in the authentification of Anne Frank's diary. These doctors and scientific experts were seeking neither money nor fame; they were professionally examining a litigant. Reche collected more than a hundred photographs of Grand Duchess Anastasia and then photographed Anna Anderson at the same angles and under the same lighting conditions. He compared the two faces, millimeter by millimeter, and concluded that "such coincidence between two human faces is not possible unless they are the same person or identical twins. Mrs. Anderson is no one else than Grand Duchess Anastasia." Becker compared more than a hundred samples of Grand Duchess Anastasia's handwriting with samples of Anna Anderson's handwriting. "I have never before seen two sets of handwriting bearing all these concordant signs which belonged to two different people," she concluded. "There can be no mistake. After thirty-four years as a sworn expert for the German courts, I am ready to state on my oath and on my honor that Mrs. Anderson and Grand Duchess Anastasia are identical." Despite the testimony of Dr. Reche and Dr. Becker, the court declared the case *non liquet*, neither established nor rejected.

During her lifetime, Anna Anderson enjoyed another scientific victory, gained in 1977 by Dr. Moritz Furtmayr, a prominent German forensic expert. Furtmayr had devised a system of mapping the human skull with grids and graphs to produce what he called a "head-print," no two of which were alike in human beings. Using this "P.I.K. Method," which had been accepted in criminal cases by German courts, Furtmayr proved that the anatomical points and tissue formations of Anna Anderson's right ear corresponded with Grand Duchess Anastasia's right ear in seventeen points, five more than the twelve required by German courts to establish identity.

Furtmayr's report provided a nasty shock for Lord Mountbatten. Despite his large investment of money, Mountbatten never met the claimant. In 1977, however, Michael Thornton, bringing with him a copy of Furtmayr's findings, visited Earl Mountbatten at Broadlands, his country estate. "He sat opposite me and he read through it twice, in German and in the English translation," Thornton remembered. "His face was an absolute study while he was reading it. What I could see in his face was recognition of the terrible possibility that this raving woman, who was so eccentric, so unlikely, who was dismissed out of hand by 90 percent of the people she met, might actually be his cousin Grand Duchess Anastasia."

The final judicial verdicts were inconclusive. The courts did not say that Anna Anderson was not Grand Duchess Anastasia; they ruled only that she had failed to prove that she was. Eight thousand pages of testimony were bound into forty-nine volumes, placed on back shelves, and forgotten. At Unterlengenhardt, Anna Anderson announced that she no longer cared. "I know perfectly well who I am," she said. "I don't need to prove it in any court of law." Meanwhile, her circumstances were deteriorating. She had retreated from the world, barred the door even to her friends, and lived alone inside with sixty cats. When the third of her great dogs died, she buried it herself in a shallow grave—too shallow, apparently, for the odor spread over the village and brought remonstrance from the district board of health. Insulted, she suddenly decided to accept an invitation arranged by her friend of forty years, Gleb Botkin.

Gleb, now living in Charlottesville, Virginia, had befriended a wealthy genealogist, Dr. John Manahan. At Gleb's suggestion, Manahan, a bachelor, had offered the claimant his hospitality in Virginia for as long as she liked. On July 13, 1968, without a word to anyone in Europe, she suddenly flew to Dulles Airport at Manahan's expense. He and Gleb met her and drove her to Charlottesville. In December 1968, her friends in Europe were shocked again when she married chubby, crew-cut Manahan, who was at least eighteen years her junior. It was a marriage of convenience, they told themselves; her American visa was about to expire. Manahan himself was amused as well as pleased. "Well, what would Tsar Nicholas think if he could see his new son-in-law?" he asked his best man. "I think he would be grateful," Gleb Botkin replied.

Anastasia and John Manahan lived together for more than fifteen years. They had separate bedrooms in his classically elegant house on a quiet street in Charlottesville, only a few blocks from the university and Thomas Jefferson's famous library and quadrangle. She called him—inexplicably—Hans; he called her Anastasia. They drove almost daily to his large farm in the nearby countryside and frequently dined at the Farmington Country Club. There, Anastasia, a tiny figure with dyed auburn hair, often dressed in a blouse and bright red pants several sizes too large for her, carefully collected scraps from the plates of everyone at the table and placed them in foil to take home to her new and growing population of cats. It did not take long for the house and garden to begin to resemble her chalet at Unterlengenhardt. Overgrown bushes, vines, and weeds filled the front yard and blocked the front door. Inside, the floor of the living room was piled high with books and covered with newspapers, spread to cover messes made by the cats. When one of the cats died, she cremated it in the fireplace. Manahan seemed not to mind. "That's the way Anastasia likes to live," he explained. The neighbors minded, however, and in 1978, the Manahans were taken to court over the smell—"I think it could be described as a stench," one friend admitted—rising from the property.

Manahan enjoyed being Anastasia's husband; he sometimes described himself as a "Grand Duke–in–Waiting." His wife seemed uninterested. "That is so far back and so dead," she said, "all so past. Russia doesn't exist." Gradually, the couple descended from eccentricity into derangement. On one occasion, Manahan told a gathering that his wife was a descendant of Genghis Khan; subsequently, he added Ferdinand and Isabella to her ancestral tree. In 1974, he sent out a nine-thousand-word Christmas card entitled "Anastasia's Money and the Tsar's Wealth," in which he accused Franklin D. Roosevelt of aiding the Marxist conspiracy to communize the world and described an episode at the end of World War II in Europe as the arrival of "American negroes with leveled guns." He and his wife, he said, were under surveillance by the CIA, the KGB, and the British Secret Service. She told a visitor that, in the Ipatiev House, the entire Imperial family except the tsarevich had been repeatedly raped, all of them being forced to watch as each was violated. In November 1983, she was institutionalized. A few days later, her husband kidnapped her, and for three days they drove down Virginia back roads, stopping to eat at convenience stores. A thirteen-state police alarm finally produced an arrest and her return to a psychiatric ward.

Three months later, on February 12, 1984, Anastasia Manahan died of pneumonia. Her body was cremated that afternoon, and in the spring her ashes were buried in the churchyard at Castle Seeon. Manahan died six years later.

At her death, the controversy over Anna Anderson's identity was unresolved. Unknowingly, however, she left behind a piece of evidence that would tell the world who she was.

CHAPTER 15

..........❖..........

A MATTER OF
FAMILY HONOR

Four and a half years before her death, Anastasia Manahan underwent a severe medical crisis. On August 20, 1979, after several days of vomiting and stubbornly refusing help, she was rushed to Charlottesville's Martha Jefferson Hospital. Dr. Richard Shrum operated immediately. He found obstruction and gangrene in the small intestine, caused by attachment to an ovarian tumor. He removed almost one foot of the intestine, resectioned the bowel, and closed the wound. Mrs. Manahan was a difficult patient. At first, after surgery, she repeatedly pulled tubes from her body. Eventually, her behavior improved. "She remained reclusive, did not like to talk to people, and smiled rarely," Shrum recalled. "She would sit around with a handkerchief held up to her nose as if she were afraid of catching something."

Immediately after the operation, Shrum followed standard hospital procedure and sent the tissue he had removed to the pathology laboratory, which retained five inches of the intestine. This tissue was divided into five one-inch segments, and each segment was bathed in a tissue preservative called formalin, sealed inside a block of paraffin wax one inch square and half an inch deep, and placed in a small blue and white box on a shelf filled with other similar boxes containing tissue specimens. The purpose of preserving excised tissue after surgery is purely medical: should the same or a similar condition recur, having actual tissue previously removed can be an invaluable diagnostic tool. In 1979, the Martha Jefferson Hospital pathology laboratory was new, having opened only the year before. "We have kept everything since it opened," said a hospital employee, "every sample from all patients, regardless of who the patient is." Once stored, tissue specimens, like written medical records, remain legally the property of the hospital. The hospital, observing a fiduciary obligation to the patient and the patient's family and heirs, guards these materials fiercely. Any release of records or specimens to anyone other than the patient, family, heirs, or executors, requires a court order.

After Dr. William Maples' July 1992 announcement that Grand Duchess Anastasia was missing from the grave in Ekaterinburg received international publicity, it was perhaps not surprising that exploratory probes as to whether Martha Jefferson Hospital possessed any of Anastasia Manahan's blood or tissue samples began. On September 22, Syd Mandelbaum, a Long Island blood analysis expert connected with several major laboratories, wrote to the hospital that he intended to write a book on the use of DNA testing as a forensic tool and wished to include a chapter on Anna Anderson. "As remote as this sounds," Mandelbaum's letter declared, "we are trying to obtain a genetic sample . . . in the form of a blood sample, follicular hair, or tissue culture" to test at Cold Spring Harbor Laboratory or at Harvard Medical School. D. D. Sandridge, the executive vice president of Martha Jefferson Hospital, replied to Mandelbaum that "we have nothing here that could be useful to you." Later the hospital explained this mistake to me as a clerical error: "The wrong person was asked to look for it."

The right person to ask was Penny Jenkins, the director of medical records, and it was she who dealt with the next two applicants who inquired about the tissue. The first of these, writing in November 1992, was Mary DeWitt, who described herself as "a student of forensic pathology at the University of Texas" and said that she would like the tissue because she was "writing a paper." Jenkins assumed that DeWitt was a young student, "writing a paper like my daughter in high school. It was not a case of 'medical need to know' or 'patient care,' " Jenkins decided, "so I said, 'No, I can't help you.' " Mary DeWitt, however, did not go away. Instead, she contacted James Blair Lovell, a Washington author who had written the last Anastasia biography, and explained to him that she knew that the hospital had the tissue but that she needed the cooperation of the Manahan family in order to obtain the required court order. Proposing to Lovell that they work together, she offered to pay for a lawyer if Lovell would approach the Manahans. Lovell agreed and obtained a letter from John Manahan's cousin Fred Manahan, granting him authority to dispose of the tissue. DeWitt retained a Charlottesville lawyer. In the spring of 1993, however, DeWitt wrote to Penny Jenkins that, henceforth, she, Mary DeWitt, would deal with the hospital on anything to do with the tissue, while James Lovell's role would be restricted to that of a historian recording the process. Lovell, hearing about this letter, became enraged and said to Jenkins, "They're cutting me out!" Jenkins had to choose. "Because I felt that Jimmy Lovell's agenda was a little bit cleaner, I decided that we weren't going to communicate anymore with Mary DeWitt," she said. Jenkins never heard again from Mary DeWitt, but later she was told that DeWitt was a woman in her forties, the wife of a private investigator.

Two days after receiving her first letter from Mary DeWitt, Jenkins received a telephone call from Dr. Willi Korte, who identified himself as a German lawyer and historical researcher. He told her that he was associated with the Forensic Institute of the University of Munich and was working as part of an international team to identify the Ekaterinburg bones and solve the mystery of Anastasia. "He was very smooth, very charming," Jenkins remembered. "He dropped a lot of names: Dr. Maples in Florida...Dr. Baden in New York...and others. He told me that his job was to wander around the world looking for comparative tissue samples. He asked whether we had any. I said, 'Yes, we do have a specimen.' A short time after that, a Washington, D.C., lawyer, Thomas Kline, of the firm of Andrews & Kurth, called to ask about the tissue. Kline said that Korte, with whom he worked, was out of the country. I repeated to him, 'Yes, we do have the tissue.' That was the last I heard from either of them," said Jenkins. "I never saw Korte again until we were sitting in court. Then he did not speak to me."

In January 1993, Thomas Kline contacted Fred Manahan, who Kline believed controlled the tissue. Manahan referred Kline to James Lovell. On April 16, after several telephone conversations, Kline wrote a three-page letter to Lovell, formally asking for help in obtaining access to Anastasia Manahan's tissue for DNA testing to be done by the Forensic Institute in Munich. He said that the institute already had access to a number of living relatives of the Imperial family whose blood could be used to make DNA comparisons. To buttress his appeal, Kline cited two scientific articles which dealt with DNA analysis. One was the work of the British Forensic Science Service team led by Dr. Peter Gill. On June 18, Kline wrote to Lovell again to clarify Dr. Willi Korte's role in the Munich institute's investigation. Korte, Kline said, was an experienced researcher, not a medical doctor. Kline added that the Munich institute had established working relationships with forensic scientists in the United States, "in particular, Dr. Mary-Claire King, [who] has agreed to work with the Forensic Institute."

James Lovell found his encounters with Thomas Kline alarming. Unsure of his own legal status, Lovell consulted Richard Schweitzer, a Virginia attorney, who, like Lovell, believed in Mrs. Manahan's claim to be the tsar's daughter. Speaking of Kline, Lovell told Schweitzer, "He's just harassing me to death. He keeps saying, 'We have to have an answer! We just can't leave it! We must act! We must have an answer from you right now!' " Lovell asked Schweitzer what he ought to do. "Jimmy, you don't have to do anything," Schweitzer advised. "You don't even have to talk to him on the phone." "So," Schweitzer said later, "the next time the man called, Jimmy—on his own, I didn't tell him to do it—did the best thing he could do. When he heard, 'You've got to answer right now, yes or no!' Jimmy said, 'Then the answer is no,' and hung up. Then Jimmy said to me, 'Do you think I did right? What can they do next?' And I said, 'Jimmy, they can't do anything. They don't have any standing. They cannot participate in a lawsuit in the State of Virginia unless they have standing. The only person I know of who's a resident of this state, who can come in and have any connection with this case, is Marina.' "

Marina Botkina Schweitzer, Gleb Botkin's daughter, is a Virginia gentlewoman with a quiet demeanor and soft southern accent. Her Russian origins, not immediately apparent to outsiders, are of profound importance to her. Her great-grandfather, Dr. Sergei Botkin, was the father of Russian clinical medicine and the friend and personal physician of Tsar Alexander II; her grandfather, Dr. Eugene Botkin, played the same role for Tsar Nicholas II and, as a consequence of his loyalty, died with the Imperial family in the cellar in Ekaterinburg. She reads and speaks Russian and German and every day sits down to watch the *Vremenya* evening news broadcast from Moscow on cable TV. The only daughter among Gleb's four children, Marina was born in Brooklyn, grew up on Long Island, and graduated from Smith College. While working in a law office in Charlottesville, she met her future husband, Richard Schweitzer.

Schweitzer, who, on his wife's behalf, was to fight a single-handed court battle with a nationwide law firm employing 250 attorneys, is of Swiss descent. His ancestors came to America from the canton of Basel in the early nineteenth century, intending, as religious missionaries, to convert Indians in Wisconsin. He graduated from the University of Virginia and served for four years during World War II on antisubmarine duty in the North Atlantic. For a while, he was a member of a secret U.S. Navy raiding team, trained to blow up German U-boat pens. Schweitzer practiced law in the field of international reinsurance and finance and retired in 1990. At seventy-three, he is feisty and, when aroused, fierce. He has a straight back, a sharp face behind rimless glasses, and thinning white hair. His language is lawyerly, but underneath there is an ironic sense of humor. In the lawsuit that was to come, Richard Schweitzer's opponents tended to patronize him and treat him as a small-town country lawyer. They made a mistake.

The woman called Anna Anderson had been a part of Marina Schweitzer's life since Marina was five, when her father visited the claimant at Castle Seeon. Marina knew the claimant slightly when Anna Anderson was in America at the end of the 1920s. In the 1950s, Schweitzer said, "when she was living in poverty in the Black Forest, we put money in envelopes and sent it to her by registered mail. Finally, somebody wrote to Gleb and said, 'Please tell Mrs. Schweitzer to stop sending money because she is taking it to buy meat for the dogs and not food for herself.' We never stopped. So she was aware of us as people who wanted to help." After Anna Anderson returned to America in 1968 and became Anastasia Manahan, Marina Schweitzer continued, "we saw her two or three times a year. But it was more because of her closeness to my father than to us."

In fact, Marina Schweitzer was always somewhat wary of Anastasia Manahan. "She talked to us on the phone a lot ... especially when she was having trouble with Jack. I purposefully kept her at a distance because she had a history of quarreling with every person who was close to her. And the truth is we never quarreled. She called me 'Marina' and she called Dick 'Mr. Schweitzer.' Another reason we did not go there often was that I could not stand the sight of Jack and the way he treated her as a prize possession, something to brag about. I think he did her case more harm than all her enemies put together. He used her to prop up his own ego. One thing that infuriated me was that, before he married her, he took my father and her to his bank and made her swear that she was Anastasia, and then made Father swear that he knew that she was Anastasia."

Whatever she did—and during her final years, the Schweitzers admit, she was often difficult—Marina and Richard Schweitzer never doubted that the woman they knew was the daughter of the tsar. Her behavior, they believed, was not abnormal for a woman who had been through the experiences she had endured. The crux was her identity. "For us," Richard Schweitzer said, "having known Anastasia all those years, it was a matter of family honor to try our utmost to fulfill her lifelong wish to have her identity as the Grand Duchess Anastasia recognized."

The Manahan family and James Blair Lovell did not realize, early in 1993, that they were not entitled by Virginia law to control of Anastasia Manahan's tissue. In Virginia, in cases where there is no will and no surviving spouse or children, an estate devolves on next of kin by blood. John Manahan's cousins were his wife's next of kin, but not by blood, and when Martha Jefferson Hospital learned that the matter was being discussed, it politely informed the Manahans of this law. If the Manahans did not have control, then, by extension, they could not assign it to James Lovell, who, in turn, could not pass it to Mary De-Witt, or Thomas Kline, or anyone else.

Informed of this by the hospital's attorneys, Penny Jenkins began to worry. She had already spoken to Richard Schweitzer when De-Witt had hired a Charlottesville lawyer to try to obtain the tissue. At that time Schweitzer had said, "Listen, if these people come to you and you don't want to give them anything, tell me immediately. I will come to Charlottesville and file an intervenor in Marina's name, insisting that nothing should be delivered unless the hospital is protected and part of the samples are kept." Intervenor is a legal term describing a court-approved intervention by an outside party in an ongoing lawsuit. Because Marina was both a citizen of Virginia and a direct descendant of one of the victims of the Ipatiev House massacre, Schweitzer felt sure that she would be permitted to intervene.

After Mary DeWitt disappeared, Schweitzer and Jenkins continued to talk. Jenkins realized that the hospital was vulnerable to an avalanche of demands for the tissue. Again Schweitzer offered to help. He looked up the appropriate statute and, working with Jenkins and the hospital lawyers, began drafting a petition which would permit Martha Jefferson Hospital to release the tissue to a qualified laboratory. The work proceeded slowly. The hospital's attorneys, Schweitzer remembered, were "hand-holding lawyers, the kind that hold the hands of the trustees, fuddy-duddy lawyers, office lawyers, fiduciary lawyers, desk lawyers who work with wills and estates and never go to court, very thorough and picky and slow. They never met a date with me. They kept changing position, and I constantly drafted and redrafted to meet their demands. Finally, they put it into the hands of a skillful litigator, Matthew Murray, and we got it done. It took from May to September, but if Matt had handled it from the beginning, we'd have been finished in June." By September, Schweitzer had satisfied everyone and written a nonadversarial document of which the hospital could say, "Yes, this is the kind of petition we want you to pose in court."

While working with the hospital, Schweitzer also began looking for a laboratory which could test the tissue once it was available. He contacted the Armed Forces Institute of Pathology in Maryland, but he and they could not agree on terms. In addition, the AFIP had no DNA materials from the Romanovs or Hessians for use in comparing the Manahan tissue. Schweitzer therefore approached Dr. Peter Gill and the British Forensic Science Service, which, of course, possessed not only the DNA profiles taken from the Ekaterinburg remains but also the blood sample from Prince Philip linking him to the bones of the purported Empress Alexandra. During the summer, Schweitzer began negotiating with Home Office solicitors to work out a private commission. Ultimately, a written agreement was signed. Schweitzer made an initial down payment of five thousand pounds and placed another five thousand pounds in escrow in an English bank to be drawn on if needed.

On September 30, 1993, Richard Schweitzer filed his wife's petition for release of the tissue with the Virginia Sixteenth Judicial Circuit Court. Marina Schweitzer, the petition declared, had standing in the court on three counts: as a Virginia citizen, as the granddaughter of Dr. Eugene Botkin, and as the only resident of Virginia having a prolonged, serious connection with the life and identity of Anastasia Manahan. The basis of his wife's suit, Schweitzer explained to the court, was that, as Dr. Botkin's granddaughter, she had a right to know what had happened to her grandfather: "Identification of a putative survivor of the murders [that is, Grand Duchess Anastasia] would assist in the more certain identification of all, including petitioner's grandfather, Dr. Botkin." In the petition, Schweitzer did not ask the court to authorize release of the tissues to his wife; he asked only that the court permit access by Dr. Peter Gill to small samples of the tissue so they could be tested. Marina Schweitzer, her husband concluded, was prepared to pay all the costs and expenses of this DNA testing.

Martha Jefferson Hospital took no position on the petition and told the court it would do whatever the court ordered. Informally, Matthew Murray declared, "If the plaintiff can prove she has a right to the tissue and that's what the court orders, we don't have any problem with that. We don't stand to gain or lose anything." Schweitzer believed that things were going smoothly. "I had even drafted the order for the judge to issue, the way the hospital wanted it," he recalled. "The judge set a hearing for November 1. I thought we'd sail right through."

On the afternoon of November 1, 1993, Circuit Court Judge Jay T. Swett, a young-looking man with blond hair, gathered his black robe around him, seated himself high above everyone else in his courtroom, and prepared to deal with the matter of Anastasia Manahan's tissue in Martha Jefferson Hospital. In front of and beneath him were three lawyers: Richard Schweitzer, attorney for his wife, Marina, who wanted the tissue made available for DNA testing in England; Matthew Murray, attorney for the hospital, who was willing that this happen providing the court approved; and an attorney for the *Richmond Times,* who wanted to make sure that the hearings were not closed to the press and public. This last matter was quickly dealt with when Schweitzer conceded that all hearings should be in open court and that no court documents should be sealed. There seemed little more to do, and Judge Swett instructed Schweitzer and Murray to get together and draft an order which he could sign. The case, apparently, was concluded; the tissue would soon be available to Dr. Gill.

"Is there anything else the court should know before we move on?" Judge Swett asked.

"Well, Your Honor, there are some other people here who want to be heard because they think they have an interest in this," replied Matthew Murray.

At this point, a young woman with brown hair pulled back in a ponytail stood up in the back of the room. She introduced herself as Lindsey Crawford, an attorney in the Washington, D.C., office of Andrews & Kurth, where Thomas Kline also worked. "Your Honor, we have a client who wishes and deserves to be heard," she said. "I have just heard from Prince Nicholas Romanov, the head of the Romanov Family Association, whom most living Romanovs accept as the legitimate pretender to the throne. He has just literally this morning asked me to come and investigate what's going on here and what effect, if any, this could have on his family." She asked Judge Swett to hold up proceedings to give her time "to protect his interest and that of the Romanov family." Crawford added that her firm also represented another client with an interest in the Anastasia Manahan tissue. This was a New York corporation called the Russian Nobility Association.

"Do you have a petition to file?" asked Judge Swett.

"No, we don't, Your Honor, because our client spoke to me only this morning."

Richard Schweitzer, recognizing the name Andrews & Kurth, objected to any delay. "The real client of this law firm," he told the court, "is not any member of the Romanov family or the Russian Nobility Association. It is a Mr. Korte." Schweitzer pulled out a copy of the letter Thomas Kline had written in June to James Lovell in which Kline described the work of Willi Korte. "This firm, Andrews & Kurth, has been representing Mr. Korte for months before this hearing date," Schweitzer told the judge. "They have been trying to get hold of this tissue for Mr. Korte's purposes and to prevent others from getting access."

For several minutes, Judge Swett pondered. Then he told Crawford that he would hold things up for three days so that she could file a petition. Penny Jenkins, sitting near Lindsey Crawford in the courtroom, heard her say in disbelief, "There's no way we can do this in three days." Jenkins also noticed a tall, curly-haired man probably nearing forty, with a sharp nose, sitting next to Crawford. He wore no necktie, had sandals on his feet, and was carrying a backpack. Jenkins realized—"I don't know how. I just knew," she said later—that this was Willi Korte. Before the hearing was over, Korte rose and quickly left the courtroom.

Looking back after the case was settled, Richard Schweitzer hypothesized what had happened up to this point: "Andrews & Kurth wanted to block Marina's access to the tissue and gain exclusive control for their real client. I believed then that this client was Willi Korte. He had worked on acquiring the tissue for months, but, once he had failed with the Manahans and Jimmy Lovell, he didn't know what to do. He couldn't come into court in Virginia on his own because he had no standing. He needed a client who would be permitted as an intervenor in our lawsuit. So he and his colleagues in Europe went swinging through the world looking for a client—or a couple of clients. They came up with Nicholas Romanov and the Russian Nobility Association."

In Europe, one of Korte's co-workers, Maurice Philip Remy, was trying to involve the Romanov princes in blocking the Schweitzers. Prince Nicholas, who lived in Rome, telephoned his cousin Prince Rostislav, who lived in London, and said he was being pressured to become involved in the Virginia case. Rostislav telephoned New York and Prince Alexis Scherbatow, the president of the Russian Nobility Association, whom he didn't know, to ask what was going on. Rostislav and Scherbatow spoke for half an hour, and then Rostislav telephoned a London friend, Michael Thornton. "When Rosti got off the phone with Scherbatow," Thornton said, "he called me and said, 'Jesus Christ! What is wrong with that man?' Then he started telling me all the things Scherbatow had said: Schweitzer was a crook...he had a very dubious background...there were things about him that, if we knew, would make our hair curl.... They saw this as a sinister conspiracy to have the claimant recognized as genuine." Scherbatow also had told Rostislav that Anna Anderson's tissue must not be tested in England. "The only place it could be properly done," Scherbatow had said, "was in California by a Dr. Mary-Claire King."

Thornton's reaction to Rostislav was "This is all rubbish! For God's sake, fax Nicholas and tell him to leave this thing in Charlottesville alone. It will be chaos." Thornton himself then wrote a letter to Rostislav, which Rostislav faxed to Nicholas, saying that it would be a disaster for the Romanovs to become involved with the case. "I said they would be very badly criticized, having rejected Anna Anderson all her life, if they now started to claim parts of her body after her death," Thornton recounted. "The media would crucify them. Furthermore, I said, it would represent a shift in the long-held policy of the Romanov family, which was that she wasn't genuine. If you now start claiming parts of her body, it's going to make everyone think that you've made a mistake. The best thing is to stay out."

Michael Thornton's message had effect. Prince Nicholas Romanov immediately withdrew as a potential client of Andrews & Kurth, and there was no mention of him or of any Romanov in subsequent court documents.

On Thursday, November 4, Lindsey Crawford was ready as instructed by Judge Swett to submit her petition to intervene. The document named only a single client, the Russian Nobility Association. Crawford had signed the petition, along with Thomas Kline of her law firm, and Page Williams, a Charlottesville attorney hired as local counsel. In the petition, the association represented itself as "an historic [*sic*] and philanthropic organization whose purpose is to protect the authenticity of the line of the Imperial family of Russia and the events prior to 1917 in Russia." The association challenged the fitness of Marina Schweitzer to petition for the tissue, saying that she was not related by blood to either "Anastasia Romanov [the daughter of the tsar] or Anastasia Anderson [the claimant]." It denied that identifying the tissue samples in Martha Jefferson Hospital would be helpful in verifying Dr. Botkin's remains. It agreed that mitochondrial DNA testing might be useful in determining the true identity of Anastasia Manahan but went on to say that "it is essential that any tests conducted on the tissue samples be of the highest scientific integrity which cannot be achieved in the manner requested by Schweitzer" (that is, in the laboratory of Dr. Peter Gill).

In a memorandum attached to the petition, the Russian Nobility Association heaped further calumny on Dr. Gill: his laboratory was said to represent "second-best scientific testing," and his samples were said to have been possibly "contaminated." Finally, the association argued (inaccurately, it turned out), "There is no scientific evidence that the tissue samples can be split so that parallel testing could be conducted at two laboratories." The Russian Nobility Association's argument was that if the court awarded the tissue to Gill, it would be throwing away any chance of proving the claimant's identity. The only solution, it urged, was for the tissue to be sent to its nominee, "the foremost genetics scientist in the United States," Dr. Mary-Claire King at Berkeley.

Attached to the Russian Nobility Association's petition were affidavits from Prince Alexis Scherbatow, the organization's president, and Dr. William Maples. Scherbatow's affidavit mostly parroted the petition. What was significant was that the scientific statements and recommendations in all three of these documents—the Russian Nobility Association petition, its memorandum, and the affidavit of Prince Scherbatow—rested on the affidavit of Dr. Maples. Maples' statement praised Dr. King and denigrated Dr. Gill. It said that Gill's finding of 98.5 percent certainty that the Ekaterinburg remains belonged to the Romanovs was "not scientifically significant." It referred to the heteroplasmy Gill and his colleagues had discovered in Nicholas II's DNA as "more likely the result of contaminated samples." It attempted to frighten the court that there would not be enough to go around: "If any blood or tissue samples from Anastasia Manahan are used in mtDNA testing, they are likely to be completely consumed in the process.... Therefore, it is unlikely that there would be sufficient genetic material for the sample to be split and tested by two different laboratories."

The Russian Nobility Association is an assemblage of descendants of the aristocratic families which once helped to rule Imperial Russia. In the 1990s, it is made up of perhaps one hundred dues-paying members, most of whom are children and grandchildren of men and women who emigrated from Russia at the time of the revolution. If they still lived in Russia under a tsar, many of these people would be called prince and princess, or count and countess. In America, they wear their honorifics only at charity events, hoping to add a little glitter and thus attract Americans impressed by titles. The organization is in threadbare financial condition. Its primary source of income is a ball every May, which brings a net profit of twelve thousand to eighteen thousand dollars. Most of this money goes to pay the rent on a second-floor apartment on First Avenue, where the association's library of crumbling Russian genealogical books is housed. The rest is doled out to children, needy old people, and the sick.

No one in the world at this time is more expert at tracing the bloodlines of the Russian aristocracy than the president of the Russian Nobility Association, eighty-four-year-old Alexis Scherbatow. Scherbatow has lived his life as an emigre. His family lost everything except their lives in the revolution. They moved to Bulgaria; he lived in Italy, graduated from the University of Brussels, came to the United States in 1938, and, during World War II, was a sergeant in the U.S. Army. After the war, he taught history at Fairleigh Dickinson College in New Jersey and translated documents in Russian and Latin for other historians and writers. His views are typical of many Russians of his generation: he hates Communism, is suspicious of post-Communist Russia, and despises England ("They are a bunch of liars in England"). He never accepted Anna Anderson's claim to be Anastasia. As an argument he cites the fact that he personally saw the grand duchess in 1916, when he was five years old.

Richard Schweitzer responded to the Russian Nobility Association's intrusion into his wife's lawsuit by saying that "the issue was not one of the comparative merits of respective scientific facilities. The real issue is whether or not the Russian Nobility Association has any standing whatsoever to participate in any way in selection of a scientific facility. There is no evidence before the court of any such standing." He pointed out that the association had not filed a certificate of its officers or certified resolution of its directors or trustees consenting to the Charlottesville court taking jurisdiction over its activities in these proceedings. Privately, Schweitzer believed that the officers and membership of the Russian Nobility Association had no idea what was going on. He also was convinced that somebody else was paying the association's legal bills.*

---

*In fact, as Schweitzer suspected, neither the members nor any of the other officers of the Russian Nobility Association were aware of their president's action. Also, as Schweitzer suspected, the association was not paying its own legal bills. In November 1994, Alexis Scherbatow admitted that the eight months of lawsuits in which the Russian Nobility Association was the nominal client had cost his organization nothing: "Not a cent! Not a cent! Not a cent!" he chortled.

Schweitzer launched a barrage of documents. He said that he never sought *exclusive* authority from the court for access to the tissue. He doubted that there was any danger of serious erosion to the tissue samples; he had been told that scientists needed only the tiniest slice, 24/10,000 of an inch thick, from each of the one-inch preserved units. On November 16, he told the court that he would not oppose tests by Dr. King at Berkeley; he would only oppose testing *exclusively* by Dr. King. On another tack, he said that the Russian Nobility Association should not be given standing in the case because Anastasia Manahan never claimed membership in the Russian nobility; she had always said that she was a member of the Russian Imperial family. Privately, both Schweitzers were contemptuous of Alexis Scherbatow for signing himself "Prince" in his sworn affidavit. "When he became an American citizen, he swore to give up foreign titles," Schweitzer said. "I find it hard to accept the oath of one who claims a foreign title in an affidavit under oath, if that same person has, on naturalization, forsworn all foreign titles and allegiances. Either one oath or the other has dubious validity." Schweitzer also poured scorn on William Maples: "Maples' affidavit is not a credible basis [for selecting a laboratory to do the testing]," he told the court. "He has categorically asserted on public television that Grand Duchess Anastasia could not have survived. He is not a disinterested scientist. Maples is an anthropologist, not a geneticist. He states no expertise qualifying him to set criteria for genetic work."

Richard Schweitzer was not the only one immediately critical of Dr. Maples' affidavit. When Mary-Claire King read the affidavit a few days after it was filed, she too was upset. On November 19, she telephoned Peter Gill in England, disassociated herself from Maples' remarks about Gill's incompetence, and told him that she would be pleased to work in collaboration with him on the Anastasia Manahan tissue. Later that day, she spoke by telephone with Marina and Richard Schweitzer. By fax that day to King, Schweitzer attempted to spell out his and his wife's position: they were issuing a privately funded commission to Dr. Gill with no control: "no strings, no spin." Gill's report, whatever its conclusions about Mrs. Manahan's claim to be Anastasia, would go directly to the court and the hospital, not to the Schweitzers. As for a role for Dr. King, Schweitzer told her, "It is not our wish to exclude you from participation with Peter Gill in what should be a purely scientific, totally disinterested series of procedures and conclusions." Indeed, Schweitzer offered to include King in his own petition to the court. "Unfortunately," he told her, "your name has been brought into court by a New York genealogical society which has attempted to have the court prevent access sought by us for Dr. Gill. In our view, this is really a law firm action by Andrews & Kurth on behalf of undisclosed parties which have been in the background since March or April 1993."

During their conversation, King asked Schweitzer to speak to Lindsey Crawford to see whether there was a way that she and Dr. Gill could work in collaboration or, at least, in parallel. The following day, Schweitzer passed this message to Crawford, proposing that Dr. King be included in his wife's petition and that Andrews & Kurth withdraw from the case. For two weeks, Schweitzer heard nothing; then, on December 4, he learned that Andrews & Kurth had no intention of withdrawing; on December 6, he was told that Thomas Kline was complaining that Schweitzer was interfering with "his" expert. Schweitzer immediately telephoned Kline, who backed down and admitted that Dr. King did not belong to him and that Schweitzer's contacts with her were entirely proper.

Subsequently, however, Crawford wrote to Schweitzer asking for copies of "all six of the facsimile transmissions to Dr. King." A week later, Crawford wrote again, sternly demanding that the six fax transmissions be sent to her "upon receipt of this letter. This incident," she continued, "emphasizes the need to centralize through me all communications concerning or in any way related to the Proceeding." Schweitzer sent copies of his faxes to Judge Swett but never to Lindsey Crawford.

Meanwhile, Mary-Claire King was putting her own views in writing. On December 7, 1993, she wrote and notarized an affidavit contradicting what Dr. Maples had said about Dr. Gill's competence. Although her affidavit had been summoned by Andrews & Kurth and was written ostensibly in support of the Russian Nobility Association,

King took a separate course. "I have been working for the past seven months on the identification of the skeletal remains of the nine individuals believed to include Tsar Nicholas II and members of his family," she said. "I have also received blood and tissue samples from descendants of Tsar Nicholas and his wife, Alexandra.* I am in the process of preparing a report on my findings. I am familiar with DNA research into the remains from Ekaterinburg being conducted by Dr. Peter Gill. If there is sufficient mtDNA bearing material, it would be ideal to have two qualified laboratories carry out the mtDNA testing and compare their results. I have spoken with Dr. Gill and would like the opportunity to work collaboratively with him in the analysis of the samples."

Because Dr. King's affidavit overturned much of the scientific argumentation on which Andrews & Kurth had based its case, it was withheld by that law firm and not submitted to the court or read by opposing attorneys until three months later.

Meanwhile, the number of parties attempting to participate in Richard Schweitzer's lawsuit was growing. On November 10, a fifty-six-year-old woman from Mullan, Idaho, Ellen Margarete Therese Adam Kailing, born in Germany on October 23, 1937, and still a German citizen, petitioned to intervene. She was, she swore, "the long-lost daughter" of Grand Duchess Anastasia and Prince Henry of Reuss. She said that in January 1993, only ten months before, she had changed her legal name to Anastasia Romanov. Her argument was "If Mrs. Manahan is proven to be the Grand Duchess Anastasia Romanov, then I, Anastasia Romanov, as her daughter, am a member of the Imperial family of Russia." Therefore, she told the court, she alone had a right to her mother's tissue, and she alone would decide whether, where, and by whom the tissue would be tested.

Mrs. Kailing-Romanov explained that her mother, later Mrs. Manahan, did not raise her because relatives believed that the grand

---

*Undoubtedly, King meant *relatives* of the tsar and his wife; all of their *descendants* were with them in the Ipatiev House cellar.

duchess was incompetent after the murder of her family. Mrs. Kailing-Romanov said that she had been saved from a concentration camp and placed in a German family: "I was told in 1964...that I was a princess." She came to the United States in 1968, married an American, and had children. "The truth of my identity was kept from me until June 10, 1990,... [when] I was told that I was the daughter of Anastasia Romanov by Mother Alexandra, abbess of the Orthodox Monastery of the Transfiguration in Ellwood City, Pennsylvania. When I did see the pictures in Peter Kurth's book, I knew this was my story.... Actually, Lovell in his book gave me the right informations [*sic*].... Now the picture was compleat [*sic*] and fitting.... The last information came from the book of Edvard Radzinsky."

To strengthen her case, Mrs. Kailing-Romanov contacted a Charlottesville company called Locators Inc., whose stationery promises "Missing Persons Located—Fast Action—Amazing Results." The company's finders fee contract stated that if it was determined that the claimant was entitled to share in the estate of Nicholas Romanov, Alexandra Romanov, and Anastasia Romanov, then Locators Inc. would receive 33 percent of the claimant's share of the estate. Further, "in the event it is determined that claimant is a lawful heir of Tsar Nicholas II and this in turn results in establishing claimant in a position of governmental authority in Russia," additional compensation would come in the form of payment of Russian government bonds issued in 1916, "together with accrued interest, as the first official act under claimant's government." Mrs. Kailing-Romanov decided that she did not trust Locators Inc. and did not sign the contract.

Subsequently, Mrs. Kailing-Romanov made other declarations to the court: "I am just overcoming arsenic poisoning. My income is below the poverty line." She asked that all court dates be fixed in advance because "the petitioner does not fly, she only travels by train or by car. The petitioner lives in Idaho, more than 2,000 miles away, and it takes by train more than three days to get to Charlottesville, Virginia. The office of the Tsar is given by God over which the earthly has no power. I, Anastasia Romanov, have a son and he continues the line."

To Richard Schweitzer, it seemed that the Russian Nobility Association and Mrs. Kailing-Romanov were turning his wife's lawsuit into a circus. Declaring that Mrs. Kailing-Romanov's pleading was "too incoherent to merit response," he suggested the court determine "the competence of the petitioner to represent her own or any other interests" and asked for immediate denial of her petition to intervene. Again, as it had done with the Russian Nobility Association's petition, Martha Jefferson Hospital, hoping to litigate the tissue matter only once, took the opposite course and asked that Mrs. Kailing-Romanov be admitted as an intervenor.

On December 7, to Richard Schweitzer's dismay, Judge Swett announced that both the Russian Nobility Association and Mrs. Kailing-Romanov were permitted to intervene in the suit.

························ ❧ ························

CHAPTER 16

THESE PEOPLE
HAVE NO
STANDING

Judge Swett's decision to admit the Russian Nobility Association and Anastasia Kailing-Romanov as intervenors into the Schweitzers' lawsuit was included in a letter to all parties, which also directed them to meet, confer, and resolve among themselves the questions of how and where the tissue should be tested. If the quantity of tissue was sufficient, he instructed that parallel tests be done by Dr. Gill and Dr. King. Further, the parties were instructed to reach agreement on payment of costs and on how the test results would be disclosed. When they had worked everything out, they were to submit a draft order for him to sign.

Richard Schweitzer and Lindsey Crawford immediately disagreed on the starting point for this process. Schweitzer wanted to begin by meeting and conferring; Crawford, on the other hand, quickly began preparing her own version of a draft order for the judge. Schweitzer wrote repeatedly, pushing for a meeting: "I am willing to come to your offices at your convenience at the earliest possible date, preferably this week, prior to the Christmas holidays," he wrote on Decem-

ber 20. Crawford replied, "We are in the process of drafting a proposed order which we hope to circulate to all parties within the next
few days. I will consult with you regarding scheduling a meeting after
I circulate this draft."

When Crawford's draft order arrived, Schweitzer was surprised to
see that it contained a major shift in his opponents' argument. Previously, Andrews & Kurth, accepting Dr. Maples' opinion, had condemned Peter Gill's laboratory as a place at which DNA evidence had
possibly been contaminated and which offered only "second-best scientific testing." Crawford's draft proposed the judge direct that the
tissue be made available to *both* Dr. Gill and Dr. King. Nevertheless,
Schweitzer was irritated. He disliked what he regarded as Crawford's
arrogant detailing of the scientific procedures to be followed; he disliked her insistence that both King and Gill work without reimbursement (Schweitzer knew that the British Forensic Science Service
would not work without a fee); and he insisted that each of the scientists be free to publish their results as soon as they had been obtained.

Schweitzer wrote to the hospital's attorneys, "These documents
are ample proof that we should first meet and confer as directed by
the court and not be limited by an attempt by Counsellor Crawford to
control the agenda by 'drafts' or otherwise." The day after Christmas,
Schweitzer, increasingly angry, returned to his fax machine and informed the hospital's lawyers that "Counsellor Crawford has dis-
dained our requests to meet as instructed and has elected to prepare
and circulate a draft of what she purports to be an 'order.' "
Schweitzer added that he now wished to go ahead and meet with the
hospital's attorneys, "with Counsellor Crawford to attend or not as
she wishes."

This got Lindsey Crawford's attention. She scheduled a conference of all the attorneys involved to discuss a response to Judge
Swett's letter. The time was January 10, 1994; the place, the Charlottesville office of Page Williams, the local lawyer whom Andrews &
Kurth had brought into the case. The Schweitzers, learning that bad
weather was predicted for the tenth, drove down the night before. On
the afternoon of the tenth, as the meeting began, the Schweitzers,
Page Williams, and hospital attorney Matthew Murray were there,

but Lindsey Crawford, who had called the meeting, was not. The weather was bad; it was impossible for her to drive, Williams explained. The weather, however, did not prevent the appearance of another figure who drove that day from Washington to Charlottesville.

As the attorneys were distributing copies of proposed consent orders to regulate distribution of the tissue, Dr. Willi Korte walked into the room. Schweitzer asked why Korte was present. Williams announced that Korte was there "to represent the Russian Nobility Association." Schweitzer demanded credentials or evidence of authority, and Korte pulled from his briefcase a document signed that day by Alexis Scherbatow. "I hereby request and authorize Willi Korte to assist the RNA and its lawyers in the litigation," the document read. "The authority granted herein authorizes Dr. Korte to work with the association's attorneys in the U.S. in conducting negotiations, reviewing documents, providing advice and otherwise taking any necessary and appropriate steps to advance the interests of the Association in these matters."

As the litigation progressed, Richard Schweitzer had a growing sense that he was battling multiple opponents, one standing behind another. For months, he had been aware of the presence of Dr. Willi Korte, but until January 10, he had not seen this antagonist in person. Even then, Schweitzer did not know much about him. Julian Nott, a British filmmaker working on a television documentary about Anastasia, learned more. "Korte is deliberately mysterious," Nott said a few weeks after Schweitzer's confrontation with him. "He won't reveal much about himself or who is paying him. He's German, but he lives near Washington, D.C. He's a very good researcher. His normal job is working undercover, tracking down stolen works of art. A few years ago, he helped locate the missing Quedlinburg Treasure, valued at $200 million to 'priceless,' stolen immediately after the Second World War by a U.S. Army lieutenant and hidden in Texas. In the Romanov case, I've bumped into him in Boston at the meeting of forensic scientists when Avdonin delivered his paper, at Harvard looking at the Sokolov documents, and in London.

"He's been very persuasive with some of these families, particularly the Hessians, and he has roped them in to help him," Nott continued. "He's scared them by saying, 'Look, do you know what's happening here? Do you realize that Gleb Botkin's son-in-law, Richard Schweitzer, and James Lovell are about to perpetrate this amazing fraud on you? And here I am. Why don't you give me a helping hand?'

"My feeling is that Korte is the brains and driving force behind this," Nott continued. "He's very determined, and he just won't compromise. He wants the whole damn thing; he doesn't want Schweitzer involved at all. But what he's really doing is simply making this thing the most terrible mess."

Nott was wrong, however; Willi Korte was not the motive force behind Schweitzer's opponents. By January, a figure behind Korte had begun to emerge. Maurice Philip Remy was a German television producer from Munich, interested, like Julian Nott, in doing a film on Anastasia. A few weeks later, Nott went to Munich to meet this competitor. "He's a wealthy man from an aristocratic family and his television company is quite successful," Nott declared on his return. "And he wants to solve seventy-six years of mystery on one television show. Unfortunately, he's got more money than decency. He's going after this, and he's not going to let go. He confirmed that he's behind Korte; he talked about Korte as if Korte was something worse than his butler: 'I sent Korte to do this, I sent him to do that.' Speaking of the Russian Nobility Association, he was much more careful. 'I have great influence with them,' he told me."

Remy's position on Anna Anderson was vehemently hostile. "He is not out to be objective," Nott declared. "He intends to prove that she was an impostor. He is in alliance with the Hessians, to whom, all along, he has presented himself as contemptuous of Anna Anderson." Remy also made a useful ally of Dr. von Berenberg-Gossler, the former attorney for Mountbatten and the Hessians, who, at eighty-five, still describes Anna Anderson as a "con artist" and a "phony."

Gradually, it became clear to Nott that Remy's objective was to gain complete control of the Anna Anderson case. He would block Richard and Marina Schweitzer, obtain the tissue for himself, have it

Dr. Sergei Abramov.
(Vladimir Soloviev)

Abramov's
superimposition
technique: a picture of
Nicholas II superimposed
on the skull of
Nicholas II.

Nikolai Nevolin (left) and Dr. William Maples in Ekaterinburg.

Dr. Mary-Claire King.

Dr. Peter Gill.

Dr. Pavel Ivanov.

Vladimir Soloviev.

Lt. Col. Michael Goleniewski, the Polish CIA agent who claimed to be Tsarevich Alexis. *(Bettmann archive)*

Eugenia Smith, the Chicago woman who said she was Grand Duchess Anastasia.

Above: The woman who was later called Anna Anderson in a Berlin hospital, 1925. *(Ian Lilburne Collection)*

Right: Anna Anderson.

Below: Anna Anderson married Dr. John Manahan and became Anastasia Manahan on December 22, 1968. She was seventy-two; he was forty-nine. *(Bettmann archive)*

Above: Richard and Marina Schweitzer.
(Tom Cogill, courtesy of Martha Jefferson Hospital)

Left: Prince Alexis Scherbatow.

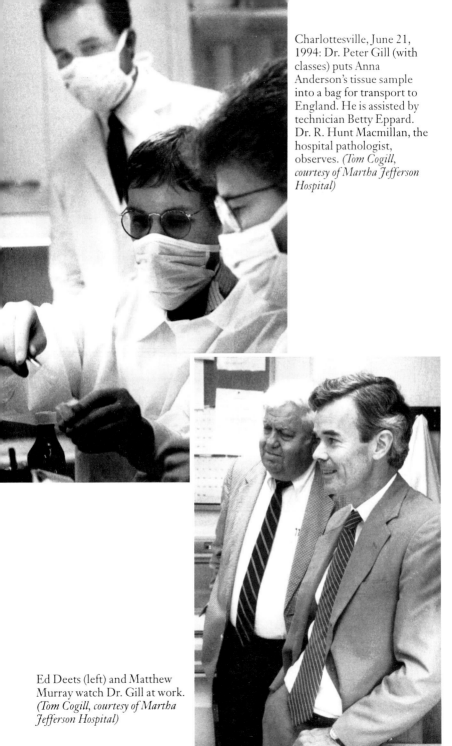

Charlottesville, June 21, 1994: Dr. Peter Gill (with classes) puts Anna Anderson's tissue sample into a bag for transport to England. He is assisted by technician Betty Eppard. Dr. R. Hunt Macmillan, the hospital pathologist, observes. *(Tom Cogill, courtesy of Martha Jefferson Hospital)*

Ed Deets (left) and Matthew Murray watch Dr. Gill at work. *(Tom Cogill, courtesy of Martha Jefferson Hospital)*

The seven Romanov princes in Paris, 1992. Left to right: Nicholas, Dimitri, Michael, Alexander, Andrew, Rostislav, Nikita.

Grand Duchess Maria, the current pretender, and her son, Grand Duke George.

Facing: Grand Duke Vladimir, pretender to the Russian throne, 1938–1992, and his wife, Grand Duchess Leonida, in Madrid. *(Bettmann archive)*

Overleaf: Prince Nicholas Romanov. *(Camera Press)*

tested, then dominate the release of information. He and his agents fanned out across Europe, not only consulting archives, letters, films, home movies, recordings, interviews, and broadcasts but trying to buy them. "No ordinary television program or station would do that; it's too expensive," Nott said. "But Remy's behind in this race so he wants to stop the Schweitzers and Gill, at least until he can arrange to have everything released simultaneously. The reason given would be that it's good science; that all the materials should be available to everyone as a public record of scientists at work. The real reason would be commercial advantage. Meanwhile, he's quietly attempting to tie up the world's supply. Then he'll go around to all the networks and stations in Europe and the world and try to presell a film with exclusive rights to the Anna Anderson DNA tests. He'll tell them he owns Anna Anderson."

In January 1994, yet another figure appeared in the case. This was Baron Ulrich von Gienanth, an eighty-six-year-old former German diplomat who had become a friend of Anna Anderson after the war and during her Unterlengenhardt years had managed her scanty finances. In a series of five wills written between 1949 and 1957, the claimant had named von Gienanth as one of her four executors. (The others, all dead by 1994, were her friend Prince Frederick of Saxe-Altenburg and her Hamburg lawyers, Kurt Vermehren and Paul Leverkuehn.) On January 21, 1994, in Bad Liebenzell, near Stuttgart, where he lived, Baron von Gienanth signed a declaration that, as the only survivor of the original four, he accepted the function of executor of Anna Anderson's last will.

Von Gienanth's declaration, if accepted by the court, would change the entire complexion of the case. Marina Schweitzer's petition to the court had been based on there being no blood relatives, no heirs, and no executors. Clearly, if he were validated as executor, von Gienanth's status would supersede Schweitzer's and, therewith, any role whatsoever for the intervenors, the Russian Nobility Association and Anastasia Kailing-Romanov. Nevertheless, Richard Schweitzer saw a legal opening and determined to exploit it. Learning that von

Gienanth wished to proceed with parallel testing of the tissue by Dr. Gill and Dr. King, Schweitzer petitioned the court to name the baron as the claimant's personal representative in Virginia. Schweitzer knew that if the court agreed, his own nonadversarial suit against the hospital would be dismissed. But, along with this, the participation of Andrews & Kurth and Anastasia Kailing-Romanov would be terminated. Trying to prevent this, Andrews & Kurth filed a motion to block von Gienanth's declaration from being presented to the court.

At this point, Schweitzer's opponents either misunderstood his objective or underestimated his legal acumen. On February 22, Schweitzer, Matthew Murray, Lindsey Crawford, and Page Williams appeared before Judge Swett ostensibly so that the judge could set a date for a hearing on the unresolved issues raised in his December 7 letter: how the two sides were going to agree on which laboratories would test the tissue and how they should deal with the publicity attending the results. The judge looked down and said, "Have you all agreed on an order?" Schweitzer said simply, "No." The judge stared at the lawyers in front of him. Then Murray said, "Your Honor, we really think that the first hearing ought to be over evidence we have received that there is someone [von Gienanth] who meets the requirements of the statute. If this other hearing can be held, anything else would be moot. I'd like to show you this request we have received from the man who purports to be the executor."

"Has that man filed any pleadings in this case?" the judge asked.

"No," said Murray.

"Is he a party in this case?"

"No," said Murray. "But if he is who he claims to be, then the hospital is entitled to have this case dismissed so we can deal directly with this man."

"Well, Mr. Murray," said the judge, "what the hospital should do is file a motion to dismiss and attach these new documents as evidence in support. This court can't rule because we don't have any motion to dismiss."

Here, Schweitzer spoke up. "Your Honor, there is a prayer to dismiss. I filed it in response to the last pleading of the Russian Nobility Association."

The judge looked surprised. "Do you understand that if I dismiss the hospital, you're in effect dismissing [the legal term is *nonsuiting*] your own case?" he asked. "Are you aware that you would be pleading a nonsuit?"

"Yes," said Schweitzer.

"Are you willing to take a nonsuit?"

"Yes," said Schweitzer.

"Counselor, do you plead nonsuit before this court?"

"Yes."

"This case is dismissed," said Judge Swett.

The other side was stunned. "Your Honor, we object to the entry of a dismissal because we are the intervenors," protested Lindsey Crawford. "We have an interest and a claim on this tissue."

"Well, if you have a claim or interest in the tissue, you can bring your own lawsuit"—Judge Swett paused—"if you have standing." When he heard this, Richard Schweitzer, who for months had been arguing the Russian Nobility Association's lack of standing, wanted to cheer.

As a result of this hearing and the entry of Judge Swett's dismissal order on March 1, Baron von Gienanth, temporarily at least, was in control of the tissue. He immediately wrote to Martha Jefferson Hospital, asking that it make the tissue available to Dr. Gill so that he could carry out the Schweitzers' commission. Von Gienanth also wrote to Lindsey Crawford urging an agreement that would make the same tissue available to Dr. King. Given this fact, the subsequent behavior of Andrews & Kurth was strange. Even as the baron was offering to do exactly what Lindsey Crawford had proposed in her draft consent order, she was vigorously attempting to undermine his credentials.

Andrews & Kurth retained counsel in Germany and learned that Anna Anderson's will had never been probated there because, at the time of her death, she did not live or own property in that country. Further, the will authorized "any two of my executors" to act, and—Crawford subsequently told Page Williams—since only one was still alive, the will "has not and cannot be probated under German law...[and] probably cannot be probated in Virginia." This led

Williams to inform Matthew Murray that, in order for Baron von Gienanth to be appointed, he would "have to appear in person...in order to probate the will and be qualified as executor." In fact, von Gienanth, elderly and deaf, was unwilling to fly.

In the meantime, attempting to deal with its sudden elimination as intervenors by Richard Schweitzer's withdrawal of his wife's case, Andrews & Kurth asked Judge Swett to review, clarify, and modify his nonsuit order; it was at a March 4 hearing on this motion that Mary Claire-King's affidavit, written on December 7, ultimately was filed. The judge rejected Andrews & Kurth's request; in effect, he told the firm, this is a nonsuit, you're out, there's no cross-claim, counterclaim, or third-party claim; that's it, this lawsuit is over. If Marina Schweitzer wants to terminate this case and cut you out, she has a right to do so.

To Lindsey Crawford and her clients, this raised the possibility that Martha Jefferson Hospital might now feel free to turn the tissue samples over to Baron von Gienanth, who then would turn them over to Dr. Gill. "Your Honor," asked Crawford, "can we have an injunction or a restraining order against the hospital pending our filing another action against the hospital?"

"If you want an injunction," said the judge, "file for an injunction."

At this stage, the Russian Nobility Association's lawyers, determined to prevent any release of the tissue and frustrated by the sudden ending of the Schweitzer lawsuit, began showering letters on Matthew Murray, telling him what Martha Jefferson Hospital should and should not do. On March 18, nearly three weeks after termination of the Schweitzers' nonadversarial suit against the hospital, the association filed its own adversarial suit, seeking an injunction against release of the Anastasia Manahan tissue before the court could rule on its challenge to von Gienanth's credentials. The petition repeated that "it is essential that the tests be of the highest scientific integrity," with the important modification that the association now sought "parallel testing of the tissue samples at two qualified laboratories" (only one, Dr. King's laboratory in California, was named). Release of the tissue samples or any part of them at this stage, it said, would cause the association "great and irreparable harm" because "any chance at ensuring the maximum degree of scientific integrity in the mtDNA testing may be lost forever... [and] posterity may never know the true identity of Anna Manahan."

Unfortunately for the Russian Nobility Association, this document, signed by Lindsey Crawford, contained a grievous error of fact, which ultimately was fatal to her case: "Upon information and belief," Crawford had written, "there is no qualified personal representative of the estate of Anna Manahan."

Once again, Richard Schweitzer was ahead of his adversaries. Around March 8, he uncovered an obscure Virginia law dealing with abandoned property. "It related mostly to farmland," Schweitzer said. "If a farmer died or disappeared and left his farm abandoned, his cattle unfed, and so forth, anybody—it didn't have to be someone with family connections—who knew about it could go into court and ask that the sheriff be appointed to take charge of the property until whoever was supposed to come and be responsible would do it. Then they changed the law—and this is the part I hadn't previously realized—because sheriffs were being overwhelmed by managing property, paying insurance, and all that, which they had to do out of the sheriff's budget. The new law says that anybody can petition the court to appoint not just sheriffs but anybody else resident of the county or town as administrator of an abandoned estate.

"So I talked to my cocounsel and 1953 University of Virginia Law School classmate Ed Deets. Ed agreed to be named, and I told him, 'I will act as your lawyer so you won't have any legal expense, and I will put up the bond,' which was about seventy-five dollars since there was no physical estate. So on March 16, with Judge Swett's approval, my former cocounsel, Ed Deets, was sworn in as personal representative and administrator of Anastasia Manahan's estate in Virginia.

"Matt Murray was aware of what I was doing. He was sick of the case, which was costing the hospital all that money, and he said, 'Hell yes! Go ahead and file it!' Baron von Gienanth was aware of it, and, as his credentials were going to be challenged, he also approved. Under the law, the administrator is entitled to medical records, including specimens and tissue. Ed promptly submitted a request for the tissue to be sent to Dr. Gill."

Ed Deets's appointment provided Matthew Murray with ammunition for a powerful attack on Lindsey Crawford's request for an injunction. Filing two court documents on March 24, Murray struck hard at the absence of court standing of the Russian Nobility Association, which, he pointed out, had never filed certified copies of its articles of incorporation or a certificate of good standing. He described the New York association as "obviously ... a mere genealogical society" which had no connection with "the person of Anna Manahan. Further," said Murray, the association failed to present any facts or grounds to support its claim that it "would suffer any injury, much less irreparable injury, were any transfer of tissue samples to take place." Finally, Murray delivered the coup de grâce: On March 16, two days before the filing of the nobility association's request for an injunction, Ed Deets had been appointed as administrator of Anastasia Manahan's estate. This made him, not the hospital, responsible for the disposal of the tissue. If you want an injunction, Murray said, sue Ed Deets.

Murray was hopeful that the matter was almost over. "If the judge rules favorably on this, then we'll never get to the issue of the injunction," he said about this time. "Before long, the Russian Nobility Association is out the window. Soon Ed Deets will file a document, as I have, saying in effect, 'Judge, these people have no standing and you have no jurisdiction.' Then the judge is going to be forced to rule on it. They [the Russian Nobility Association] could appeal, but I doubt they will. If they do, they have to post a bond to prevent us in the meantime giving up the tissue. They'd have to go to the Supreme Court of Virginia and to get the Supreme Court to issue an injunction has a snowball's chance in hell. The real question now is who they are and what they are doing in Virginia."

On the afternoon of March 30, 1994, a group of people gathered again in Judge Swett's courtroom in the colonial red brick Circuit Courthouse in Charlottesville. The attorneys, Matthew Murray for the hospital and Lindsey Crawford and Page Williams for the Russian Nobility Association, sat in front at opposite tables. Alexis Scherbatow of the Russian Nobility Association sat beside his two lawyers. In back, on benches on one side of the room, were Marina and Richard Schweitzer, Ed Deets, Penny Jenkins, the English documentary filmmaker Julian Nott, a local newspaper reporter, Ron Hansen, and me. On the other side sat Dr. Willi Korte and an editor of the scientific journal *Nature Genetics*, Dr. Adrian Ivinson.

The subject of the hearing was to be the nobility association's request for an injunction, but Murray immediately asked the judge to rule on his challenge to the association's standing. Judge Swett decided, however, that Ed Deets's new role and the fact that Deets had not yet asserted his wishes or filed any papers justified postponing the issue of standing. On that day, said the judge, he would listen only to arguments for and against a temporary injunction.

The significant event of the afternoon was the public display of Andrews & Kurth's reversal of its position on Peter Gill and parallel testing. The Washington lawyers had no choice. Mary-Claire King's affidavit, withheld at the time she wrote it but now a part of the court record, had made clear the fallacies in William Maples' attack on Gill. Now, with Deets in command of the disposition of the tissue, Andrews & Kurth had to face the fact that, in the near future, Peter Gill probably was going to receive and begin to test a piece of Anastasia Manahan. The best Crawford now could hope for was that the tissue not be sent to Gill until, at the same time, it went to King. Therefore, she who had opposed parallel testing became its advocate.

The instrument of this reversed advocacy was Adrian Ivinson, a young Englishman with a doctorate in clinical and molecular human genetics. He appeared as an expert witness on behalf of the Russian Nobility Association. Taking the witness stand, Dr. Ivinson declared that consigning the tissue to parallel testing at two laboratories would be scientifically more significant than testing in only one laboratory.

Judge Swett wanted Ivinson's opinion of two famous DNA scientists. "I take it you hold Dr. King in the highest esteem as an international scientist," he said.

"Yes," said Ivinson.

Then Judge Swett asked whether Ivinson would put Dr. Peter Gill and the Forensic Science Service laboratory on the same level as Dr. King's laboratory.

"Yes," said Ivinson.*

At the end of that day, Judge Swett did not grant the temporary injunction the Russian Nobility Association had requested because, during the hearing, Matthew Murray promised voluntarily to have the hospital hold on to the tissue a little longer—for "the next several days or weeks"—until conclusion of the litigation. In the meantime, the judge instructed the association to deal with Ed Deets, the new administrator of Anastasia Manahan's estate.

Deets immediately focused on the nobility association's relationship with Mary-Claire King. He asked Page Williams whether the association had a written agreement with King and, if so, what it was. He also asked for a copy of King's report on the work she had done on the Ekaterinburg remains. Williams wrote back that the Russian Nobility Association had no written agreement with King. Deets tried telephoning Dr. King. At first, his calls went unanswered. Eventually, when they spoke, neither was impressed by the other. Deets said that if she was going to test the tissues, he thought there ought to be a definite time schedule. King, apparently offended by this suggestion, hung up.

The final court hearing on Anastasia Manahan's tissue took place on May 11, 1994. By then, both Martha Jefferson Hospital (Matthew Murray) and the administrator of Anastasia Manahan's estate (Ed Deets) had filed papers demanding that the lawsuit of the Russian Nobility Association be dismissed because the court lacked jurisdic-

---

*Subsequently, Dr. Kevin Davies, the editor of *Nature Genetics* and Ivinson's superior, made an even stronger statement: "Gill's lab is, obviously, the leading lab in this kind of thing in the world." Davies also explained that Andrews & Kurth had, at Mary-Claire King's suggestion, solicited his participation as an expert witness. Because he was unavailable that day, Ivinson had traveled to Charlottesville in his stead. Davies was surprised that Andrews & Kurth had not only not paid his colleague the customary expert witness fee but "didn't even give him lunch."

tion and the association lacked standing. In reply, Lindsey Crawford of Andrews & Kurth argued one last time that the association's interest in noble lineage and "protecting the history of Imperial Russia" automatically gave it standing.* Despite Crawford's plea, Judge Swett accepted the arguments of the hospital and Deets and dismissed the case. His court order was entered on May 19, 1994, and gave the Russian Nobility Association and Andrews & Kurth thirty days to file an appeal. If no appeal was filed, the case was over.

Richard Schweitzer waited until the exact day that time ran out on the Russian Nobility Association's power to appeal Judge Swett's decision. Then, on June 19, Peter Gill arrived in Charlottesville to collect a sample of Anastasia Manahan's tissue. He came in secrecy; Schweitzer still feared that Willi Korte or Andrews & Kurth might attempt to intercept Gill or interfere with his access to the tissue. "Gill might be served with a process to prevent his acting," Schweitzer wrote to Matt Murray, objecting to the hospital's plan to publicize the visit. "Attempts may be made under obtuse regulations to prevent him taking these [human] materials out of the U.S. He or his specimens may be subjected to physical interference, although I have arranged for an escort to accompany him."

Gill had lunch that day with the Schweitzers and then went to the hospital to collect the tissue. He was greeted there by Ed Deets, Matthew Murray, Penny Jenkins, and Dr. Hunt Macmillan, director of the hospital pathology laboratory. While the lawyers and nonscientists watched from the back of the room and a documentary film crew recorded everything that happened, the process got under way. Macmillan, Gill, and Betty Eppard, a registered histology technician

---

*This interest in Russian history failed to sustain Crawford when she wrote in her final memorandum to the court that Anastasia Manahan claimed "that along with her brother Nikolas [*sic*], she survived the murders in the cellar." In fact, Anastasia Manahan never said that any other member of the Imperial family survived. And, of course, the brother of Grand Duchess Anastasia was named Alexis.

who actually cut the tissue, appeared wearing sterile masks, gowns, and gloves. The five blocks of paraffin containing the embedded tissue of Anastasia Manahan were produced, and the same procedure was repeated five times: Macmillan handed Gill a tissue block and identified it. Gill sterilized it and handed it to Eppard. Eppard mounted it on a microtome, a machine resembling a bacon slicer, and deftly sliced three to six dark brown pieces, each equal in thickness to two hairs. Gill, using tweezers, gently lifted the sliced tissue and placed it in sterilized vials. Macmillan placed the sterilized vials in tamper-proof, transparent plastic bags and sealed and labeled each bag. After each block, the microtome was wiped with absolute ethanol and its cutting blade was changed. Afterward, at a hastily summoned press conference, Gill warned that "I can't be sure at the moment how likely it is we'll get DNA from the samples." He had no idea, he said, what effect the age of the tissue or the use of the chemical preservative formalin would have had on the DNA. If the DNA extraction process went well, he hoped to have a comparison between Anastasia Manahan's DNA and the DNA profiles of the Imperial family taken from the Ekaterinburg bones within three to six months.

On June 29, ten days after Peter Gill collected the tissue in Charlottesville, Maurice Remy wrote Richard Schweitzer a remarkable confessional letter. In the letter, in a subsequent press release, and in a mass of other documents which he forwarded to Schweitzer, Remy revealed everything that had happened in his camp before and during the long court battle. His enterprise began, he said, when he met Geli Ryabov in Moscow in 1987 and decided to produce a documentary on the murder of the tsar and his family. In July 1992, he was present at the Ekaterinburg conference on the remains of the Imperial family. There he met Dr. Maples and his team, who told him that the skeletons of Alexis and Anastasia were missing. At that moment, Remy said, he decided to concentrate his efforts on the missing grand duchess and to expand his research to include a DNA test on Anastasia Manahan.

Learning that Anastasia Manahan had been cremated, Remy began searching for a blood or tissue sample she might have left behind. He asked Dr. Willi Korte to investigate Martha Jefferson Hospital in Charlottesville. Having found that, indeed, a tissue sample existed, Remy next asked Thomas Kline, of Andrews & Kurth, to approach the Manahan family and James Lovell for permission to analyze the tissue. This approach foundered. Meanwhile, on Remy's behalf, Korte was busy in Germany and Greece, collecting comparative blood samples from Princess Sophie of Hanover and Xenia Sfiris. In this same period, tracing an alternative identity for Anastasia Manahan, Remy located a niece of Franziska Schanzkowska and persuaded her to donate blood.

Remy revealed the reason for William Maples' attack on Peter Gill. In June 1993, Korte, as Remy's agent, had signed a contractual letter of agreement with Maples and Lowell Levine. Maples and Levine promised to use Dr. King to do DNA tests on the Romanov and Hessian comparative materials which Korte would supply. They also promised to keep Korte's work "in strict confidence."* The only consideration promised by Korte in return was payment of travel expenses, but, the letter said, "all travel will have to be approved in advance by Dr. Korte." Maples, thereby, became a part of Remy's team. When, in November 1993, scientific testimony was needed to support the Russian Nobility Association's petition to intervene in the Charlottesville case, Maples supplied his aggressive, ill-informed affidavit.

Learning that Richard and Marina Schweitzer were filing a court petition seeking access to the Martha Jefferson Hospital tissue on behalf of Dr. Gill, Remy recruited Scherbatow and the Russian Nobil-

---

*Although there was nothing in Maples' agreement with Korte that prohibited Maples from revealing their professional relationship, the anthropologist was eager to keep it a secret. I first heard of Willi Korte from Dr. Michael Baden in one of my initial interviews for this book. "You ought to talk to Willi Korte," Baden told me expansively. "He knows everything that's going on." When, in January 1994, I asked Maples about Korte, Maples seemed alarmed: "Korte is extremely knowledgeable, but he won't talk to you. He would be rabid if he knew that Michael had been talking to you. He and the German outfit he works for are extremely secretive." After the lawsuit was over, when I knew about the agreement with Korte, I asked Maples about it. He denied that an agreement ever existed.

ity Association. Throughout the two lawsuits which followed, the nominal client of Andrews & Kurth, proclaimed in every court document, was the Russian Nobility Association, although Remy stressed that Prince Scherbatow was not told exactly how he was being used. But the direction of the case and the payment of all legal expenses came from Remy, locally managed by Korte.

Remy also described to Schweitzer his relationship with Dr. King: In the summer of 1993, he said, the Forensic Institute of the University of Munich withdrew from the investigations and, as a replacement, Maples suggested King. An oral agreement with King was struck, supplementing the written agreement between Korte and Maples, and Korte thereafter carried to California the blood samples from Sophie of Hanover and Xenia Sfiris. But, with the Anastasia Manahan tissue still locked in a fierce court battle, Remy had no comparative material from the primary claimant, the woman in whom he was most interested.

In his confession to Schweitzer, Remy attempted to smooth over the court battles of the previous winter. This unpleasantness, Remy told Schweitzer, was the result of misunderstanding, bad advice, and loose organizational discipline. Korte had reported inaccurately what was happening in America, he said, and he blamed himself for not maintaining tighter control. He and Korte, Remy added, had severed their relationship.

When the tissue went to England, seventeen months of legal maneuvering and battling in Charlottesville came to an end. In retrospect, one significant question pertaining to the case remained unanswered. It was the role of Dr. Mary-Claire King. Originally, Dr. King, a famous scientist, deeply involved in research into the causes of breast cancer, agreed at the persuasion of Dr. Maples and Dr. Levine to accept bones and teeth from the Ekaterinburg skeletons and to attempt to establish whether these were the remains of the Imperial family. This report, despite increasingly urgent telephone calls from Maples, was never released. Nevertheless, King accepted a second Romanov assignment, orally agreeing to receive, test, and compare a slice of

Anastasia Manahan's tissue to material from Romanov relatives and descendants brought to her by Korte. Over many months, wearied, perhaps even disgusted, by the seemingly endless squabbling in Charlottesville, King remained unwilling to make any commitment on paper as to how the tests should be performed and how, when, and where the results should be released.

The question arises as to why, busy as she was with critical research into a disease which threatens and takes the lives of millions of women, King agreed to involve herself and her laboratory in Romanov identities in the first place. She did not do it for money; in order to retain absolute control, King refuses to accept money in cases of this kind. If she did it to enhance her reputation or because she was intrigued, why did she not follow through? The fact is that without King's name and reputation behind them and the prospect that she was available to test the tissue, the Russian Nobility Association and Andrews & Kurth would have found it almost impossible to block the testing arrangements agreed on by Richard Schweitzer, Peter Gill, and Martha Jefferson Hospital. In the end, many people spent many months and many thousands of dollars waiting for Dr. King. She did not deliver.

CHAPTER 17

AS GOOD
AS THE PEOPLE
USING IT

During the summer of 1994, while Peter Gill and his colleagues at the Forensic Science Service were working to extract DNA from the Anastasia Manahan tissue slices which Gill had brought from Charlottesville, Maurice Philip Remy was still trying to acquire for himself some source of Anastasia Manahan's DNA. The dismissal of the Russian Nobility Association's suit against Martha Jefferson Hospital for lack of standing did not, in itself, prevent Remy from obtaining from the hospital a piece of tissue identical to the one taken by Gill. Indeed, Judge Swett's dismissal of the case left Remy entirely free to apply to Ed Deets, the administrator of Manahan's estate, for a tissue sample to send to Mary-Claire King in California. Remy was dubious, however, about Dr. King's reliability. In deciding what to do next, he turned unexpectedly to his recent adversary, Richard Schweitzer. How did Schweitzer think he ought to handle King? Schweitzer tried to be helpful. "Mary-Claire King didn't do the actual work on those materials," he told Remy. "It was done by a man named Charles Ginther. He's now persona non grata in her lab, but he continues in another lab out there, and I can give you his number." Remy promptly called Ginther. Soon, he found himself in further difficulties.

Charles Ginther, a young DNA scientist working in Dr. King's laboratory, had extracted mitochondrial DNA from the Ekaterinburg materials brought by William Maples and from the Xenia Sfiris and Princess Sophie blood samples supplied by Remy. Ginther, King explained to Richard Schweitzer, "has finished his report and turned it in, but I can't release it. He's a good scientist, but he's not a good report writer. I've had to send it back to him to work on so that I feel that we can put it out as a regular report of this laboratory." This may be true, but another circumstance also may have contributed to King's failure to release this report: that is that the tests on the Ekaterinburg bones in King's laboratory produced results which were the same as or inferior to those already announced by Dr. Gill. If this was the case—as another DNA scientist has pointed out—King would not want to say, "Here are our results. They are not as good as Gill's results." Probably, she felt it was better to say nothing.

In any case, as the Charlottesville lawsuit was coming to an end, King and Ginther had a disagreement, and Ginther moved across the hall, into the laboratory of Dr. George Sensabaugh. "Dr. King put their falling-out in the harshest terms to me," said Richard Schweitzer. "I have never heard one scientist degrade another that way. She said, in essence, that she had to put Chuck Ginther out of her laboratory. For a scientist to say that to a layperson seemed to me extraordinary." Ginther, junior to King at the same university, speaks of this relationship with circumspection: "Mary-Claire King is a very famous scientist. She is the right person, at the right time, working on the right disease [breast cancer]. She is a woman, working on a woman's disease, at a famous university. And a lot of people very much want her to succeed. But she is very difficult to work for."

It was in this context that Remy turned to Schweitzer. "Remy didn't know how to go about writing a commitment letter from a lab," Schweitzer recalled. "And he also had problems about how to get the Ekaterinburg specimens out of the hands of Mary-Claire King and transferred to Ginther across the hall. So I helped him. I drafted documents for him." Why did Schweitzer, who had just concluded a grueling seven months' battle with Remy in court, try to help his former antagonist make an arrangement with Ginther? "Because I wanted to get more testing done, comparing the Manahan tissue with the Hessian," Schweitzer explained. "I knew that Charles Ginther was an excellent scientist and technician in that field. I had no objection to Remy being the person to get it done. My problem all along with Remy and his group was that they did not care what damage they did as long as they could get their way. They didn't understand that they could get their way without doing a lot of damage. I told Remy that I thought that was his major flaw."

In June, Remy—with Schweitzer's help—asked Ginther to accept a commission so that he could make a proper request to get a tissue sample from Ed Deets. Except for the Manahan tissue, Ginther already had what he needed to go ahead. He had done Hessian and Romanov profiles in King's laboratory; by that time he also had the same profiles published in *Nature Genetics* by Peter Gill. Had Ginther received tissue from Charlottesville, he could have smoothly completed Remy's commission.

But Ginther (who was not being paid for his work) posed two preconditions: First, he wanted Mary-Claire King to state unequivocally in writing that she was not willing to accept the proposed commission from Remy and that she had no objection to his doing so. Also, Ginther asked that Remy arrange for King to release to him the comparative Romanov and Hessian materials in her lab. In an attempt to do this, Remy telephoned Dr. King. He had difficulty reaching her, and, when he did, he failed to persuade her.

Remy thereupon hired the Los Angeles law firm of O'Melveny and Myers to intercede. The lawyers told him that when they called King, she said she would be happy to release the blood samples if she could find them...she didn't know exactly where they were...this was just one of many projects in her laboratory. She also complained that she could not deal with Remy, who had ranted and raved on the telephone, telling her what to do. She was not going to waste her time on somebody like that, she said. Remy's response was "I don't know what she's talking about."

Ultimately, King did turn over the comparative samples to Ginther. Subsequently, however, Remy complained to Schweitzer that she gave Ginther very little material to work with. "She just threw most of it away," Remy said, "the stuff we had worked so hard to get." Whether, in fact, she had failed to save the blood samples or whether she wanted to keep some for future purposes, no one knew. Remy believed that her motive was spite. Schweitzer disagreed. "I just don't think she gave a damn anymore. She was doing something else, and she just didn't care."

Ginther, like Remy, felt that Mary-Claire King did not permit him to take enough material by volume or weight from her laboratory. Gill, Ginther told Schweitzer, was working with a gram and a half of DNA material, whereas he had less than a gram. Nevertheless, Ginther started over. He already had done most of this work in King's lab, but he wanted to do it over in order to avoid being accused of using her work. Once again, he derived mitochondrial DNA from the Hessian and Romanov materials. Once again, he extracted mtDNA from a blood sample, sent to him by Remy, taken from a woman named Margaret Ellerick. (Mrs. Ellerick was a niece of Franziska Schanzkowska, the Polish woman who disappeared in Berlin about the time that Fräulein Unbekannt was pulled from the canal.) Nevertheless, even as he did this work in July 1994, Ginther still had no material—no tissue, no blood, no bone or hair—from which to extract the DNA of the woman Remy had commissioned him to identify, Anastasia Manahan.

Remy, frustrated by his inability to get results from Mary-Claire King and by the time it was taking to meet Charles Ginther's conditions to work, got busy elsewhere. He realized that, for all the words uttered in court regarding the benefits of parallel testing, any results Ginther obtained from testing Charlottesville tissue would provide only a duplicate of the tests already being done by Peter Gill. Coming in second in this race was not Remy's objective. "I think by then Remy decided to circumvent the Gill sample by finding his own sample somewhere else," said Ginther.

Remy and his assistants began searching in Germany, through hospitals, sanatoria, and doctors' offices, for stored samples of Anna Anderson's blood which might have resulted from medical examinations during her four or five decades of living in that country. One of his researchers located a trace of blood in a canule (a tube) used during a routine examination in the late 1950s and kept by her local physician as a curiosity. But nothing useful could be derived from this canule.

In July, Remy found Professor Stefan Sandkuhler, a former hematologist from Heidelberg University, who had examined Anna Anderson on June 6, 1951. She had been brought to him to be tested as a carrier of hemophilia, presumably to reinforce her claim to be a daughter of Empress Alexandra. After taking a blood sample, Sandkuhler had followed the usual procedure and smeared a drop of blood on a glass plate, where it dried and was preserved. The professor located the sample and gave it to Remy. Scratched into the glass was its only source of legitimacy, the patient's name. Remy said he read there "Anastasia." The result of the 1951 test for hemophilia carriership, Sandkuhler told Remy, had been inconclusive.

Remy divided the slide he had acquired from Sandkuhler into two pieces. One half was sent to Professor Bernd Herrmann, a specialist in short tandem repeat (STR) identification of nuclear DNA at the Anthropological Institute of Göttingen University. The other half of the slide went to Dr. Ginther in Berkeley. The only clue to identity was the name Anna Anderson (not "Anastasia," as reported by Remy) etched in the glass. Ginther tried and failed to extract DNA from the dried blood. Subsequently, however, Herrmann managed to get DNA from his half of the slide. He sent this DNA material to Ginther to sequence and obtain a profile. Ginther found that this DNA did not match the Hessian profile (that is, the donor of the blood was not related to Empress Alexandra), nor did it match the Schanzkowska profile as derived from Margaret Ellerick. Because the blood on the slide did not match, as Ginther put it, "any of the characters of interest," he wondered about the integrity and origin of the slide. "It was an open slide. It could have been contaminated. It didn't even have a cover slip on it. Somebody had just smeared blood which dried," he said.

✣

Over the summer of 1994, Peter Gill's findings about the Charlottesville tissue were awaited anxiously in English palaces and German castles. The earlier report that Anastasia's skeleton was missing from the Ekaterinburg grave had stirred uneasiness in dynastic families in both countries. Almost without exception, royal Britons and Germans had always firmly rejected Anna Anderson's claim to be the daughter of the tsar. The British Royal family, following the lead of Prince Philip's patriarchal uncle Lord Mountbatten, habitually referred to Mrs. Manahan as "the false Anastasia." The Hessian cousins of Prince Philip used stronger language. Now, as Gill was about to give his report, a ghastly pit opened before these families. What if a morally appalling and politically embarrassing injustice had been committed against a helpless Royal cousin?

For several years, Maurice Remy had done his best to involve the Hessians—that is, the descendants of the family of Empress Alexandra and her brother, Grand Duke Ernest Louis—in the attempt to block the Schweitzers. Prince Philip's elder sister, Princess Sophie of Hanover, now eighty-one, had given blood to Remy, which he sent for comparative purposes to Mary-Claire King. Remy also had approached Princess Margaret of Hesse, the eighty-two-year-old widow of Prince Louis of Hesse, whose father, Grand Duke Ernest, had been the claimant's nemesis in the 1920s. Born Margaret Geddes in Scotland, Princess Margaret inherited Wolfsgarten, the Rhineland castle where Empress Alexandra spent her childhood. She also controlled the private Hesse family archives, which, for a while, she opened to Remy's researchers. A third concerned Hessian was Prince Moritz, who would inherit Schloss Wolfsgarten after the death of the childless Princess Margaret.

Remy's effort was thwarted primarily by Prince Philip and his private secretary, Sir Brian McGrath. The prince had no objection to his sister providing a blood sample—after all, he had given his own blood to Peter Gill to help verify the Ekaterinburg bones. But when Remy went further and tried to draw Sophie, Margaret, and Moritz into the Charlottesville litigation, McGrath, speaking for Prince Philip, sternly "advised" these German relatives to stay away. It was not that the British Royal household was seriously worried that the claimant might turn out to be Anastasia; in fact, they were unflappably convinced that she was not. Rather, their concern was that the controversy over Anastasia Manahan's identity and the resulting lawsuits in Charlottesville might somehow compromise Queen Elizabeth II's upcoming state visit to Russia. No one wanted this diplomatic event overshadowed by a pronouncement—especially while Elizabeth was actually in Russia—that Anna Anderson had been Tsar Nicholas II's daughter. The queen's advisers, therefore, favored a solution to the claimant's identity before Her Majesty left for Moscow on October 17.

Early in September, Peter Gill told Richard Schweitzer that he was close to achieving results. Schweitzer and the Forensic Science Service mutually agreed on a date, October 5, on which Gill would announce his findings at a press conference in London. Simultaneously, Ed Deets would file the results in court and hold a press conference in Charlottesville. The FSS made it clear to Schweitzer that, as this was a private commission, he, not they, was responsible for arranging and presiding over the press conference.

Neither Gill nor Schweitzer sought exclusivity for Gill's tests. On the contrary, said Schweitzer, "from the day Peter Gill came to Charlottesville to take the tissue, he insisted that the Armed Forces Institute of Pathology do another set of tests to verify what he is doing. Gill wanted this confirmation before he made his own public announcement. Actually, he hoped to have a joint news conference with these other scientists." During this same period, Schweitzer—also with Gill's encouragement—began arranging a third test of the Manahan tissue, with Dr. Mark Stoneking, a mitochondrial DNA specialist at Pennsylvania State University. An agreement with AFIP was finally worked out on September 21, only two weeks before the London press conference. Susan Barritt, an AFIP scientist, drove to Charlottesville and collected two sets of Anastasia Manahan tissue slices, one for AFIP and one for Dr. Stoneking. Thereafter, Dr. Gill did everything possible to help AFIP accelerate its testing. Rather than leave the U.S. government scientists to work only with his published results, he dispatched all his protocols and codes to Maryland; the same data went simultaneously to Dr. Stoneking. Schweitzer was enormously pleased by this exhibition of scientists working together and wholeheartedly approved Gill's proposal of joint publication of the results of their mutual investigations.

Maurice Remy continued to wish to play a dominant role in solving the Anastasia mystery. After Richard Schweitzer assisted him in June in working out an agreement with Charles Ginther, Remy and Schweitzer lost contact with each other. Nevertheless, Schweitzer and Gill heard rumors that Remy had commissioned further tests on the 1951 blood slide, and Remy picked up the news that Gill's press conference was scheduled for October 5. Remy reacted to this in two ways: he began pressing Schweitzer to allow him to attend and participate in the press conference, and he readied plans to release new information apparently obtained by Dr. Herrmann from the 1951 blood slide.

Remy's request to participate in the London press conference met with partial acceptance from Schweitzer, who, having paid for Gill's testing, had the right to make this decision. "I told him I'd be happy for him to come," Schweitzer said. "I told him that we fully intended to acknowledge that he was the original discoverer of the tissue at Martha Jefferson Hospital, and that we intended to speak of his many years of work. And I said that I would announce that he would be available afterward. But it was not to be a joint press conference." However, a secondary role was not what Remy envisaged. Unless his demands were met, Remy warned, he might release his own findings before October 5. He mentioned that the London *Sunday Times*, which routinely pays thousands of pounds for exclusives on premium stories, was interested. Schweitzer and Gill were unwilling to make the arrangements Remy demanded.

On Sunday, October 2, the *Sunday Times* trumpeted its scoop: Anna Anderson had been "unmasked as the conwoman [*sic*] of the century," said the newspaper. "Genetic tests have established beyond all doubt that Anna Anderson... was one of the biggest imposters the world has known.... The news came at the end of a global race to solve the mystery.... Yesterday's results beat a British team led by Dr. Peter Gill who is to announce his findings on Wednesday.... The existence of the sample was discovered by Maurice Philip Remy, a German television producer who has spent five hundred thousand pounds to find the genetic keys that would unlock Anastasia's past." The *Sunday Times* reported that the test had been done by Professor Bernd Herrmann of the Anthropological Institute of Göttingen University; otherwise, there were no scientific details. Essentially the same story appeared that weekend in the German newsmagazine *Der Spiegel.*

The rest of the London press ignored the *Sunday Times* and crowded into Dr. Gill's press conference. Richard and Marina Schweitzer were on the dais with Dr. Gill and his colleague Dr. Kevin Sullivan. Facing them in the front row, Prince Rostislav Romanov, grandnephew of Nicholas II, sat next to his friend Michael Thornton, who had once had power of attorney for Anna Anderson in Britain. Next to Thornton sat Ian Lilburne, a supporter of the claimant who had attended every session of the grueling Hamburg court battles in the 1960s. Against a side wall sat a tall, white-faced, bespectacled man with slicked-down blond hair. He was Maurice Philip Remy.

Schweitzer introduced himself and his wife, and, before anything else, credited Remy with discovering the tissue samples at Martha Jefferson Hospital. Then, assisted by photographs and charts projected onto a screen behind him, Peter Gill described what he had done: he had extracted both nuclear and mitochondrial DNA from the Charlottesville tissue (which, he always said carefully, was "said to have come from Anna Anderson"). He had compared the DNA profile of the Charlottesville tissue with DNA profiles of the presumed tsar and empress (obtained from the Ekaterinburg bones), with the blood sample donated by Prince Philip, and with a blood sample obtained from a German farmer named Karl Maucher, who was a grandnephew of Franziska Schanzkowska. Using the short tandem repeat technique on nuclear DNA, Gill said he determined that "if you accept that these samples came from Anna Anderson, then Anna Anderson could not be related to Tsar Nicholas or Empress Alexandra." Gill then compared mitochondrial DNA from the tissue to the DNA sequence obtained from Prince Philip; if Anna Anderson was Grand Duchess Anastasia, her mitochondrial DNA sequence would match Philip's. In this case, in one distinctively hypervariable area, there were six base pair differences. This was enough for Gill to conclude that "the sample said to have come from Anna Anderson could not be associated with a maternal relative of the empress or Prince Philip. That is definitive." Finally, Gill compared the mitochondrial DNA profile of the Charlottesville tissue with that of Franziska Schanz-kowska's grandnephew, Karl Maucher. He achieved "a one hundred percent match, an absolute identity." Again speaking cautiously, Gill said, "This suggests that Karl Maucher may be a relative of Anna Anderson."

At the press conference, Peter Gill never flatly said that Anna Anderson was not Grand Duchess Anastasia and that she was Franziska Schanzkowska. He explained that he had used his own database of three hundred Caucasian sequences along with additional DNA sequences supplied by AFIP and Mark Stoneking. He said that while he had found the Maucher and Anderson DNA profiles to be identical, he had found no similar profiles in his own database. Therefore, he said, the odds that Anna Anderson was not a member of the Schanz-kowska family were three hundred to one, perhaps more.*

The journalists had other questions. Gill was asked how certain he was that the tissue he tested had come from Anna Anderson. He answered carefully. "I can't really speak for procedures at Martha Jefferson Hospital," he said. "But when I was there, they showed me pretty

---

*The language of scientists, cautious and replete with qualifiers, often moves backward toward its goal. Thus, in this case, Gill actually said, "The chance of finding matching profiles if Anna Anderson and Karl Maucher are unrelated is less than one in three hundred." Later, in his published report, Gill was more direct: "This finding supports the hypothesis that Anna Anderson and Franziska Schanzkowska were the same person."

good documentation; the numbers on the wax blocks tied up perfectly with numbers on the case notes." He was asked whether he thought that DNA profiling was infallible. "A technique always is only as good as the people using it," he said. "But providing you always put your findings into the correct context, then, yes, it should be infallible." He was asked to compare his work with the studies done in Germany. "When I compared our results with their results, they were"—Gill paused—"different. And from that I concluded that the sample which I analyzed and the sample they analyzed almost certainly came from different people."

This was a surprise. Immediately, Michael Thornton stood up and stared at Maurice Remy across the room. Thornton was a friend of Richard Schweitzer and had not appreciated Remy's attempt to overshadow Dr. Gill's research and press conference. Gill's revelation that the DNA extracted from Remy's blood sample did not match the DNA extracted from the Charlottesville tissue left them, Thornton declared, "with the fact that the blood sample used for *Der Spiegel* and the *Sunday Times* is false. It is not from Anna Anderson."

Remy, his face coloring, rose to defend his tests and his blood sample. Apparently, he had known before he flew to London that the DNA profile his scientist had obtained differed from that achieved by Peter Gill. "I don't want to bore you with some problems whether the sample is right or not right," he told the audience. "We've done our work properly. I think the best way now is it should be solved by the scientists. While leaving Germany yesterday, my scientists told me that there are ten reasons the DNA might be different. One might be the provenance [chain of custody] of the sample and nine other possibilities could lie in the examining of the samples. I am an intermediary between scientists and we will work it out. But to me there is no doubt of the provenance of the blood sample we used."

Thornton persisted. "Then why do you have a different DNA?" he asked.

"I'm not a scientist, so I'm maybe not the right one to answer this question," Remy said, "but we'll try to work it out. Anyway, the results are the same."

"No," said Thornton implacably, "they are not the same. The DNA is different."

"The DNA is not so different. And I don't want to bore you."

"The DNA is different," Thornton repeated. He turned to Peter Gill. "Will you confirm that it is entirely different DNA, Dr. Gill?"

"They looked pretty different to me," Gill admitted.

"So the DNA is different and the blood sample is false," Thornton said.

Remy tried again: "Let's leave it to the scientists and not start a war between an intestine and a blood sample."

"There is no war," said Thornton. "It's a question of the truth."

Remy, badly flustered, wanted Thornton to leave him alone. "We'll find out at the end," he said hurriedly. "We'll hand it over to the scientists. We have nothing to hide. We will show all of our results at the end. They will be published. Then we'll see."

"We look forward to that," Thornton said coolly and sat down.

When the press conference concluded, many journalists remained, interviewing principals. Schweitzer told one group that while he accepted the science of Dr. Gill's findings, it was "contrary to the rational experience of all the people who knew Anna Anderson, talked to her, and stayed with her, to believe that she was a Polish peasant." Remy moved through the room handing out a five-page press release claiming that he and his German scientist had achieved "the breakthrough... a result of almost 100% significance. Not one of the four DNA particles obtained from the cell nucleus... tallied with the DNA of the Tsar and his wife." On another side of the room, Thornton continued his criticism of Remy: "He tried to undermine Dr. Gill's announcement with a scoop of his own, which has failed to stand scrutiny. It is also the worst kind of bad manners to come to someone else's press conference and distribute his own self-glorifying press release, which, incidentally, is riddled with factual errors."

CHAPTER 18

THE CLEVEREST
OF THE FOUR
CHILDREN

"Game, set, match! Anna Anderson is out! This is the scuppering of the pro-Anna party!" exulted Sir Brian McGrath, who was with Prince Philip at Sandringham when the news got out. "It's over," declared Prince Rostislav Romanov in London. "It's about time," said Prince Nicholas Romanov in Switzerland. No one was happier than Prince Alexis Scherbatow. "I've been vindicated," he rejoiced in New York. "From the beginning I knew she was a fraud."

On the other side, Anna Anderson's supporters and Anastasia Manahan's friends were shocked, dismayed, and incredulous. "I knew her for twelve years," said Peter Kurth, the author of *Anastasia: The Riddle of Anna Anderson*. "I was involved in her story for nearly thirty years. For me—just because of some tests—I cannot one day say, 'Oh, well, I was wrong.' It isn't that simple. I think it's a shame that a great legend, a wonderful adventure, an astonishing story that inspired so many people, including myself, should suddenly be reduced to a little glass dish."

Brien Horan, a Connecticut lawyer who first met Anna Anderson in 1970 and subsequently produced a never-published dossier of all the evidence, pro and con, pronounced himself "stunned" by the Schanzkowska identity. "You have to forgive me," he said. "I've learned about the Schanzkowska results so recently that, after so many years, it's virtually impossible for me to process this information. But it is just not possible that a Polish peasant in the 1920s, long before television made us all so similar, could have become this woman. I would have had much less trouble if they had found simply that she was not Anastasia. But for them to say that she was a Polish peasant, that's difficult for me to swallow."

Richard and Marina Schweitzer, like Brien Horan, refused to accept the Schanzkowska identity. "I know one thing for certain," said Schweitzer immediately after the London press conference. "Anastasia was not a Polish peasant." Schweitzer made clear that he did not challenge Peter Gill's findings that the Charlottesville tissue Gill had tested was unrelated to Empress Alexandra and probably was related to the Schanzkowska family. Instead, he challenged the legitimacy of the samples Gill had tested.

"To say that Gill was correct, but that Anna Anderson was not Schanzkowska, means that the tissue tested was not Anna Anderson's," Schweitzer explained while he was still in London. "We now feel that there had to be some form of manipulation or substitution. Specifically, that means that somehow, somebody got in and switched or substituted tissue at Martha Jefferson Hospital. The first thing I will do is go back to the hospital and get the documentation on all of their procedures: how the hospital kept its archives, how certain their security system was, how sure they were that it could not have been breached. Then I want to investigate various potential scenarios. When Willi Korte came to see Penny Jenkins in November 1992, how much material did she have on her desk in front of her at the time? Did she have files out that might have had numbers that showed? Were the files arranged in a way that somebody might have read the numbers upside down? Or were the files in her office so that somebody could slip in later, open the file drawer, and say, 'Here it is,' take it out and get the numbers themselves? Penny did tell me that when the doctors first went to find the tissue, they couldn't find it and she had to get up and together they found the right box in the right hole. Then the hospital put it under special guard, in 'proprietary custody.' "

What could be the motive for such a conspiracy? Schweitzer suggested two: "When it looked as though they were going to be thwarted by Lovell from getting access to the tissue by legal means, they took the real tissue away and put something else there [the "something else" would have been Schanzkowska family tissue]. Then, later, after feigning a long search, they could come up with the lost tissue, the real tissue, produce the right results, and get credit for solving the mystery. Or, if their objective was to make sure that she was recognized as Schanzkowska, a substitution would achieve that nicely. Who might 'they' have been? Many people had many reasons—family reasons, almost hereditary reasons—for not wanting her to be Grand Duchess Anastasia. Money would not be a problem for these people."

Schweitzer intended to ask other questions: "Can we determine the sex and the age of the person from whom the tissue was taken? [Gill subsequently informed Schweitzer that the tissue had indeed come from a woman.] Can we determine how old the specimen was as a specimen? That is, was it about fifteen years old, as it would have been as a result of a 1979 operation? What part of the human body was it from, the lower bowel or somewhere else? Was the same kind of preservative used by the hospital at that time? Do the medical records support the fact that the tissue brought out was gangrenous?"

Richard Schweitzer's friends, even those who shared his views, believed that the odds against him were great. Brien Horan, a loyal Anna Anderson supporter, said, "The conspiracy theory is not going to be taken seriously. It's just too hard to imagine that a substitution could be pulled off. It boggles the mind!" But Schweitzer was not backing away. Asked if he minded being called a conspiracy theorist, he said, "I'm seventy years old. I don't care what anybody thinks. I don't have a theory. All I have is a series of conjectures. I'm looking for the truth."

Penny Jenkins, who was responsible for keeping Martha Jefferson Hospital's medical records, including blood and tissue samples, had great respect for Richard Schweitzer, as he did for her. Knowing that he was focusing on a possible substitution of the tissue at the hospital, she telephoned him and said, "That's not possible and here's why." Later, she repeated what she had said to him: "We have two separate backups. In 1979, when Dr. Shrum did surgery on Mrs. Manahan, we took slides of the tissue, in addition to preserving in paraffin the larger blocks of excised tissue. Taking slides when doing surgery is routine; you take it, look at it, and say, this is cancer, or it's not cancer, or it's an infection, or whatever. We preserve these slides in one place and the tissue in paraffin wax in a totally different place.

"Further, when we moved this tissue from storage back to the hospital early in 1993, Dr. Thomas Dudley, the assistant pathologist, cut some new slides from one of the blocks. We compared these new slides cut in 1993 with those original slides cut in 1979. They were identical. If someone had swapped them in storage during the last couple of years, they would not have matched. And the chance that somebody was able to get to both locations and switch both slides without access to specimen numbers is impossible. I don't think Dick wanted to hear this, but I had to tell him."

While he was in London, Richard Schweitzer learned the results of two other DNA tests, one on tissue, the other on hair, both alleged to have come from Anastasia Manahan. Neither was encouraging to Schweitzer's belief that she was Grand Duchess Anastasia. The tissue report came from the Armed Forces Institute of Pathology. Scientists there had extracted mitochondrial DNA from the tissue sample which Susan Barritt had brought to Bethesda from Charlottesville. This profile was compared to Peter Gill's published profile of Prince Philip. The result was the same as that achieved by Gill: there was no match. Thus, AFIP's Charlottesville tissue, like Gill's, was excluded from a relationship with Prince Philip and Empress Alexandra. The institute did not make a comparison with the Polish profile obtained from Karl Maucher. They did not report, therefore, who the donor might be, only who she was not.

Further confirmation of Gill's results came from a surprising source. Susan Burkhart, a thirty-one-year-old Blue Cross–Blue Shield supervisor in Durham, North Carolina, had been intrigued by the Anastasia mystery since she was twelve. In 1992, learning that John Manahan's large library had been sold to a Chapel Hill rare book store, she began spending time in the basement of the store, going through hundreds of boxes of old books. One day, the store's owner, Barry Jones, discovered in one of these boxes an envelope on which Manahan had penciled, "Anastasia's hair." Inside was a matted clump of hair, which appeared to have been removed from a hairbrush. The hair was "salt and pepper with some strands of auburn" and, significantly, still had follicles attached at the roots. Burkhart, married to a DNA researcher, knew the importance of follicles and bought the envelope and its contents for twenty dollars. Eventually, Peter Kurth put Burkhart in touch with DNA enthusiast Syd Mandelbaum, who arranged for Dr. Mark Stoneking at Penn State to test the hair for DNA.

On September 7, 1994, Susan Burkhart sent six strands of hair to Stoneking. He managed to extract mitochondrial DNA and confirmed that it had the same DNA sequence as that obtained from the Charlottesville tissue by Peter Gill. Stoneking then compared the profile obtained from the hair with the published Hessian profile taken by Peter Gill from the blood sample provided by the Duke of Edinburgh. Stoneking found that the two did not match; therefore, not being related to Prince Philip, the owner of the hair could not be related to Empress Alexandra. Stoneking concluded that "if the hair samples are from the claimant Anna Anderson, this analysis indicated that she could not be the Grand Duchess Anastasia."*

Stoneking's results on the hair greatly reassured Peter Gill about the accuracy of his own DNA tests. The Armed Forces Institute of Pathology had used the same source, the Charlottesville tissue, and derived the same results; Mark Stoneking, using a different source, had come up with the same DNA sequence and the same results. For

---

*Mark Stoneking did not test the Charlottesville tissue sample which had been sent to him. After Dr. Gill and AFIP both came up with similar results, Stoneking advised Richard Schweitzer that a third test on the same tissue would be unlikely to produce a different result. This tissue remains in Dr. Stoneking's laboratory, preserved and frozen, for use in future research.

Richard Schweitzer's theory of tissue substitution, however, Stone-king's hair results were harmful: how likely was it that conspirators had not only penetrated Martha Jefferson Hospital to substitute Schanzkowska tissue for Anastasia Manahan's but also had planted a clump of hair in an envelope with John Manahan's writing on it and left it to be found years later in the basement of a North Carolina bookstore?

As Schweitzer continued to fight, he was criticized for his refusal to accept the findings of science. The London *Evening Standard* described him as "displaying the tireless enthusiasm of the sort which keeps the Flat Earth Society in business." *Nature Genetics,* a usually authoritative journal, editorialized, "Why is it that Schweitzer and his supporters refuse to accept the results and are even now exploring other ways of proving themselves and the late Anna Anderson right? What, given such reluctance, does the scientific community have to do to convince the public that it knows what it is talking about?" Unfortunately for its own reputation, *Nature Genetics* stumbled badly in handling the editorial. The writer was the same Dr. Adrian Ivinson who had testified on behalf of the Russian Nobility Association in the Charlottesville courtroom. In addition to displaying an ill-tempered bias against the Schweitzers (Richard Schweitzer was described as being "married to a woman who claimed to be the granddaughter of Dr. Botkin"), the editorial was marred by numerous errors involving the persons concerned in the case, the sequence of events, the findings of various scientists, and even the science of genetics. Eventually, the journal apologized.

Maurice Philip Remy continued through the winter and spring of 1995 to look for a way to make his own contribution to resolving Anna Anderson's identity. Ironically, after two and a half years of intensive effort, he had achieved little. He never obtained access to the Charlottesville tissue. He did not possess any of the Chapel Hill hair. His only source of what he believed was Anna Anderson DNA was the

1951 blood slide from which Charles Ginther at Berkeley was unable
to extract DNA. Remy's scientist, Dr. Bernd Herrmann of Göttingen
University, did find nuclear DNA on the slide. Comparing short tandem repeats taken from this slide to the published STRs of Nicholas
and Alexandra, Herrmann declared that Anna Anderson could not
have been Anastasia. Unfortunately for Remy, Peter Gill declared at
the October 5 London press conference that the DNA from Remy's
slide and the DNA from the Charlottesville tissue did not match. No
one, therefore, knew who the donor of Remy's blood slide had been.
In addition, Gill has quietly expressed doubt about Dr. Herrmann's
technique. An attempt to get DNA from a slide which is highly vulnerable to contamination is almost certain to go wrong, Gill believes;
a scientist is more likely to get DNA from his own breath or his own
saliva. Finally, Dr. Gill said that, until the name came up in connection with Remy's claim of triumph in the *Sunday Times,* he had never
heard of Dr. Herrmann.*

Nevertheless, in May 1995, Remy was still urging his scientists to
try to extract more DNA from the blood slide and send it to Ginther
for comparison with his Hessian profiles. If Ginther were to obtain a
match (indicating that the donor was related to Empress Alexandra),
this would indeed be news, and all previous test results would have to
be reevaluated. The irony is that this result would delight Remy's
erstwhile antagonists, the Schweitzers, and dismay his former allies,
the Hessians and Prince Scherbatov.

A new result would not, at this stage, have greatly concerned Dr.
Willi Korte, who, no longer employed by Remy, had returned to
tracking stolen art. The relationship between Remy and Korte was
distant. Korte, a professional investigator, was not pleased that Remy
had claimed credit for most of the original thinking in the case.
(Korte told the *Abendzeitung* of Munich that the idea of identifying
Anna Anderson by tracking down samples of remaining tissue or
blood—which Remy had claimed was his—had come to him in Au-

---

*Pavel Ivanov also is unfamiliar with the work of Dr. Herrmann. "You know, we
read all the papers in our field and we know pretty much who is doing what,"
Ivanov said. "No, I have never heard of him."

gust 1992 as he was sitting in the lobby of Moscow's Slavanskaya Hotel.) "To make a long story short," Korte said, "I set this whole thing up. But I don't consider it one of my better cases. It did fall apart. I had too many amateurs running around. At the end, certain people sort of lost their nerve. They were all over the place, trying to save their skins."

Who was Franziska Schanzkowska, the woman who for over sixty years had claimed to be Grand Duchess Anastasia? She was born in 1896 in the Prussian province of Posen, adjacent to the border with Poland, which was then a part of the Russian Empire. Two hundred years before, her family had belonged to the lesser Polish nobility, but by the end of the nineteenth century, the family were farmworkers. Franziska's father, an impoverished alcoholic, died when his children were young. In the village where she grew up, Franziska always was different and solitary. She did not make friends, and she tried especially to distance herself from her sisters by assuming what they considered an affected, upper-class manner. At harvesttime, when the entire village was out in the fields bringing in hay, Franziska would be found lying in a cart reading books on history.

"My Auntie Franziska was the cleverest of the four children," said Waltraud Schanzkowska, a resident of Hamburg. "She didn't want to be buried in a little one-horse town. She wanted to come out into the world, to become an actress—something special." In 1914, shortly before the outbreak of the First World War, Franziska, at age eighteen, left the Polish provinces for Berlin. She worked as a waitress, met a young man, and became engaged. Before she could marry, her fiancé was called up for military service. Franziska began working in a munitions factory. In 1916, the young man was killed on the western front. Soon afterward, Franziska let a grenade slip from her hands on the assembly line. It exploded nearby, inflicting splinter wounds on her head and other parts of her body and eviscerating a foreman, who died before her eyes. She was sent to a sanatorium, where her physical injuries healed but the shock remained. Franziska was declared "not cured, but not dangerous," and discharged. She was taken in, almost as a charity case, by Frau Wingender, who gave her a room of her own. Incapable of working long periods, Franziska was in and out of sanatoria; in between, she remained bedridden at the Wingenders' apartment, complaining of headaches, swallowing pills, and reading history books from the local library. In February 1920, her favorite brother, Felix, received a last message from her. On February 17, 1920, she disappeared.

According to Peter Gill, DNA is infallible, and therefore we know that Fräulein Unbekannt, Anna Tschaikovsky, Anna Anderson, and Anastasia Manahan all evolved from Franziska Schanzkowska. Her Polish family identity explains the central flaw in her claim: that is, her ability to understand Russian but not to speak it as a native. Nevertheless, it was an astonishing and brilliant performance. Almost certainly, she did not start out as an impostor. She was in Dalldorf asylum for two years; she had a strong resemblance to one of the tsar's daughters; people around her wanted to believe. Then she went out and lived among the emigres. Here was an interesting new life. People paid attention to her; some bowed and curtsied and called her Your Imperial Highness. In time, her mind absorbed this alternative identity and she was transformed.

After Peter Gill's press conference, some of Anna Anderson's supporters said that perhaps she was not the daughter of the tsar but she could not possibly have been a Polish peasant. Yet many famous professional actresses, of equally humble origins, have convinced audiences playing the roles of majestic grandes dames. A great lady is not necessarily a woman of ancient pedigree and expensive schooling; she can be someone accustomed to a certain milieu for a long time and confident of her position. Anna Anderson had sixty-three years to learn the part.

She had a strong and emphatic personality, and she was sure of the role she had found for herself. Even her enemy Dr. Gunther von Berenberg-Gossler, who opposed her claim for years in the German courts, paid tribute to that "exceptional" quality and to her "life achievement." "Be prepared," he said to a young man about to meet her for the first time. "She will win you over. She has the greatest suggestive power of any person I have ever met." In fact, after the early years, she herself never attempted to persuade people of her identity. Instead, it was others who adopted her cause, took her claim to court, and demanded of the world that she be recognized.

Now, more than a decade after her death, the mystery of her identity has been solved. The woman pulled from a Berlin canal was not Grand Duchess Anastasia; she was an impostor with astonishing physical similarities to the young woman who died in an Ekaterinburg cellar in 1918. Nevertheless, her life *was* exceptional. If, once upon a time, she was a Polish factory worker, she became—in her own mind and the minds of her supporters—a princess. Her performance, still so vivid that some cannot put it aside, lent color to the twentieth century. Many real grand dukes and grand duchesses survived the revolution and then lived and died in relative obscurity. Against this backdrop, only one woman will be remembered: Anna Anderson.

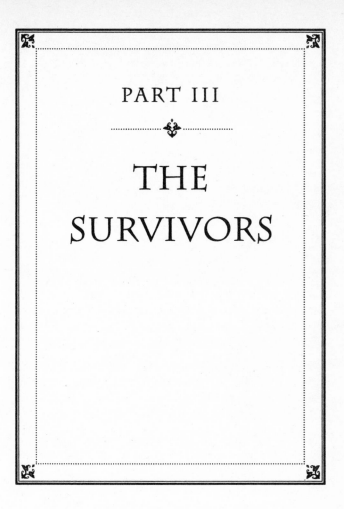

PART III

❖

THE
SURVIVORS

········· ❖ ·········

CHAPTER 19

THE
ROMANOV
EMIGRES

The slaughter of the Romanovs neither began nor ended with the tsar's immediate family. The first Romanov to die after Lenin's seizure of power was sixty-eight-year-old Grand Duke Nicholas Constantinovich, who, as a result of banishment to Central Asia by Tsar Alexander II, had lived most of his life in Tashkent. Here he was killed by the Bolsheviks in unknown circumstances in February 1918. The second Romanov murdered was Nicholas II's younger brother forty-year-old Grand Duke Michael. Arrested at Gatchina, near Petrograd, Michael and his English secretary, Brian Johnson, were interned in a hotel in Perm in the Urals. For six months Michael was treated liberally, granted "all the rights of a citizen of the republic," and allowed to stroll in the town and go to church. Then, on the night of July 13, 1918—three days before the murders in Ekaterinburg—three men burst into Michael's hotel room, seized him and his secretary, ordered them into two small carriages, and drove them into the countryside. Turning off the road into the forest, they stopped and offered the grand duke a cigarette. As he smoked, one of the captors pulled out a revolver and shot Johnson in the temple. Michael, arms outstretched, ran toward his secretary and friend, as if to protect him. Three bullets were fired into Michael. The bodies were covered with twigs to be buried later. Andrew Markov, chief of the murderers, then went to Moscow, where, at Yakov Sverdlov's suggestion, he was taken to tell his story to Lenin.

Less than twenty-four hours after the Imperial family was murdered in Ekaterinburg, six more Romanovs were killed 120 miles away, at Alapayevsk. They included Grand Duchess Elizabeth, age fifty-four, sister of Empress Alexandra; Grand Duke Sergei Mikhailovich, forty-nine; three sons of Grand Duke Constantine: Prince John, thirty-two, Prince Constantine, twenty-seven, and Prince Igor, twenty-four; and Prince Vladimir Paley, twenty-one, the son by a morganatic marriage of Nicholas II's uncle Grand Duke Paul.

Grand Duchess Elizabeth, like her sister, had been born a German princess in Hesse-Darmstadt. A widow and a nun since the 1905 assassination of her husband, Grand Duke Sergei Alexandrovich (Nicholas II's uncle), she almost seemed to be seeking martyrdom. After the tsar's abdication and even after the Bolshevik assumption of power, Elizabeth turned down all offers of security and escape. In March 1917, the Provisional Government had asked her to leave her convent and take refuge in the Kremlin. She had refused. Early in 1918, Kaiser Wilhelm II, who had loved her before either he or she was married, had tried several times though diplomatic channels to bring her to safety in Germany. Again, she refused. Transferred by the Bolsheviks to Alapayevsk, east of the Urals, she spent the winter of 1917–18 in a former provincial school called the House by the Fields. The day after her sister's death, Elizabeth and the other Romanovs interned with her were forced into peasant carts and taken into the country to the opening of an abandoned mine shaft.

Accounts differ as to how they died. Until recently, Nicholas Sokolov's version was widely accepted: the victims were blindfolded and ordered to walk across a log placed over the top of the sixty-foot pit. All obeyed except Grand Duke Sergei, a former artilleryman, who struggled and was shot immediately. The others, unable to see as they walked out onto the log, inevitably toppled into the pit. To complete the work, hand grenades and heavy timbers were thrown down on top of them. Not all died immediately, however. A peasant, creeping to the edge of the pit after the assassins departed, reported hearing hymns being sung at the bottom of the shaft. When the Whites found the bodies—this is according to Sokolov's story—a wound on the head of one of the young men had been bound up with the handkerchief of the grand duchess. Autopsies, Sokolov wrote, revealed that the mouths and stomachs of some of the victims were filled with dirt, indicating that some had actually died of exposure, thirst, and starvation. Now this story is contradicted by other evidence discovered by the investigating officer Vladimir Soloviev. The grand duchess, the grand duke, and the four young men, Soloviev believes, were simply taken to the mouth of the pit, shot in the head, and tumbled into the shaft.

Six months later, on January 28, 1919, four more grand dukes, including the tsar's uncle Paul (who was the father of Prince Paley killed at Alapayevsk), were executed in Petrograd in the courtyard of the Peter and Paul Fortress. Their bodies were dumped into a mass grave in one of the fortress bastions. (So many prisoners were executed at this time in this place and the bones became so intermingled that no attempt to separate them has been—or is likely to be—attempted.) One of these murdered grand dukes was Nicholas Mikhailovich, a distinguished liberal historian. On the basis of his reputation as a scholar, the writer Maxim Gorky pleaded with Lenin that this grand duke be spared. Lenin refused. "The revolution does not need historians," he said.

Along with Tsar Nicholas II and Empress Alexandra, the Bolsheviks massacred seventeen other Romanovs, including eight of sixteen grand dukes living at the time of the revolution, five of seventeen grand duchesses, and four young princes of the blood. After this carnage, there remained the dowager empress, eight grand dukes, and twelve grand duchesses, four of whom were foreigners who received the title on marrying Russian grand dukes.

❧

By 1919, the largest concentration of Romanov survivors was in the Crimea, where a cluster of family summer palaces provided familiar places of refuge. The tsar's mother, Dowager Empress Marie, was at the Imperial palace of Livadia, overlooking the Black Sea resort town of Yalta. With Marie was her daughter Grand Duchess Olga, accompanied by Olga's new husband, Colonel Nicholas Kulikovsky, and their infant son, Tikhon. Nearby, Marie's older daughter, Grand Duchess Xenia, her husband, Grand Duke Alexander, and six of their seven children were at the palace of Ai-Todor. Also nearby, in his own palace, was Grand Duke Nicholas Nicholaevich, commander in chief of the Russian Army at the outbreak of war. Nicholas Nicholaevich's brother, Grand Duke Peter, was with him, along with their wives, the Montenegrin sisters, Grand Duchesses Anastasia and Militsa. Grand Duke Nicholas had no children, but Grand Duke Peter's twenty-one-year-old son, Prince Roman, was present.

For eighteen months, while the Russian civil war swayed back and forth, the band of imperial refugees sheltered uneasily in these comfortable but insecure surroundings. Their suspense ended in April 1919, when the British battleship HMS *Marlborough* arrived in Yalta and offered to remove the dowager empress. Marie refused to depart unless the British agreed to embark all the Romanovs, their servants, and a number of others who wanted to go. When the large warship sailed for Malta, her broad decks were crowded with Russians, none of whom would see their country again. From the *Marlborough*, the refugees scattered across Europe and the world. The dowager empress returned to her native Denmark, where her nephew Christian X was king. Eventually, Grand Duchess Xenia, separated from her husband, moved to London, where she lived from 1936 to 1960 in a small mansion provided by the British Crown and named, appropriately, Wilderness House. Grand Duchess Olga and her husband remained in Denmark until after the Second World War, when they moved to Canada. After her husband died, Olga moved in with a Russian couple in an apartment over a barbershop in Toronto. She died there in November 1960, seven months after the death of her sister, Xenia.

Another family of Romanovs survived because the revolution found them at their summer estate in Kislovodsk in the Caucasus. This was Grand Duchess Marie Pavlovna, the German-born widow of Nicholas II's eldest uncle, Grand Duke Vladimir, and her two younger sons, Grand Duke Boris and Grand Duke Andrew. Each of these men was accompanied by his mistress; Boris by Zinaida Rachevsky and Andrew by Mathilde Kschessinska, the former prima ballerina who, before Nicholas II's marriage and assumption of the throne, had been the tsar's first and only mistress. Once out of Russia, both grand dukes married their companions and settled down in Paris and its suburbs.

Their elder brother, Grand Duke Cyril, his English-born wife, Grand Duchess Victoria, and their two young daughters were the only Romanovs who left Russia by a northern route. This was not difficult because they left in June 1917, when the moderate Provisional Government was still in power. They asked permission of Alexander Kerensky, then a leading minister, received their papers, boarded a train in Petrograd, and departed for Finland. Later that summer, while they were still in Finland, their son Vladimir was born. Grand Duke Dimitri, the twenty-six-year-old murderer of Rasputin and a first cousin of both Nicholas II and Grand Duke Cyril, left Russia by an extreme southerly route. He had been exiled to the Caucasus for his role in the assassination, and soon after the tsar abdicated he escaped over the mountains into Persia.

Over the past seventy-five years, the surviving Romanovs have subdivided into five subclans, each named, in Russian fashion, for a patriarch. They are the Mikhailovichi, the Vladimirovichi, the Pavlovichi, the Constantinovichi, and the Nicholaevichi. The Mikhailovichi, descended from Michael, a son of Tsar Nicholas I, are closest by blood to Tsar Nicholas II and also the most numerous. These were and are the children and grandchildren of Nicholas's sister Grand Duchess Xenia and her husband, Grand Duke Alexander, a son of the aforementioned Michael. Xenia had seven children, born around the turn of this century. Her eldest child was Irina, who married one of Rasputin's assassins, Prince Yussoupov. The Yussoupovs settled in Paris, where they lived for almost fifty years until they died. They had one child, a daughter, who had a daughter, who has a daughter. It was Yussoupov's granddaughter Xenia Sfiris who provided a blood sample to Peter Gill which helped him to identify the femur of Nicholas II.

Grand Duchess Xenia also had six sons. These boys and young men grew up in the West, living first with their mother in Denmark and London, then scattering to Paris, Biarritz, Cannes, Chicago, and San Francisco. Germany, the usual source of Romanov brides, was barren for this purpose after the First World War, so these youthful princes married young women from the aristocratic Russian families they knew—Kutuzovs, Galitzines, Sheremetyevs, Vorontsov-Dashkovs—the oldest and most glittering names of the Russian nobility. Xenia's sons were well spoken, well mannered, well educated, and well tailored, but not ambitious or energetic. "They spoke six languages," says Rostislav Romanov, whose father, also named Rostislav, was one of the six brothers. "But nobody ever said anything, so they were always referred to as being silent in six languages. I remember taking my father to see his brother Nikita. They said hello to each other and the conversation died. Another day one of Nikita's sons suggested, 'Why don't we drive over and see Uncle Rostislav?' Nikita said, 'Why? I already know him.' " Grand Duchess Xenia's youngest son, Prince Vassily, who was born in 1907 and left Russia at twelve, spent most of his adult life in Woodside, California, near San Francisco. He raised award-winning tomatoes and held a number of jobs, including selling (and delivering) champagne and wine. His private joke was to arrive at the back door of the estate of a friend, deliver the cases ordered, then put on his coat and tie, go around to the front door, ring the bell, present his card, which announced Prince Vassily of Russia, and ask whether madame was at home.

Prince Vassily died in 1987, and Xenia's grandchildren now are men and women in their sixties and seventies. The men, all referred to in society and the press as Prince Romanov, have followed varied careers. Prince Andrew, who served as a Royal Navy seaman on the arctic convoy route during World War II, is a painter who lives in Inverness, California. Prince Michael, whose grandfathers both were grand dukes, has spent most of his life as a film director in France and now lives in Paris and Biarritz. Prince Nikita, a historian with a Ph.D. from Stanford, lives in New York, as does his brother Prince Alexander. The youngest and most active of these princes is Rostislav, who speaks English with a wholly American accent. This is unsurprising, as he was born and grew up in Chicago, went to an American prep school, and was graduated from Yale. In New Haven, none of his classmates cared that he was a Romanov, and he himself cared mostly about crew. Today, he is a London merchant banker commuting daily from Sussex to Waterloo Station. Although he has worked in England for fourteen years, the British Royal family—like his Yale class—has not noticed his presence. Rostislav does not mind. He is an Anglophile. He does not want to go back to Russia except to visit. "Life in this country suits me," he says.

After Nicholas II's sisters, nephews, and nieces, the tsar's closest surviving relatives were the Vladimirovichi, then comprising his four first cousins, Grand Dukes Cyril, Boris, and Andrew and their sister, Grand Duchess Helen, all children of Nicholas's eldest uncle, Grand Duke Vladimir. In normal times, the near-simultaneous deaths of a tsar, his son, and his brother, as happened in 1918, automatically would have promoted the eldest of these cousins, Cyril, who was forty-two in 1918, to the Imperial throne. In 1918, however, there was neither empire nor throne, and, consequently, nothing was automatic. Succession to the Russian throne followed the Salic law, meaning that the crown passed only to males, through males, until there were no more eligible males. When an emperor died and neither a son nor a brother was available, the eldest eligible male from the branch of the family closest to the deceased monarch would succeed. In this case, under the old laws, this was Cyril. After Cyril stood his two brothers, Boris and Andrew, and after them the only surviving male of the Pavlovich line, their first cousin Grand Duke Dimitri, the son of Nicholas II's youngest uncle, Grand Duke Paul. Nicholas II's six nephews, the sons of the tsar's sister Xenia, were closer by blood than Cyril but were ineligible because the succession could not pass through a woman.

Cyril, living in France, was cautious about putting forth his claim as pretender. The Dowager Empress Marie would not believe that her son and his family were dead and refused to attend any memorial service on their behalf. A succession proclamation by Cyril would have shocked and deeply offended the old woman. Further, there was another, not very willing pretender: Grand Duke Nicholas Nicholaevich, former commander in chief of the Russian Army, was from the Nicholaevichi, a more distant branch of the Romanov tree, but, among Russians, he was far more respected and popular than Cyril. Nicholas Nicholaevich was forceful and Russia's most famous soldier whereas Cyril was a naval captain, who, having had one ship sunk beneath him, refused to go to sea again. Nevertheless, when emigre Russians spoke to Grand Duke Nicholas about assuming the throne in exile, he refused, explaining that he did not wish to shatter the hopes of the dowager empress. Besides, Nicholas agreed with Marie that if Nicholas II, his son, and his brother really were dead, the Russian people should be free to choose as their new tsar whatever Romanov— or whatever Russian—they wished.

In 1922, six years before the death of Marie and while the old soldier Nicholas Nicholaevich still had seven years to live, Cyril decided to wait no longer. He proclaimed himself first Curator of the Throne and then, in 1924, Tsar of All the Russias—although he announced that for everyday use he still should be addressed by the lesser title Grand Duke. He established a court around his small villa in the village of Saint-Briac in Brittany, issued manifestos, and distributed titles. Although, technically, his daughters and son were princesses and a prince, he—in his new capacity as tsar—elevated them to grand duchesses and grand duke. When his cousin Grand Duke Dimitri supported his claim, Cyril responded by ennobling Dimitri's American wife, Audrey Emery, as Princess Romanovsky-Ilyinsky; in 1929, Dimitri and Audrey passed this name and princely title to their infant son, Paul.

Cyril was sixty-two when he died in October 1938 in the American Hospital in Paris and passed his claim to his twenty-one-year-old son, Vladimir. This young man, privately tutored at home and then in a Russian lycée in Paris, spent his summers tinkering with motorcycles and zooming them down the narrow roads of Brittany. At one point he spent six months working in a machine shop in England, in order "to experience the life of a working-class person." In 1946 he moved to Madrid, and two years later, at thirty-one, he married a

Georgian princess, Leonida Bagration-Moukhransky. Leonida had previously been married to an older, wealthy, expatriate American, Sumner Moore Kirby, by whom she had a daughter, Helen. In 1937, twenty-three-year-old Leonida divorced Kirby. He remained in France during the Second World War, was seized by the Gestapo, and died in a German concentration camp.

For the four and a half decades of their marriage, Vladimir and Leonida lived quietly. They occupied a villa in Madrid during the winter, moved to Saint-Briac in the summer, and maintained an apartment in Paris. Occasionally, they visited New York, where monarchist friends rented limousines, gave dinners, and listened while Vladimir addressed them in impeccable English, Russian, French, and Spanish. I met him several times on these occasions. He was a handsome, pleasant, soft-spoken man, who, in the tradition of royalty, said little that was remarkable. His real passion was for machinery: the construction and operation of cars, motorcycles, and helicopters. He was neither scholar nor historian; when his boyhood friend Alistair Forbes prodded him to investigate the Anna Anderson identity, Vladimir replied amiably, "Oh, yes, Ali, I daresay all you say is true, but I shan't let you see the papers I have on the subject, so let's talk of something else." Vladimir had no occupation other than being pretender, and most people assumed that the couple was supported by Helen Kirby, who had inherited her father's American fortune and lived with her mother and stepfather.

Grand Duke Vladimir and Leonida had only one child, Maria, born in 1953, when her mother was thirty-nine. In 1969, when it was obvious that he would never have a son, Vladimir acted to ensure that the succession would remain within his line. He issued a manifesto which proclaimed, to the chagrin of most other Romanovs, that upon his death his daughter would become Curatrix of the Throne. Maria had been brought up to fulfill a significant dynastic role. She was educated in Madrid and Paris and eventually spent several terms studying Russian history and literature at Oxford University. In 1978, she married a Hohenzollern prince, Franz Wilhelm of Prussia, a great-grandson of Kaiser Wilhelm II. Before their marriage, Franz Wilhelm converted to Orthodoxy, took the Russian name Michael Pavlovich, and was awarded the title of grand duke by his new father-in-law. In 1981 Maria and her husband produced their only child, George, whose grandfather also gave him the title of grand duke.

Vladimir never expected to return to Russia as tsar, although he frequently announced that he was ready. By the time of *glasnost* and *perestroika*, he was seventy, and when Yeltsin was elected president he had reached seventy-four. Suddenly, events accelerated. A few weeks after Yeltsin's inauguration in July 1991, the president and the pretender exchanged letters. That autumn, the city of Leningrad voted to take back its name St. Petersburg. The mayor, Anatoly Sobchak, invited the Romanov pretender to attend the celebration. Vladimir and Leonida flew to the former Imperial capital and looked down from a balcony of the former Winter Palace (now the Hermitage Museum) on sixty thousand people filling the Palace Square. Subsequently, when Vladimir entered a room to hold a press conference, three hundred journalists, Russians and foreigners, rose to their feet. Five months later Vladimir flew to Miami to give a speech to fifteen hundred business and financial leaders. Answering questions during a press conference, he slumped in his chair and died soon afterward. Two days later Yeltsin signed a decree permitting the first funeral mass for a Romanov in Russia in three quarters of a century. On May 29, 1992, Vladimir was buried in a vault in the Cathedral of St. Peter and St. Paul in St. Petersburg.

Vladimir's status as pretender to the Russian throne appeared to have been endorsed by Sobchak and perhaps even by Yeltsin, but it was hotly contested by the majority of Romanovs. The schism that has divided the family—that plagued Vladimir while he was alive and today bedevils his daughter—did not begin with either of them. It began with Vladimir's father, the first pretender, Grand Duke Cyril.

The Russian Law of Succession to the throne, established by Emperor Paul in 1797, set five criteria for succession: First, the monarch must be Orthodox. Second, the monarch must be a male as long as there are any eligible males in the Imperial house. Third, the mother and wife of a male monarch or male heir close in the line of succession must be Orthodox at the time of marriage. Fourth, the monarch or heir must make an "equal marriage" to a woman from another "ruling house"; an unequal marriage to a woman of lesser rank, even a woman from the highest level of the aristocracy, disqualified that couple and their offspring from reaching the throne. Fifth, the future monarch could marry only with the permission of the reigning tsar. (Unlike Britain, Russia did not make a woman's previous divorce an impediment to her marrying into the Imperial family or even eventually becoming the consort of a tsar.) Grand Duke Cyril failed to meet two of these requirements: Neither his mother nor his wife was Orthodox when she married. And Cyril married without the permission of—indeed, in defiance of—Tsar Nicholas II.

Cyril's mother, Grand Duchess Marie Pavlovna, a German princess from Mecklenburg-Schwerin, had insisted on remaining Lutheran when she married Cyril's father, Grand Duke Vladimir. She remained Lutheran for thirty-four years after her marriage. In 1908 she realized that, because of the illness of the little Tsarevich Alexis, her husband and her son Cyril were close in line of succession to the throne. In order to promote their chances, Marie Pavlovna belatedly converted to Orthodoxy. By then, however, Cyril's affairs were wretchedly tangled on other accounts. As a young man he had fallen in love with his cousin Victoria Melita, a granddaughter of Queen Victoria. But the old queen, constantly arranging marriages for her dozens of progeny, decided that Victoria Melita should marry her grandson on another side, Grand Duke Ernest of Hesse. Victoria Melita, although she was in love with Cyril, obeyed her grandmother. Her marriage to Ernest was unhappy—Ernest's feelings about women were ambivalent—and Victoria Melita began spending weeks at a time with Cyril in Russia and Germany. From a distance, Cyril's appeal for the Hessian grand duchess is difficult to understand; he was described by Victoria Melita's sister, later Queen Marie of Rumania, as "the marble man...extraordinarily cold and selfish...he seems to freeze you up and has such a disdaining way of treating...people." Nevertheless, within months of Queen Victoria's death in 1901, Victoria Melita and Ernest were divorced, and she looked forward to marrying Cyril.

There were, however, obstacles to the marriage. Victoria Melita's dynastic credentials were splendidly in order: she was of the House of Saxe-Coburg, which occupied the throne of England. And although the Russian Orthodox Church prohibited marriage between first cousins—as she and Cyril were—Victoria Melita did not become Orthodox until three years after her marriage. Ironically, this fact, while helping her avoid one pitfall, plunged her into another: it violated the rule of the Russian Imperial house that men in line for the throne may marry only women who were Orthodox at the time of their marriage. Most significant, however, was that the marriage lacked the permission of the reigning tsar. Here the problem was that Victoria Melita's former husband, Ernest of Hesse, was the brother of Nicholas II's wife. The puritanical empress was infuriated by Victoria Melita's rejection of her brother and her open affair with Cyril. Alexandra, having the ear of the tsar, was determined to block the marriage.

One can only sympathize with Nicholas II, overwhelmed by the political problems of ruling an empire and also afflicted by marital upheavals in the extended Imperial family. Real love matches, like the tsar's own, were rare. Some Romanovs married stolid German princesses and settled down to a lifetime of tedium; others, like Boris and Andrew, and Sergei Mikhailovich, took lively, near-permanent mistresses; still others, like the tsar's brother Grand Duke Michael and his uncle Grand Duke Paul, married previously married Russian women beneath their rank. Michael had a son before a morganatic marriage to his lover; Paul had two children by the woman he married morganatically. Nicholas II, attempting to enforce the law, banished his brother and uncle from Russia.

Cyril and Victoria Melita, in the tsar's view, were guilty of similar illegal conduct when, in 1905, they secretly married in Germany. When Cyril returned home, hoping to carry the day by presenting a fait accompli, he was instead stripped of his rank and command in the navy, deprived of the allowance he received as a member of the Imperial family, and ordered to leave Russia within forty-eight hours. His wife was denied the title of Grand Duchess. The couple lived in a small apartment on the avenue Henri-Martin in Paris, until, in 1909, on the death of Cyril's father, their banishment was revoked. Nevertheless, despite official reconciliation, antagonism between the families ran deep.

During the First World War, Cyril, promoted to rear admiral for no reason other than his name, remained in St. Petersburg commanding the Garde Equipage, an elite unit of sailors which in peacetime provided crews for the Imperial yachts. At the moment of crisis, in February 1917, Nicholas II was at Army Headquarters, five hundred miles from the capital. Empress Alexandra and her five children, all but Marie confined to darkened rooms with measles, were at the Alexander Palace at Tsarskoe Selo, fifteen miles from the city. A hostile crowd of mutinous soldiers from St. Petersburg was looting and drinking in the town, shouting its intention to seize "the German woman" and her son. The most reliable unit guarding the palace was a battalion of the Garde Equipage which established its campfires and soup kitchens in the palace courtyard. On the night of March 13, Alexandra, throwing a cloak over her shoulders and accompanied by her daughter Marie, went out among the sailors.

"The scene was unforgettable," wrote Baroness Buxhoevden, who watched from a window above. "It was dark, except for a faint light thrown up from the snow and reflected on the polished barrels of the rifles. The troops were lined up in battle order...the figures of the Empress and her daughter passed from line to line, the white palace looming a ghostly mass in the background." Walking from man to man, Alexandra told them that she trusted them completely and that the life of the heir was in their hands. Returning to the palace, she was exuberant. "They are all our friends," she said. In relays, she brought the men into the palace to drink hot tea.

Thirty-six hours later, when the empress looked out on the morning of March 15, the courtyard was empty. Grand Duke Cyril had ordered the Garde Equipage to return to St. Petersburg, leaving the tsar's wife and children undefended. The previous day Cyril had—in the words of French ambassador Maurice Paléologue—"come out openly in favor of the revolution." Sporting a red cockade on his naval uniform, he had placed himself at the head of his men and marched down the Nevsky Prospect to the Duma, where he had offered his services to Duma president Michael Rodzianko. Nicholas II was still on the throne, and Rodzianko was struggling to retain the monarchy in some form. Disgusted by Cyril's breach of his oath to the tsar, he told the grand duke, "Go away. Your place is not here." A week later Cyril compounded his betrayal. In an interview with a Petrograd newspaper, he said, "I have asked myself several times if the ex-empress were an accomplice of Wilhelm [the kaiser] but each time forced myself to recoil from the thought." At that time Ambassador Paléologue went down Glinka Street and, he said, "saw something waving over [Grand Duke Cyril's] palace: a red flag." For the remainder of Cyril's life, many Russian monarchists, even those who admitted that, despite his mother's Lutheranism, he should be the legitimate pretender, considered that his abandonment of the empress and her children, his breach of oath to his sovereign, and his display of a red cockade and a red flag disqualified his claim to the throne.

Grand Duke Vladimir's life was free from the shame that disgraced his father, but it was, nevertheless, filled with disputation. Vladimir's marriage, like Cyril's, transgressed a rule of the Imperial family. Leonida Bagration-Moukhransky was unquestionably Orthodox. Leonida certainly had the "tsar's" permission, for the "tsar" was Vladimir himself. She had previously been married and divorced, but divorce was not objectionable to the church and had not been raised as an argument against Cyril. The sticking point in Vladimir's marriage to Leonida was whether she was descended from a "ruling house." The argument here is arcane, but, within the family, bitterly contested. Leonida Bagration-Moukhransky descends from a branch of the family which ruled the kingdom of Georgia for three centuries. In 1800 Tsar Paul annexed Georgia into the Russian Empire and, in the opinion of *Burke's Royal Families of the World,* "the Georgian kingdom ceased to exist...the princes of the blood royal were deported to Russia [and] their descendants were assimilated into the Russian aristocracy." The Bagrations quickly became a leading family of the Russian nobility; Marshal Peter Bagration became a hero in the war against Napoleon and died on the field of Borodino. For over a hundred years, the Bagrations—like the Galitzines, the Sheremet-yevs, and others—served the tsars in the Russian Army and at the Imperial court. Vladimir and Leonida, however, insisted that the Bagrations remained "a ruling house." Thus, they contended, she was fully qualified to become the wife of a man who claimed the throne, to carry the title Grand Duchess of Russia, and to provide children and grandchildren who could become future sovereigns.

Vladimir and Leonida, feeling the weakness of their own position, were always aggressive on questions of "equal marriage" and "ruling houses" when these applied to other Romanovs. In their view, since the revolution no Romanov male except Vladimir had made an equal marriage to a woman from a ruling house. By marrying unequally, all these others had disqualified their children not only from succession to the throne but from membership in the Imperial family, from using the title Prince, and even from calling themselves by the family name of Romanov. In Vladimir's view, it was this dynastic horizon, barren of eligible males, that gave him the right to elevate his sixteen-year-old daughter to the succession.

This 1969 proclamation stirred opposition among the several dozen people to whom the news that they were neither princes nor Romanovs was surprising and disagreeable. The leading members of the three other extant branches—Prince Vsevolod of the Constantinovichi, Prince Roman of the Nicholaevichi, and Prince Andrew of the Mikhailovichi, all born in Russia before the revolution (as Vladimir was not)—banded together to protest in writing. In this letter, they addressed Vladimir not as Grand Duke but merely as Prince, which would have been his prerevolutionary title. They declared that Leonida, having married Vladimir unequally, had no higher status than the wives of other Romanov princes and that she was not entitled to be called Grand Duchess. They said that they did not recognize Maria as a grand duchess and declared her proclamation as future curatrix of the Russian throne and head of the Russian Imperial house illegal.

Intrafamily warfare continued in 1976, when Maria married Prince Franz Wilhelm of Prussia and Vladimir promoted his son-in-law to grand duke. It became even worse in 1981, when Maria's son George was born and Vladimir named his new grandson a grand duke. Prince Vassily, a nephew of Nicholas II, responded that "the Romanov Family Association hereby declares that the joyful event in the Prussian royal house does not concern the Romanov Family Association since the newborn prince is not a member either of the Russian Imperial house or of the Romanov family. All questions of dynastic importance can only be concluded by the great Russian people on Russian soil." Attempting to secure young George from the damaging (in Russia) allegation that the boy was a Hohenzollern, Vladimir legally changed his grandson's name to Romanov and registered him with the French authorities as Grand Duke George of Russia. This infuriated George's father, Prince Franz Wilhelm, now separated from Maria ("He came home one day and found his things in the hall," explained a friend). In March 1994, Franz Wilhelm, who had shed his own Russian name and title of grand duke, said of his son, "I have his German passport right here"; he tapped the breast pocket of his jacket. "I always carry it with me. It says he is Prince George of Prussia."

The family argument about who is and is not qualified to claim a nonexistent throne, who is or is not a grand duke, a prince, or a Romanov is fueled by bitterness on both sides, but the more aggressive hostility has come from Cyril, Leonida, Vladimir, and Maria. Since the revolution, there has been no claimant or line of claimants other than this branch of the family. For them, this has not been enough. They have demanded acquiescence and support for their claim, and when these are denied they have retaliated. In 1992 Grand Duchess Maria wrote to President Yeltsin on the burial of the Ekaterinburg bones. Speaking of cousins closer by blood to Nicholas II than she, the grand duchess informed Yeltsin that "members of the Romanov family, heirs of morganatic marriages, not having any connection to the Imperial house, do not have the slightest right to speak their mind and wishes on this question. They can only go and pray at the grave, as can any other Russian who so wishes."

That summer, the seven senior Romanov princes in the Mikhailovich and Nicholaevich lines gathered in Paris to create a charitable Romanov Family Foundation, whose purpose was to provide medical and other assistance to Russia. Infiltrating a press conference announcing this foundation, partisans of Maria handed out their own press release, signed by Maria, declaring that "the other living members of the House of Romanov have lost all rights of succession as a result of the morganatic marriages of their parents."

In 1994 four Romanov princes were invited, along with Maria, to St. Petersburg to attend a Nicholas and Alexandra exhibition at the Hermitage. Maria refused to come. And a message from Leonida's secretary stated that Her Imperial Highness Grand Duchess Leonida of Russia was shocked by the misuse of titles and protocol involved in the invitations to the princes. Earlier, at a press conference in Ekaterinburg with Maria, Leonida, and George sitting on the dais, the master of ceremonies announced, "There are only three Romanovs in the world. They are all in this room."*

Grand Duchess Maria, the forty-two-year-old Curatrix of the Russian Throne, lives with her son in a tree-shaded villa in the wooded hills outside Madrid. They share the house with Maria's sister, Helen Kirby, now approaching sixty. (Maria and Helen's mother, Leonida, lives mostly in Paris.) In the entry hall of the Madrid villa, there is a

---

*There are, of course, many more than three Romanovs. One of them, whose existence makes some of the others uncomfortable, is Paul R. Ilyinsky, an American citizen, a former colonel in the U.S. Marine Corps, and the current mayor of Palm Beach, Florida.

Ilyinsky, sixty-seven, is the son of Grand Duke Dimitri and Cincinnati heiress Audrey Emery. He was born in England and, as a child, was given the title Prince Paul Romanovsky-Ilyinsky by the pretender, his father's cousin Cyril. Because his parents divorced when he was nine and his father died when he was fourteen, Paul's youthful life revolved around his American mother. He went to a Virginia prep school and the University of Virginia. Setting out on his own, he took the name Paul R. Ilyinsky, entered the Marine Corps as an enlisted man (thereby becoming an American citizen, which entailed renouncing his foreign title), was promoted to officer, served in Korea, and remained in the Reserve to the rank of colonel. He married in Palm Beach, has four children and

portrait of Maria's great-great-grandfather, Tsar Alexander II, beneath which the grand duchess likes to pose with guests. In the parlor, a large portrait of Miss Kirby hangs over the fireplace.

Maria is the central figure in the household. She is short and heavy, and her round face is surmounted by dark hair coiled on top of her head. Her English is fluent and Oxford accented; her Russian is equally fluent. In interviews both in Russia and in the West, she begins with caution, her answers rehearsed, feeling her way. Occasionally, she may shed the careful phraseology in which she has been schooled and speak more openly. Many Russians abroad who did not support Vladimir's claim to the throne nevertheless liked him as a person. The same is true of his daughter.

She answers straightforwardly that she cannot say when or whether the Russian government and people will restore the monarchy. "I don't know. It's difficult to tell," she says. "Probably they say, 'She might come back. She might not. Let's just keep in touch and be nice to them because one never knows.' They always treat us with kindness and respect when we go to Russia. In the summer of 1993, we made a two months' trip along the Volga, stopping in thirty towns. The piers and riverbanks were covered with people. Many of them said, 'When will you come back?' and 'Will you forgive us?' I think in the back of their minds they have the idea of a monarchy. But I am

---

numerous grandchildren, and worked in real estate and as a professional photographer. Building on a collection left him by his father, Ilyinsky has marshaled an enormous army of miniature lead soldiers; and in a wing attached to his waterside house in Palm Beach is one of the world's great private collections of electric trains.

Paul Ilyinsky was friendly with his cousin Vladimir, who visited him in Palm Beach, and is equally at ease with the other Romanov princes whom he has met. He himself is not interested in the Russian throne. Nevertheless, by whatever name he calls himself, he is a Romanov. And by interpreting the old Russian laws of succession in his own favor—a practice of all other contemporary Romanovs—he could make a claim to be the pretender. He, as a male, would come before Vladimir's daughter, Maria. Ilyinsky is the great-grandson in the male line of a tsar (Alexander II), whereas Prince Nicholas Romanov is the

not a prophet. Our return might be in a few months, or next year, or in ten years. So we just go there to find out about our country and to see whether we can help, with no desire—no immediate desire—to put on a crown." Maria has no interest in going back over the past. "It is necessary to forgive, but never to forget," she declares. As to the burial of the Ekaterinburg bones, she says that she "will be bound by the findings of the Russian government commission and the decision of the Russian government. I hope that the patriarch will canonize the family soon, along with all the martyrs of the revolution."

Maria has a good relationship with the present patriarch of the Russian Orthodox Church, Alexis II. "Every time we go to Russia, he receives us kindly," she says. "I think he really thinks that we can make a nice team and work together." She is not bothered by continuing accusations from the Orthodox Church Abroad that the church in Russia is dominated by former agents of the KGB. "Somebody had to keep our church alive during that era, and it is thanks to these churchmen who lived in Russia that there still is a church in Russia," she says. "For a small number of priests from abroad to say to them, 'Well, you can just walk out now and we'll come back and take your place,' is absurd. I think that at one time the Church Abroad had a raison d'être. It doesn't anymore."

When the schism in the Romanov family comes up, Maria is uncomfortable and testy. "If they want to abide by the family laws, then nobody will deny that they are Romanovs," she says, speaking of her cousins. "That they are. Whether they have a title or not, that's another matter. If they want to be Romanovs and carry the name with dignity, that's fine, but one doesn't need a title to do that. The family name is good enough. I understand that it is a very sad situation they find themselves in because their parents did not do the right thing.

---

great-great-grandson of a tsar (Nicholas I). Ilyinsky's father was a prerevolutionary grand duke; this is not true of any of the other living male Romanovs. The flaw in his claim is that he is the product of an unequal marriage. But so, it would seem, are all the other living Romanovs. Contemplating this, Paul Ilyinsky smiles and says, "I am an American and I already have a public office to which I was elected. I am the mayor."

Their parents said that they didn't give a damn and just went ahead and contracted these unequal marriages. Then their wives became Mrs. Romanov and their children Mr. Romanov and Miss Romanov. And that's it. I can't change our laws. My feeling about them is that now that something important is happening in Russia, they suddenly have awakened and said, 'Ah ha! There might be something to gain out of this.'"

While we talked, Miss Kirby and Grand Duke George sat with us, quietly listening. Then George had some tea and a piece of cake and politely excused himself. From the sun parlor, I could see him riding his bicycle back and forth in the garden. I asked about his future. "He knows very well that he is the tsarevich," his mother said. "He talks about it often to me. Right now, he is at an English school here in Madrid where his classmates are the children of diplomats and businessmen. I have asked that they treat him as a normal boy, and he is called George. Someday, I hope he will do his military service in Russia." In a surprising revelation, however, Maria says that George may have to wait his turn to mount the Russian throne. "As you know, I am head of the family," she says. "We shall have to see what our country wants. Right now, the one who is supposed to have the post would be me. So [before George could succeed], my country would have to say, 'We don't want a woman.'"

Prince Nicholas Romanov, recognized by everyone in his family except Maria and Leonida as head of the Imperial house, stands at the train station in Gstaad, Switzerland, on a warm early spring day, extending his hand. He is tall, robust, and smiling. "We will need a taxi to get to my house," he says. "And here we have one: the taxi Romanov." We get into a battered elderly red car, so small that Nicholas fills most of the two front seats, and drive to the small chalet apartment to which he and his wife have retired from Italy. In moving he discovered that this apartment was not large enough for his library, so he bought a one-room studio on the floor below, which now is submerged in piles of books. Most are works of Russian history.

If Grand Duchess Maria is not the legitimate pretender to the Russian throne, then Nicholas Romanov, now seventy-three, occupies that position. His parents married unequally; so, also, in his opinion, did Maria's parents. Given equality on this count, Nicholas takes precedence because he is a male. The irony is that Nicholas neither wishes to be pretender nor believes that monarchy is suited to Russia's current needs. A St. Petersburg television interviewer recently asked him what sort of a tsar he thought he would make. "My dear fellow," Nicholas replied. "You haven't heard? I am a republican."

He was born in the south of France in 1922, not far from the house of his great-uncle the tall soldier Grand Duke Nicholas Nicholaevich. The grand duke had no children, and Nicholas and his brother, Dimitri, four years younger, became the only males in their generation of the Nicholaevich branch of the Romanov family. In 1936 his family moved to Rome, where his grandmother's sister was queen of Italy. Nicholas was eighteen in 1940, when Italy entered the war, but, holding a stateless passport, he was not drafted into the army. In 1944, after the Allies entered Rome, Nicholas joined an Anglo-American psychological warfare unit. "Look here, Romanov, will you please learn English," said his English colonel. Nicholas, who already spoke Russian, French, and Italian, did his best.

In 1946, just before the referendum that transformed Italy from a kingdom into a republic, Nicholas, his parents, and his brother left for Egypt. There Nicholas fell in love with an Egyptian woman whose language was English. "My English improved immensely," he remembers. In 1950, on his way to Geneva to look for work with one of the new United Nations offices, he passed through Rome and met Countess Sveva della Gherardesca. Within a month he proposed marriage. She accepted, but her father told him, "First, get a job." He began selling Austin automobiles in Rome. Three years later his father-in-law and his wife's twin brother died at almost the same time, leaving their vineyards in Tuscany unmanaged. "Not very large but quite good wine," says Nicholas. "So I took over and went into the fields and learned to farm. And that is what I have done most of my life."

Along with farming Nicholas Romanov has devoted his life to reading history. In retrospect, he has great sympathy for his namesake, Nicholas II. "He was a charming, extremely considerate, very unlucky man," Prince Nicholas says. "He had a reputation for being indecisive, for changing his mind too easily, for never keeping his word. Part of this was his character, but part was the system. Let us say you are the minister of education and you come to see the tsar. 'Your Majesty,' you say to him, 'we must build a dozen Russian-language schools in Tajikistan; otherwise all the boys will listen only to the mullahs.' And Nicholas would say, 'An excellent idea. All right. Let's do it.' The tsar's next audience is with the minister of finance, and Nicholas says, 'Oh, by the way, I've ordered twelve new schools in Tajikistan.' And the minister of finance says, 'Good idea. But where are the funds?' 'Ah, well,' says the tsar, 'we can arrange that.' 'Not so easily, Your Majesty,' says the minister. 'You know, the French loans are coming due. And remember that we have decided to reequip the artillery. Frankly, we don't have the money.' The tsar is distressed. 'You mean we can't do it?' 'Not now,' says the finance minister. 'Perhaps later. It is an excellent idea.' So when the tsar next sees the minister of education, he says, 'Oh, by the way, an excellent idea, those schools of yours, but we can't do it just now.' And the minister of education goes out and writes in his diary and later in his memoirs that, once again, the tsar has gone back on his word.

"The problem," continues the Nicholas Romanov of the 1990s, "was the system. If Nicholas II had presided over a Council of Ministers, he would have learned, at the same session, of the need for schools and of the unavailability of money. Perhaps then he would have said, 'Let's start with three schools and try for more later.' But under the autocracy, Nicholas had to know everything and make every decision. Autocracy in Russia may have been logical in the time of Peter the Great, but it was unworkable in the time of Nicholas II."

This leads Nicholas Romanov to the question of monarchy today. "The only thing I know is that whoever speaks of monarchy in Russia today doesn't know what he's talking about. We cannot even think of it. First of all, because it's out of step with the times. The idea that it could be a symbolic thing which will unite all Russians—that's nonsense. It will unite all Russians for a while, and very soon—the minute the first problems arise—all that will collapse. People will blame whoever is the head of state, and there will be no way of getting rid of him. So this is the reason I personally favor a presidential republic now in Russia. Because we need to be able to change the man at the top periodically. It has happened with Gorbachev. It will happen with Yeltsin. The important thing is that the changes are made without trauma for the country, without bloodshed."

What about a constitutional monarchy? "No, I don't think a constitutional monarch, who is a mere symbol of the nation's unity, can work, because Russia does not have a constitutional tradition. We Romanovs took care of that in our time, and our Communist successors made sure after we were gone. This constitutional tradition is born now, it is struggling to grow. There are elections, there is give-and-take in Parliament. Yes, sometimes the wrong people get elected. That is democracy. Everyone gets upset because a madman named Zhirinovsky suddenly gets 25 percent of the vote and starts making frightening pronouncements. Does anybody in the West understand why his supporters voted for him? It's very simple. Take a Russian of my age, seventy-three. As a soldier, he was twenty-two or twenty-three when he beat the greatest army in the world, the German Wehrmacht. He fought his way from Moscow to Berlin, he climbed the Reichstag and put the red flag on the summit. All his life, he has been proud of that. Today, fifty years later, where is this old soldier? Living on a pension which provides a living for only two or three days a month. Do you expect him to be happy seeing Russia begging for deutsche marks and seeing foreigners and Russian criminals racing down streets in Mercedeses and BMWs?

"What I really want," says Nicholas Romanov, "is that my country come out of this historical period and stop dwelling on it. So I'm ready to say that I don't give a damn whether it was Lenin, Sverdlov, Smith, or Jones who ordered the murder of my family. Somebody did. The stigma lies on the men of that era. But, for heaven's sakes, after seventy-five years, we are living now in a new Russia. We have colossal problems to face. Let's forget the political aspect of the past. Let's leave that to the historians. Whether Lenin was responsible or not is extremely interesting, and I'm not in favor of bottling it up, but let's not make that more important than what happens today and tomorrow."

What about the burial of the Ekaterinburg bones? "I believe that they are valid, but what is more important is that we today—all the people of Russia—make a gesture of atonement for this crime and go and express that feeling of atonement at the grave of the victims. If somebody says, 'Look, you are repenting over the wrong bones and the wrong grave,' does that make my repenting less valid? It is the repentance which is important, not the grave. Then it will be over. Finished. Russia can go forward."

Mention of the family schism causes Nicholas to shake his head. "Look, Vladimir married a commoner," he says. "Leonida comes from the most exalted family of the Caucasus, a great, esteemed family of the Russian nobility, but she was not royalty. So what? Our parents married commoners. So what? We have married commoners. Again, so what? There was nobody to ask us to renounce our rights, so we married without renouncing them, and we and our children still have rights to the throne of Russia. That is our position. Cyril would not admit it; Vladimir would not admit it; Maria does not admit it. And we don't give a damn, because we don't want to reign in Russia. We do say, however, that Maria cannot, in her pursuit of a throne, take away who we are and what we are. She cannot put herself out in front. If, when the bones of the Imperial family are buried, Maria insists on being treated differently from us, then my advice to the rest of the family would be not to go. Because then what should be a religious service of repentance and reconciliation would become a political event.

"It is ironical, you know, our Russian law about unequal marriages. Our family in exile is more restrictive in this matter than are the royal families still on their thrones. In England, Sweden, Belgium, the Netherlands, and Denmark, when the monarch or heir marries a commoner, most people think it is politically healthy." Ultimately, Nicholas accepts the view held by the Dowager Empress Marie and by Grand Duke Nicholas Nicholaevich that only the Russian people can decide. "It is up to them whether or not they want a monarch and, if so, who that monarch should be," he says. "If they want a Romanov, they should choose any Romanov they like. If they want someone from another family, they should choose that person. It's not up to us."

Nicholas, in his own view, is Prince Nicholas Romanov, head of the family, president of the Romanov Foundation, historian and retired farmer. That he might be something more was suggested not long ago by the behavior of an expert on royal genealogy and proto-col. Traditionally, the queen of England stands up only for other monarchs or heads of state. Not long ago in London, at an exhibition of jewelry by Fabergé, Nicholas Romanov approached Elizabeth II to be introduced. Seeing him coming, the queen stood.

In Russia in 1995, the symbols of the tsars have begun to reappear. The flag of Russia is the flag of Peter the Great. The double-headed eagle of the Romanovs appears on visas issued by the Russian gov-ernment and on caps worn by Russian generals. In Copenhagen, the Russian ambassador, a former Soviet diplomat, threw up his hands be-fore a Romanov prince and said, "Imagine! They killed not just the tsar and the empress but the children too! All murdered! How terri-ble!" At a dinner in Chicago, Anatoly Sobchak, the mayor of St. Pe-tersburg, told his table partners that he supports the claim of Grand Duchess Maria and that it is only a matter of time before a constitu-tional monarchy under Grand Duke George is established in Russia.

Despite this revival of symbols and interest, however, the time of which Sobchak speaks is unlikely to be soon. Russians, for the most part, do not want a Romanov restoration. "The Romanovs are of no interest to anyone here," said Geli Ryabov, the film director who helped find the grave of the Imperial family. "Why? People are tired. Tired! They want to live quietly, to eat, drink, dress, rest, and sleep and not have to think that tomorrow, once again, someone will be shooting at government buildings." Pavel Ivanov, the DNA expert who helped identify the Romanov bones in England, agrees. "Know-ing how life is in Russia today, I can only laugh," he said about a restoration. "The Russian people have other cares, other problems. It is dangerous to live in Moscow now; the most profitable business in this city is selling steel doors. A life in Russia now is worth five thou-sand dollars; that is what it costs to arrange an assassination. Talk about royal families and thrones is ridiculous."

Irina Pozdeeva, a professor of religious history at Moscow Univer-sity, expressed the same opinion more philosophically: "Believe me, for the people in Russia today, the tsarist idea does not exist at all. The

people today do not remember the *Batushka Tsar* [Little Father].
Three generations of people, even four, have grown up without this
image. It has remained only in fairy tales and in historical memory.
For the intelligentsia, for certain circles of an intellectual spirit, this
idea has been preserved, it has a magnificent color, but it is very small.
The return of the Romanovs? No. It would be an attempt to turn the
river back in the opposite direction."

Practically speaking, a restoration of the Russian monarchy would
require that the Russian president and Parliament—two institutions
which now rarely agree on anything—combine to perform the deli-
cate operation of grafting a third institution, the monarchy, onto the
top of an already enfeebled government structure. A dictator, a Russian Francisco Franco, might do it, but Franco held absolute power in
Spain for forty years, and he prepared his country by announcing his
intention to bring back the king many years before it happened. Russia has no Franco and does not want one; its experiment with democracy is not yet concluded. But democracy has given Russia weak and
divided government, balanced so precariously that no one dares upset
its fragile equilibrium. Bodies and bones remain unburied for fear that
the act of burial would stir political antagonism: Lenin's corpse,
swimming in preservatives, lies untouched in the mausoleum on Red
Square for fear of outraging the Communists; the bones of the Imperial family lie exposed on morgue tables in Ekaterinburg for fear of
offending the Orthodox Church. A government powerless even to lay
to rest these remains of the overthrow of monarchy cannot expect—
or be expected—to find the strength to re-create it.

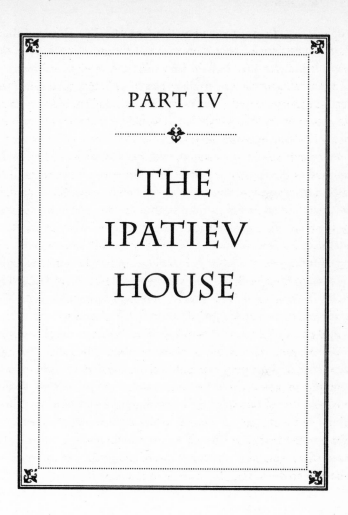

PART IV

THE
IPATIEV
HOUSE

CHAPTER 20

SEVENTY-EIGHT DAYS

For seventy-eight days, the tsar, his family, and members of their household were confined in a part of the upper, main floor of the Ipatiev House. Nicholas and Alexandra had the front corner bedroom, furnished with pale yellow wallpaper, two beds, a couch, two tables, a lamp, a bookcase, and a single armoire, which held all of their clothing. Their four daughters and thirteen-year-old son shared another room with wallpaper of pink and green flowers (eventually, Alexis's bed was moved into his parents' room). The maid, Anna Demidova, had a small room in the back of the house. Dr. Botkin slept in the salon, Trupp and Kharitonov were in the hallway. Two or three armed guards were always present on the main floor with the family, and, to get to the washroom and toilet, the captives had to walk past these men. A wooden fence or palisade, fourteen feet high, masked the house and its windows from the street. Looking out from their rooms, the prisoners could see only the tops of the trees.

The family settled into a monotonous routine. They rose at nine o'clock and at ten had black bread and tea. Every morning and evening they said prayers and read from the Gospel together. Lunch was at one, dinner between four and five, tea at seven, supper at nine. Usually, Nicholas read aloud to the family after tea and in the evening; in the days just after their arrival in Ekaterinburg, he read from the Book of Job. Those who wished were permitted to walk outside twice a day, thirty minutes in the morning, thirty minutes in the afternoon.

Siberia was still in early spring. When Nicholas, Alexandra, and Maria, who traveled from Tobolsk ahead of the others, arrived in Ekaterinburg, Alexandra was happy that the long winter seemed over. "Weather was glorious, so warm and sunny," she wrote on April 30, the day they entered the Ipatiev House. Thereafter, most days were pleasant: "Beautiful, warm, sunny, but windy...glorious bright sunshine...sunshine and changing clouds...beautiful warm morning... sat in the garden, warm wind.... Fine, bright morning." On May 25, however, she reported that it was "snowing hard" and the next day that "everything [was] covered by snow."

After May 15, it was not easy for them to see the sun, clouds, or snow from inside the house. "An old man painted all the windows white from outside," Alexandra wrote that day in her diary, "so only at the top can see a bit of sky and it looks [from inside] as though there were a thick fog." The following day another man painted over the outside thermometer so that they were unable to read the temperature. Four days later the commander of the guards "scratched off the paint covering the thermometer; so now can see again the degrees," the empress wrote.

On May 23, Olga, Tatiana, Anastasia, Alexis, and the sailor Nagorny (who for five years had carried the tsarevich when he could not walk) arrived from Tobolsk. "Such joy to have them again," Alexandra wrote. That night, there were not enough beds, and the four grand

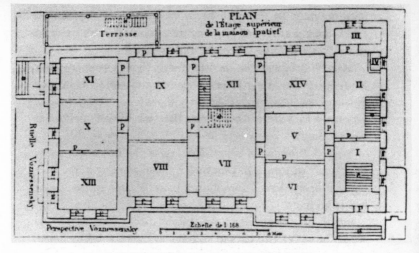

PLAN OF THE MAIN FLOOR OF THE IPATIEV HOUSE

Room XIII: bedroom occupied by Nicholas, Alexandra, and Alexis; room X: bedroom occupied by Olga, Tatiana, Marie, and Anastasia; room XI: bedroom occupied by Demidova; room VIII: salon occupied by Dr. Botkin; room XII: hallway occupied by Kharitonov and Trupp; room IX; dining room; room XIV: kitchen; room III: bathroom; room IV: toilet; room VI: occupied by guards.

duchesses slept on cloaks and cushions on the floor. The family's joy at being reunited was quickly shadowed by the illness of the tsarevich. "Baby woke up every hour from pain in his knee, slipped and hurt it when getting into bed," the empress wrote. "Cannot walk yet. One carries him. [He has] lost fourteen pounds since his illness."

From that day to the end, Alexis's illness dominated his mother's thoughts:

> May 24: Baby and I had meals in our bedroom; his pains varied.... Vladimir Nicholaevich [the tsarevich's physician, Dr. Derevenko, who was allowed to live in the town and make occasional visits to his patient] came to see Baby and change his compresses.... Baby slept in the room with Nagorny.... Baby had a bad night again....
>
> May 25: Swelling a wee bit less but pains off and on very strong.
>
> May 27: Baby had again not a good night. Eugene Sergeivich [Dr. Botkin] sat up part of the night [with him] so as to let

Nagorny sleep. On the whole better, though very strong pains. At 6:30 Sednev [a cook] and Nagorny were taken off; don't know the reason.*... [Dr. Botkin] spent the night with Baby.

May 28: Baby slept on the whole well, though woke up every hour—pains less strong. I asked when Nagorny will be let in again as don't know how we shall get on without him.... Baby suffered very much for a while. After supper, Baby was carried to his room. Pains stronger.

May 30: Baby had a better night, spent the day in our room. Very rarely in pain. [Dr. Derevenko] found swelling in the knee one centimeter less. Before dinner, pains became stronger, took him to his room.

June 2: Baby slept some time—played cards with him.... After supper he was carried back to his room by Trupp and Kharitonov.

June 4: Knee much less swollen. He may be carried out[doors] tomorrow.

June 5: Glorious morning. Baby did not sleep well, leg ached because... [Dr. Derevenko] took it yesterday out of plaster of Paris cast which held the knee firm.... [Dr. Botkin] carried him out and put him in my wheelchair and Tatiana and I sat out with him in the sun. Went back to bed as leg ached from dressing and carrying about. 6:00 P.M. [Dr. Derevenko] came and made him again a plaster of Paris cast as knee more swollen and hurts again so.

Thereafter, as the bleeding stopped and the fluids in Alexis's knee were reabsorbed, his pain subsided and his leg began to straighten. When the weather was good, he was carried outdoors to sit in the sun. "Sat with Baby, Olga, and Anastasia before the house," Alexandra wrote. "Went out with Baby, Tatiana, and Marie... wheeled Baby into the garden and we all sat there for an hour. Very hot, nice lilac bushes and small honeysuckle."

Most of the time, Alexandra, like Alexis, was immobilized. Unable to walk because of sciatica, she lay in her bed or sat in her wheelchair in

*Four days later Sednev and Nagorny were shot. The family never knew.

the pale yellow bedroom. Confronted by the white-painted windows, she embroidered, drew, or read her Bible, her prayer books, or the *Life of Saint Serafim of Sarov*. On May 28 she recorded that "I cut Nicholas's hair for the first time," and on June 20, "Cut N's hair again." Alexandra was cared for by her daughters: "Marie read to me after tea.... Marie washed my hair.... Tatiana read to me.... Anastasia read to me.... the others went out, Olga stayed with me." The empress suffered from recurring migraines: "I remained in bed as feeling very giddy and eyes ache so.... Lay with eyes shut as head continued to ache.... Remained the whole day with shut eyes, head got worse towards evening."

The strain on Nicholas was that of an outdoor animal caged. Unable to go out when he wished, he paced his room, back and forth, back and forth. One warm evening in June, he wrote in his diary, "It was unbearable to sit that way, locked up, and not be in a position to go out into the garden when you wanted and spend a fine evening outside." He was tired, and the pouches deepened under his eyes. "The tedium," he wrote, "is incredible." Suffering from hemorrhoids, he went to bed for three days, "since it is more convenient to apply compresses." Alexandra and Alexis sat by his bed for lunch, tea, and supper. After two days and nights, he sat up, and the next morning got up and went outside. "The green is very fine and lush," he wrote.

Immersed in tedium, isolated from the world outside, unaware even of events like Nagorny's death, the prisoners found variety mainly in the ups and downs of illnesses and the capriciousness of the weather. Birthdays were scarcely noticed, although four occurred while the family was in the Ipatiev House: On May 19, Nicholas was fifty; on June 6, Alexandra was forty-six; on June 18, Nicholas recorded, "dear Anastasia has turned seventeen"; on June 27, "Our dear Marie has turned nineteen." Occasionally there were breaks in their routine. Early in May a package arrived. "Received chocolate and coffee from Ella [her sister, Grand Duchess Elizabeth]," Alexandra noted. "She has been sent from Moscow and is at Perm." The following morning the empress wrote: "Great treat, a cup of coffee." Sometimes the electricity failed. "Supper, 3 candles in glasses; cards by light of one candle," she wrote. On June 4 she noted that the new ruler of Russia had exercised his power even over the clock: "Lenin gave the order that the clocks have to be put two hours ahead (economy of electricity) so at ten they told us it is twelve."

As the days passed, the captives, from emperor to cook, merged into an extended family. Botkin, an old friend rather than a servant, frequently sat with Nicholas and his wife after supper to talk and play cards. During the day when Alexandra and Alexis could not leave the house, Botkin remained inside with them for card games. After Nagorny was removed, Botkin sometimes slept in the room with the tsarevich, and he shared with Nicholas, Trupp, and Kharitonov the task of carrying Alexis out of doors. On June 23 Botkin himself became violently ill with colic, requiring an injection of morphine. He remained sick for five days; when he was able to sit up in an armchair, Alexandra sat with him. Sednev, the cook, became ill, and Alexandra kept watch over his temperature and progress.

The four grand duchesses, now young women, did what they could. Tatiana and Marie read to and played bridge with their mother. Tatiana also played cards with Alexis and, during the peak of his illness, slept near him at night. Olga, closest to Nicholas, walked beside her father twice a day. All four helped Demidova darn stockings and linen. At the end of June, Kharitonov, the cook, proposed that the five children help him make bread. "The girls kneaded the dough for the bread," recorded Alexandra. "The children continued rolling and making bread and now it is baking.... Lunched: excellent bread.... The children help every day in the kitchen."

In June summer and heat were upon them. This was a season of storms with thunder and lightning, sheets of rain, and then, quickly, bright sunshine and more heat. On June 6 Alexandra noted, "Very hot, awfully stuffy in rooms." Heat from the kitchen made things worse: "Kharitonov has to cook our food now," she wrote on June 18. "Very hot, stuffy as no windows open and smells strong of kitchen every-where." On June 21, she reported, "Out in the garden, fearfully hot, sat under the bushes. They have given us...half an hour more for being out. Heat, airlessness in the rooms intense."

Closed windows made the heat stifling. In order to keep the pris-oners from escaping or signaling to the outside, all of the white-painted, double windows in the family rooms were kept shut by order of the Ural Soviet. Nicholas set himself to overturn this decree. "Today at tea, six men walked in, probably from the Regional Soviet, to see which windows to open," he wrote in his diary on June 22. "The resolution of this issue has gone on for nearly two weeks! Often vari-ous men have come and silently in our presence examined the win-dows." On this issue the tsar triumphed. "Two of the soldiers came and took out one window in our room," Alexandra wrote on June 23. "Such joy, delicious air at last and one window no longer white-washed." "The fragrance from all the town's gardens is amazing," wrote Nicholas.

In the sunlight, Alexis sat quietly while the tsar and his daughters walked under the eyes of the guards. In time impressions of the fam-ily began to change. "I have still an impression of them that will al-ways remain in my soul," said Anatoly Yakimov, a member of the guard who was captured by the Whites.

The tsar was no longer young, his beard was getting grey.... [He wore] a soldier's shirt with an officer's belt fastened by a buckle around his waist.... The buckle was yellow...the shirt was khaki color, the same color as his trousers and his old worn-out boots. His eyes were kind and...I got the impression that he was a kind, simple, frank and talkative person. Sometimes, I felt he was going to speak to me. He looked as if he would like to talk to us.

The tsaritsa was not a bit like him. She was severe looking and she had the appearance and manners of a haughty, grave woman. Sometimes we used to discuss them amongst ourselves and we de-cided that she was different and looked exactly like a tsaritsa. She seemed older than the tsar. Grey hair was plainly visible on her temples and her face was not the face of a young woman....

All my evil thoughts about the tsar disappeared after I had stayed a certain time amongst the guards. After I had seen them several times, I began to feel entirely different towards them; I began to pity them. I pitied them as human beings. I am telling you the entire truth. You may or may not believe me, but I kept saying to myself, "Let them escape ... do something to let them escape."

On July 4, a "lovely morning, nice air, not too hot," a man whom Nicholas called "the dark gentleman" appeared and took control of the Ipatiev House. This man, who had black eyes, black hair, and a black beard, and who wore a black leather jacket, was the Chekist Commander, Yakov Yurovsky. Ironically, that same day Alexandra recorded that Alexis was getting better: "Baby eats well and is getting heavy for the others to carry. He moves his leg more easily. Cruel they won't give us Nagorny back again."

Yurovsky's arrival heralded minor improvements in the prisoners' situation. The new guards he brought were better disciplined; petty harassment of the young grand duchesses on their way to the toilet ceased. Alexandra's diary entry for July 13 ended with an optimistic note about Alexis: "Beautiful morning. I spent the day as yesterday lying on the bed, as back ached when move about. Others went out twice. Anastasia remained with me in the afternoon. One says Nagorny ... has been sent out of the ... [region] instead of giving ... [him] back to us. At 6:30, Baby had his first bath since Tobolsk. He managed to get in and out alone, climbs also in and out of bed, but can only stand on one foot as yet."

On Sunday, July 14, Alexandra recorded "the joy of a vespers—the young priest for the second time." Father Storozhev had come before, in May, and Yurovsky had agreed that he could come again. The priest found the family waiting together: Alexis sitting in his mother's wheelchair; Alexandra, wearing a lilac dress, sitting beside him; Nicholas, in khaki field shirt, trousers, and boots, standing with his daughters, who were dressed in white blouses and dark skirts. When the service began, Nicholas fell on his knees.

A poem, dedicated to Olga and Tatiana, had been sent to Tobolsk by a friend of Alexandra. In the Ipatiev House, Olga copied it in her own hand and inserted it into one of her books. It was found there by the Whites:

> Give patience, Lord, to us Thy children
> In these dark, stormy days to bear
> The persecution of our people,
> The tortures falling to our share.
>
> Give strength, Just God, to us who need it,
> The persecutors to forgive,
> Our heavy, painful cross to carry
> And Thy great meekness to achieve.
>
> When we are plundered and insulted
> In days of mutinous unrest
> We turn for help to Thee, Christ-Savior,
> That we may stand the bitter test.
>
> Lord of the world, God of Creation,
> Give us Thy blessing through our prayer
> Give peace of heart to us, O Master,
> This hour of utmost dread to bear.
>
> And on the threshold of the grave
> Breathe power divine into our clay
> That we, Thy children, may find strength
> In meekness for our foes to pray.

On Tuesday, July 16, after a gray morning, the sun came out. The family gathered, prayed together, and had tea. Yurovsky arrived to make his inspection and, as a special treat, brought fresh eggs and milk. Alexis had a slight cold. Nicholas, Olga, Marie, and Anastasia went out for half an hour in the morning while Tatiana stayed behind to read to her mother from the prophets Amos and Obadiah. At four in the afternoon, Nicholas and his four daughters walked again in the garden. At eight the family had supper, prayed, and then separated; Olga, Tatiana, Marie, and Anastasia went to their room; Alexis went to his bed in his parents' room. Alexandra stayed up to play bezique with Nicholas. At 10:30 she made an entry in her diary. It was cool, she wrote: "15 degrees" (58 degrees F). Then she turned out the light, lay down next to her husband, and went to sleep.

SOURCES AND
ACKNOWLEDGMENTS

Most of the written sources of my understanding of Nicholas II, his family, and his era are listed in the bibliography of my earlier book *Nicholas and Alexandra*. For this new book, I carefully reread Nicholas Sokolov's *Enquête Judiciaire sur l'Assassinat de la Famille Impériale Russe* and Pavel M. Bykov's *The Last Days of Tsardom*. The Yurovsky note was unavailable when my first book appeared, and I, like many others, put too much faith in Sokolov's conclusion that the bodies had been destroyed. Yurovsky's account of the murders, first revealed by Edvard Radzinsky in 1989 and later included in his book *The Last Tsar*, described what actually happened and helped Alexander Avdonin and Geli Ryabov discover where the bodies were.

Essentially, the source material for the present book was not in written form; it came from over one hundred interviews with people in Ekaterinburg, Moscow, London, Birmingham, Paris, Copenhagen, Madrid, Gstaad, Ulm, New York City, Albany, Hartford, Boston, Washington, Charlottesville, Durham, Gainesville, Palm Beach, Austin, Phoenix, Berkeley, and Jordanville, New York. Helping me with the first part of the book, "The Bones," were many Russians, including Dr. Sergei Abramov, Alexander and Galina Avdonin, Dr. Pavel Ivanov, Nikolai Nevolin, Geli Ryabov, Vladimir Soloviev, Sergei Mironenko, Prince Alexis Scherbatow, Metropolitan Vitaly, Archbishop Laurus, Bishop Hilarion, Bishop Basil Rodzianko, and Father Vladimir Shishkoff. I am very grateful to all of them. I wish to thank Dr. Peter Gill, Karen Pearson, Prince Rostislav Romanov, Michael Thornton, Julian Nott, Nigel McCrery, and Barbara Whittal for the help I received in England. In the United States, I was assisted by James A. Baker III, Margaret Tutwiler, Grace and Ron Moe, Bill Dabney, Mike Murrow, Dr. William Maples, Dr. Michael Baden, Dr. Lowell Levine, Dr. William Hamilton, William Goza, Cathryn Oakes, Dr. Charles Ginther, Dr. Alka Mansukhani, Dr. Walter Rowe, Dr. Richard Froede, Dr. Bill Rodriguez, Matt Clark, Mark Stolorow, Marilyn Swezey, and Robert Atchison.

On Romanov impostors in general, Alexander Avdonin, Edvard Radzinsky, Vladimir Soloviev, Prince Nicholas Romanov, Ricardo Mateos Sainz de Medrano, Pavel Ivanov, Bishop Basil Rodzianko, Marilyn Swezey, and Victor Dricks all told me interesting stories. In *The Romanov Conspiracies,* Michael Occleshaw describes the escape and subsequent life of Larissa Feodorovna Tudor.

On Michael Goleniewski and Eugenia Smith, I was greatly assisted by Countess Dagmar de Brantes, Brien Horan, Bishop Gregory (formerly Father George Grabbe), Father Vladimir Shishkoff, Dr. Richard Rosenfield, David Martin, David Gries, Leroy A. Dysick, and Denis B. Gredlein. David Martin's *Wilderness of Mirrors* and Guy Richards's *The Hunt for the Tsar* contained useful information about Michael Goleniewski.

The literature on Anna Anderson is extensive and, undoubtedly, will continue to expand. It includes a purported autobiography, *I Am Anastasia* (or, in England, *I, Anastasia*), of which Anna Anderson had no knowledge until she was presented with a finished copy of the book. Most of the early witnesses and disputants put their opinions in writing; among these works I read *Anastasia,* by Harriet Rathlef-Keilman, *La Fausse Anastasie,* by Pierre Gilliard and Constantin Savitch, *The Real Romanovs* and *The Woman Who Rose Again,* by Gleb Botkin, *The Last Grand Duchess* (Olga, Nicholas II's sister), by Ian Vorres, *Anastasia, Qui Êtes-Vous?,* by Dominique Auclères, and *The House of Special Purpose,* by J. C. Trewin (compiled from the papers of Charles Sidney Gibbes, the English tutor of the Imperial children). There are two relatively recent biographies of Anna Anderson: *Anastasia: The Riddle of Anna Anderson,* by Peter Kurth, and *Anastasia: The Lost Princess,* by James Blair Lovell. In depth of research, style of writing, and seriousness of purpose, Kurth's book is infinitely superior. Brien Horan was kind enough to give me a copy of his unpublished manuscript on the evidence on both sides of the Anna Anderson case. I am grateful to Dr. Gunther von Berenberg-Gossler for permitting me to see a chapter of his unpublished work on Franziska Schanzkowska.

Michael Thornton was generous, not only with his vast collection of Anna Anderson correspondence and memorabilia, but with his time and counsel. Similarly, Brien Horan helped me greatly with his knowledge of Anna Anderson and of the Romanov family schism. John Orbell of Baring Brothers, William Clarke, author of *The Lost Treasures of the Tsar*, and H. Leslie Cousins of Price, Waterhouse assisted me in grappling with the disputed story of Romanov money in English banks.

The account of the legal proceedings in Charlottesville is drawn exclusively from interviews and conversations. In this respect, Richard and Marina Schweitzer, whose integrity and honorable effort I greatly admired although I never was able to share their belief, were indispensable. In addition, I am grateful to Susan Burkhart, Mary DeWitt, Mildred Ewell, Baron Eduard von Falz-Fein, Dr. Peter Gill, Dr. Charles Ginther, Vladimir Galitzine, Ron Hansen, Penny Jenkins, Dr. Willi Korte, Peter Kurth, Syd Mandelbaum, Matthew Murray, Ann Nickels, Julian Nott, Maurice Philip Remy, Dean Robinson, Rhonda Roby, Prince Alexis Scherbatow, and Michael Thornton.

My chapter on the Romanov survivors and the possibility of a restoration of the dynasty in Russia benefited from conversations with Marina Beadleston, Prince Dimitri and Princess Dorrit Romanov, Grand Duke George, Grand Duchess Leonida, Grand Duchess Maria, Prince Michel Romanov, Prince Nicholas and Princess Sveva Romanov, Prince Rostislav Romanov, Paul R. and Angelica Ilyinsky, Xenia Sfiris, Prince Franz of Prussia, Prince Giovanni di Bourbon-Sicilies, Prince George Vassiltchikov, Professor Irina Pozdeeva, Dr. Pavel Ivanov, Geli Ryabov, Jose Luis Lampredo Escolar, Ricardo Mateos Sainz de Medrano, and Albert Bartridge.

Edward Kasinec, chief of the Slavic and Baltic Division of the New York Public Library, gave me invaluable assistance, and his colleague Sergei Gleboff also helped me. Deborah Baker was the first to mention to me the link between DNA fingerprinting and the Romanov bones. Edmund and Sylvia Morris made me feel at home in Washington, taking time from their own books to give counsel on mine. Hannah Pakula loaned me a rare book from her library. Ian Lilburne permitted me to use his pictures. Howard Ross dropped everything for several days to help with other pictures. Annick Mesko, Jacques Ferrand, Julia Kort, Victoria Lewis, and Petra Henttonen contributed comments, questions, and multilingual translations. Ken Burrows, Jeremy Nussbaum, and Nancy Feltsen stepped forward in times of trouble. I am greatly indebted to Dolores Karl, who listened to several hundred hours' of taped interviews and turned what she heard into several thousand pages of clean, workable transcript. In addition, she rescued me whenever I was losing a battle with my new (and first) computer word processor.

I had not really known Masha Tolstoya Sarandinaki and Peter Sarandinaki before I began working on this book. Peter and I went to Ekaterinburg together, where we lived with Alexander and Galina Avdonin, walked through magnificent forests of birch and pine, saw the places where the unspeakable had happened, and looked at the unburied bones of the Russian Imperial family. Once we were home, Masha translated Russian tapes into English, answered questions, offered suggestions, and repeatedly telephoned Russia to keep me abreast of events. To them, and to Olga Tolstoya, my heartfelt thanks.

I am grateful to Harry Evans at Random House, who enthusiastically embraced this story, and to Robert Loomis, whose patience, skill, and unerring eye for what works and what does not have guided authors for almost forty years. Deborah Aiges, Susan M. S. Brown, Sharon DeLano, Benjamin Dreyer, Emily Eakin, Barbé Hammer, Ivan Held, J. K. Lambert, Tom Perry, Kathy Rosenbloom, and Walter Weintz helped to turn my manuscript into a book and put it in the hands of readers. Dan Franklin, Caroline Michel, Arnulf Conradi, and Elisabeth Ruge believed in the book from the beginning.

Many friends gave me encouragement while I was writing this book. Among these I would particularly like to thank Kim and Lorna Massie, Art Spiegelman and Françoise Mouly, Harold Brodkey and Ellen Schwamm, Melanie Jackson and Thomas Pynchon, Fred Karl, Sheldon and Helen Atlas, Elsa Jobity, Janet Byrne and Ivan Solataroff, Jeff Seroy and Doug Stumpf, Peg Determan, Lance Balk, Jan and Carl Ramirez, Christina Haus and Paolo Alimonti, Steve and Ann Halliwell, and Giovanni and Cornelia Bagarotti. I also remember an evening in November 1993 when my friends in Nashville patiently listened to my presentation of the arguments for and against writing this book. With a single exception, they said, Do it. For this advice, I am grateful to Jack and Lynn May, Herb and May Shayne, Gil and Robin Merritt, George and Ophelia Payne, and Henry Walker.

My wife, Deborah Karl, who is also my literary agent, is primarily responsible for seeing that this book was written. In the beginning, she warmly encouraged the idea and negotiated the contract. She read every chapter before I went on to the next. The manuscript was late, and as the pressure rose she protected me. Of course, not everything in life is agreeable. Near the end of the writing, she and I suffered a blow from a professional colleague. After many days, during which my thoughts were of outrage and a hundred forms of vengeance, she restored sufficient rationality and calm so that I was able to finish.

INDEX

THE LAST TSAR

Edvard Radzinsky

'A masterly touch'
New York Times Book Review

The sensational biography of Nicholas II, his wife
Alexandra and their five children, and the truth behind their
brutal murders at the hands of the Bolsheviks on the night
of July 16–17, 1918.

The mass execution at Ekaterinburg brought to an end the
three-hundred year rule of the house of Romanov and set
the tone for the Stalinist atrocities which followed.

For more than seventy years layer upon layer of myth,
legend and speculation buried the dark secrets surrounding
their deaths. Now, in a story that could not have been
written before *glasnost*, acclaimed Russian playwright and
historian Edvard Radzinsky has unearthed vital documents –
including the Tsar's personal diary with its last entry written
only hours before his death – and eyewitness accounts of the
killings to bring riveting solutions to long unanswered
questions. Utterly fascinating are his minute-by-minute
reconstruction of the Tsar's terrifying last days, the
documentation linking the execution order directly to
Lenin, and, perhaps most astonishing, the new evidence
suggesting the survival of two family members.

The Last Tsar is a brilliant historical record and a hauntingly
personal narrative that evokes the epic sweep of Tolstoy and
disturbing insights of Dostoevsky. It will stand as the
definitive account of the terrible last days of one of history's
most powerful and ultimately doomed dynasties.

'Vivid, enthralling, fascinating'
Nikolai Tolstoy, Daily Telegraph

'Remarkable . . . absorbing . . . the ultimate in last-days-of-
the-Romanovs books"
New York Times Book Review

'Radzinsky's book makes vivid, as no other does, the
screaming horror of the murders themselves'
Peter Kurth, Vanity Fair

'Unforgettable'
Time Magazine

A QUESTION OF CHARACTER

Thomas C. Reeves

The book that finally exploded the Kennedy myth

No American president has been admired or respected by his country as John F. Kennedy. His charisma, energy and sincerity were without equal and his popularity has never been surpassed.

But Kennedy was a man of great contradictions: behind his ostensible fidelity and love of family he was a lascivious womaniser and, despite his religious upbringing, he lacked the commitment and conviction to be a true moral leader.

In this expertly-researched account of Kennedy's life and presidency, Thomas C. Reeves examines the public image and the private man and finds the two very much at odds. Reeves discusses the role of the media in the making of Kennedy's saintly image and the influence of his father in creating a man who risked exposure, blackmail and a sensational career for momentary excitement.

'Takes a scholarly axe to the Kennedy myth'
Daily Telegraph

'A respected academic has now published a life of Kennedy for the lay reader . . . puts an accurate version of the Kennedy story between the covers of one, not-too-long book, and what we learn is that the worst excesses of the irresponsible tabloid press were exactly on target'
Independent

DE VALERA
Long Fellow, Long Shadow

Tim Pat Coogan

'Imposing and provocative . . . compelling . . . few will fail to be impressed by Coogan's cool, deep handling of the material'
Independent

Eamon de Valera – 'The Long Fellow' – remains a towering presence whose long shadow still falls over Irish life. The history of Ireland for much of the twentieth century *is* the history of de Valera.

From the 1916 Rising, the troubled Treaty negotiations and the Civil War, right through to his retirement after longer in power than any other twentieth century leader, de Valera both defined and divided Ireland. Any one of his three major achievements – the Irish Constitution, Ireland's largest political party *Fianna Fail*, and the Irish Press Group – would have ensured his fame.

Yet many of the challenges he confronted still trouble the peace of Ireland and Britain, and some of today's problems are his legacy. For de Valera was a world figure who remade Ireland, and yet attempted to confine his nation of disciples to the narrowest of cultural and intellectual horizons. Tim Pat Coogan's comprehensive study of this political giant is a major addition to the history of Irish–British relationships.

'[Coogan] has a natural story-teller's skill . . . always readable . . . absorbing, even gripping'
Colm Toibin, Sunday Times

'This important book [offers] a conscientious encyclopaedic survey of a career that has not hitherto been properly treated with anything like the objectivity of an encyclopaedia'
Robert Kee, Times Literary Supplement

OTHER TITLES AVAILABLE IN ARROW